PERSONALITY AND DANGEROUSNESS

Genealogies of Antisocial Personality Disorder

David McCallum

Victoria University, Melbourne

CAMBRIDGE
UNIVERSITY PRESS

PUBLISHED BY THE PRESS SYNDICATE OF THE UNIVERSITY OF CAMBRIDGE
The Pitt Building, Trumpington Street, Cambridge, United Kingdom

CAMBRIDGE UNIVERSITY PRESS
The Edinburgh Building, Cambridge CB2 2RU, UK
40 West 20th Street, New York, NY 10011–4211, USA   www.cup.org
10 Stamford Road, Oakleigh, Melbourne 3166, Australia
Ruiz de Alarcón 13, 28014 Madrid, Spain
Dock House, The Waterfront, Cape Town, 8001, South Africa

http://www.cambridge.org

First published 2001

Printed in the United Kingdom at the University Press, Cambridge

Typeset in Plantin 10/12pt   System 3b2   [CE]

A catalogue record for this book is available from the British Library

Library of Congress Cataloguing in Publication data

McCallum, David.
Personality and dangerousness: genealogies of antisocial personality disorder /
David McCallum.
    p.   cm.
Includes bibliographical references and index.
ISBN 0 521 80402 7 (hardback) – ISBN 0 521 00875 1 (paperback)
1. Antisocial personality disorders – History.
2. Antisocial personality disorders – Etiology.
3. Dangerously mentally ill – Government policy.
I. Title.

RC555.M28 2001 616.85'82–dc21 2001025234

ISBN 0 521 80402 7 hardback
ISBN 0 521 00875 1 paperback

In memory of my brother
Peter McCallum
MB, BS, DPM, FRANZCP
1943–1999

Contents

Acknowledgements

I am greatly indebted to Jennifer Laurence for her role as research assistant for this project. Her scholarship and care in preparing primary source material and her immense knowledge and understanding of the research field has contributed enormously to this work.

The project was supported in the form of an Australian Research Council Large Grant for which I am most grateful. I would like to thank Victoria University for allowing me to undertake periods of leave to concentrate on the book, and to acknowledge the help and advice from colleagues at Goldsmiths College, University of London, the Australian Centre at the University of Melbourne, and the Research School of Social Sciences at the Australian National University, where as a Visiting Fellow I had an opportunity to be influenced by a broad range of thinkers in social and political theory.

The head librarian Jillian Hiscock and staff at the Mental Health Services Library, Royal Park Psychiatric Hospital in Parkville Victoria were very helpful indeed, as were Dorothea Rowse and other staff at the Brownless Medical Library, University of Melbourne. Thanks as well to the Royal Australian College of Physicians History of Medicine Library in Sydney, the Heritage Office, Department of Planning and Development in Victoria, to Elizabeth Willis, Curator of Public and Institutional Life at the Museum of Victoria, to staff in Special Collections at the Baillieu Library at Melbourne University and the La Trobe Collection in the State Library in Victoria, and to Emily Wark and other staff at Victoria University Library at Footscray Park.

I have had the privilege over several years of being able to share ideas with friends and colleagues and I especially want to acknowledge David Burchell, Graham Burchell, Mitchell Dean, Margaret Goding, Barry Hindess, Ian Hunter, Gavin Kendall, Peter McCallum, Denise Meredith, Jeffrey Minson, Nikolas Rose, David Silverman, Gordon Tait, Deborah Tyler, John Uhr and Garry Wickham. The responsibility for any of the strengths and weaknesses of the book rests, of course, with me.

I would like to thank several anonymous reviewers and Sarah Caro for help, support and suggestions about improvements to the work over its various stages of development. Finally, I am grateful to staff and students in the Faculty of Arts at Victoria University for the opportunities for ideas, debate and encouragement.

Note: parts of chapter 2 have earlier appeared in draft form as 'Mental health, criminality and the human sciences', in A. Petersen and R. Buntine (eds.), *Foucault, Health and Medicine*, London: Routledge, 1997; sections of chapters 5 and 6 draw on material published as 'Dangerous individuals: government and the concept of personality', in B. Hindess and M. Dean (eds.), *Governing Australia*, Melbourne: Cambridge University Press, 1997, pp. 108–24, and 'Law, psychiatry and antisocial personality disorder', *Law in Context*, 15, 1 (1997), 29–52.

Introduction

On a mild autumn Sunday morning in the quiet tourist hamlet of Port Arthur in Tasmania, on the southern tip of Australia, Martin Bryant drove his yellow Volvo station wagon into the grounds of the old convict prison. He sat and chatted with a tourist outside the Broad Arrow Cafe, and mumbled something about the number of 'wasps' (White Anglo-Saxon Protestants) visiting the old gaol on that morning. After eating his lunch, Bryant walked into the cafe, removed an AR15 semi-automatic rifle from the tennis bag he was carrying, and began to open fire on staff and customers, including children. In the space of a few minutes, the slightly built, fair complexioned, 'innocent-looking' 26-year-old had shot and killed thirty-five people and seriously injured another dozen. A witness said he 'wasn't going bang bang bang bang – it was bang and then he'd pick someone else out and line them up and shoot them'.[1] The following morning, after an all-night siege in a local guesthouse, Bryant ran injured from a burning building which he had apparently set alight, and was taken into custody and to a hospital.

We would prefer to think of this kind of event as a terrible anomaly. But there is evidence showing an increased incidence of multiple killings over the past twenty years in most parts of the Western world, and most often carried out by men acting alone and seemingly at random. After the Port Arthur shootings and in the aftermath of Dunblane in Scotland or the schoolyard killings in the United States, as the cases move through the protracted legal processes and communities seek to come to terms with the private and public trauma, there is a demand to know how this event could happen – what kind of person commits these terrible acts. People begin to ask whether there is a dark and evil side to modern social life. Are the links which bind a community being undermined by misguided mental health or sentencing policies? Or is there a crisis of ethics being experienced in commercial culture, or by a radical form of economic individualism which seems to have abandoned notions of community responsibility? The answers to these kinds of questions are mostly put to one side against the more compelling

question of how we recognise 'dangerous persons' and what kinds of
governmental and institutional action can be taken to protect against
dangerousness, in the context of liberal democratic societies. The
problem of how to understand dangerousness centres on the role of
both the mental health and criminal justice systems, and it is out of the
intersections of these two institutional locations that knowledges about
particular categories of dangerous persons have emerged.

As might be expected, the status of these categories is unclear. In a
recent television documentary on the Port Arthur killings, psychiatric
and psychological views were sought on the question 'What kind of
person?' by giving a portrait of the typical mass killer. One forensic
psychologist attempted to sum up the current state of knowledge with
the somewhat disarming statement that '. . . what we don't know is why
other lonely, isolated, angry men at the fringe of society don't become
mass killers'. Other experts argued that it was possible to predict
dangerousness by taking account of early warning signals in children,
such as unhappiness, narcissism, self-centredness, uncertainty, and an
inability to form relationships. A common set of signals in children –
'prolonged bed-wetting, cruelty to animals, setting fires' – were the
precursors of something more serious down the track. In television
interviews, people who had known Martin Bryant described him as 'a
strange young boy'; 'shy, sad, no friends'; 'simple, not "retarded
simple", but you know . . .'; 'a loner'. Doctors had told his lawyer that
Bryant '. . . can't empathise with people and I'm not sure a person in
that situation is capable of remorse'. These were all described as being
the antecedents, the classic symptoms, of a condition known as antisocial personality disorder.[2]

Antisocial personality disorder is the element which figures most
frequently in the description of these kinds of offenders. The latest
edition of the standard taxonomy of mental disorders, the *Diagnostic and
Statistical Manual of Mental Disorders* (*DSM–IV*) published by the American Psychiatric Association, devotes almost fifty pages to personality
disorders but we are given a summary definition of antisocial personality
disorder: 'a pervasive pattern of disregard for, and violation of, the
rights of others that begins in childhood or early adolescence and
continues into adulthood'.[3] This certainly seems to fit the bill as a
description of the multiple-murderers, sex offenders and those who
threaten violence, who have come to inhabit this category in recent
times. But the *DSM–IV* offering is limited, and deliberately so, in terms
of aetiology or causes of the condition. The sensible person interested in
community safety and good government would want to ask the questions, 'What can be done to prevent this violence?' 'Is it possible to take

steps to ensure the development of more "ordered" personalities?' 'Is there a program we can implement?' But if we take the case of Bryant, experts were quite divided on what causes antisocial personality disorder, and especially on whether the causes are physiological or social. A Canadian authority on disorders, R. D. Hare, testified that the brainwaves of psychopaths can be distinguished from the rest of the population in brain imaging experiments, which reveal almost no activity at all in the front parts of the brain. Dr Paul Mullen on the other hand, a forensic psychiatrist in Melbourne, responded that it was '. . . cheaper to say they're ill than to provide every child in our community with a decent education – a chance of success'. Clearly, the experts are divided on the causes of disorders, and the implication seems to be that a program, intervention or remedy depends on the type of explanation for the existence of the problem – that some explanations might even serve to close off possible (expensive) interventions.

Antisocial personality disorder, or psychopathy as it is known in some jurisdictions, is recognised as a diagnosable mental disorder, but it is not accepted in the legal defence of insanity. It does not by itself qualify under the McNaghten rules which have existed in one form or another since 1843; that is, that the defendant did not know the nature and quality of his actions, or if he did, that he did not know that what he was doing was wrong. These rules followed the case of Daniel McNaghten in the early nineteenth century who was tried for the murder of Drummond, Private Secretary to the Prime Minister of England, Robert Peel. McNaghten was given a not guilty verdict on the grounds of insanity, after evidence was led that McNaghten, who mistook Drummond for the Prime Minister, suffered from the delusion that he was being persecuted by 'the Tories'. So, while on medical grounds some psychiatrists might accept that antisocial personality disorder is a mental disorder, according to legal criteria it is not recognised as a mental illness within the terms of the insanity defence.

In his summing up at the Martin Bryant trial, Chief Justice William Cox pointed to the differences of opinion offered in his court over the diagnosis of Bryant's disorder. But he did point to certain key criteria of the disorder and its relation to dangerousness upon which most psychiatrists would agree. Bryant's disorder, according to evidence given by the psychiatrist who examined Bryant, left him with a limited capacity for empathy or for imagining the feelings and responses of others, and evidence was provided that Bryant's parents had endeavoured, unsuccessfully, to have the condition corrected. It was submitted that Bryant had a severely disturbed childhood, which, it is agreed, is a key precursor to antisocial personality disorder. Unlike a mental illness, which one acquires in one's lifetime (and from which one usually recovers), antisocial personality disorder is almost invariably experienced from early life whence it is classified as a conduct disorder. At present, it is fair to say that psychiatric opinion is divided on whether antisocial personality disorder is treatable or whether it is possible for a person to 'recover' from it. Bryant, whom Justice Cox described as 'a pathetic social misfit' perhaps with an eye to minimising the possibility of others seeking to achieve notoriety in this fashion, was sentenced to life imprisonment and never to be released.

The history of antisocial personality disorder traced out in this book parallels the development of the disciplines of psychiatry and psychological medicine, from the founding texts by Sydenham, Thomas Arnold and Prichard in the early part of the nineteenth century, along with the way in which law and legal process over time has responded to medical diagnosis. Some historians claim that antisocial personality disorder has simply undergone name changes over time, variously called moral mania, moral imbecility, and more recently sociopathy and psychopathy. Many early theorists believed the disorder was inherited, and during the past one hundred years it has appeared as a sub-category of the mentally deficient and defective, or the group which at one time was referred to as the feebleminded. At various points, psychiatry gave over the field of mental deficiency to psychology and its attendant new methods of measurement, care and education which evolved during the early twentieth century. From the 1880s Australia was recognised as a world leader in the care of the mentally deficient, as evidenced by the Kew Idiot Cottages built in Melbourne from this period. But for researchers in Europe, North America and Australia, the category of moral imbecility within the high-grade feebleminded was a different matter altogether. High-grade imbecility was notoriously difficult to measure, it was not picked up in intelligence testing which had begun in most countries from the 1920s, and moral imbeciles were often cunning, manipulative and highly intelligent. These difficulties gave psychologists reason to develop further tests which would measure moral or affective traits in individuals. The psycho-physiology of mental functions, which was receiving attention in anatomy and physiology departments world wide, failed to be a reliable indicator of certain types of mentality. Indeed, personality disorder only came into being after personality studies in the United States and the United Kingdom had been able to produce a statistical account of the co-relations between disorderly behaviour and psychological traits. Significantly, the closer that moral imbeciles approximated the normal in these tests, the more dangerous they were considered to be.

The connections which can be drawn between institutional sites and modes of calculating is a major focus of this study, because it was in the educational institutions, special schools, psychological clinics, children's homes, clinics of the Children's Court, as well as the precincts of lunacy and mental hygiene authorities that the statistical measures of individuals were carried out. In Australia, the links between behaviours and certain kinds of personality were fabricated during the late 1940s with the pioneering work of newly opened psychological clinics attached to institutions like the Children's Court and special homes built for children with mental and behavioural problems. In broad terms, these kinds of developments provided the theoretical and practical underpinnings of a mental hygiene strategy in the first half of this century, linking psychiatry, psychology and the education professions in a forward program of assessment and preventative measures. These were an important plank in government-supported public health programs linked to creches, kindergartens, school health and children's welfare services. In policy terms the professional link-ups were not just a nice idea; they were an essential element of what was basically a system of risk management. They were also an early strand in the now familiar shift from asylum to community-based mental health services.

Thus, in contemporary law and psychiatry the term antisocial personality disorder has become the centre of considerable controversy. Many doubt that it can be usefully thought of as a mental illness. Others point out that even if it is a good description of mental pathology, it may be so contiguous with criminality itself as to be of no use in individualising sentences. This study provides an alternative approach to this problem. It focuses on the borderlines between jurisprudence and the 'psy' sciences by means of a genealogy of antisocial personality disorder. The study shows that personality disorder, and indeed the larger concept of personality, arose as a product of efforts to know and govern certain categories of disordered persons who came to be seen in the course of the late nineteenth and early twentieth centuries as particularly dangerous.

The dangerousness of this group lay in part in their inability to fit easily into existing categories like idiocy, insanity or imbecility. The study suggests that the main imperative was an administrative one rather than a question of either science or social control. From the perspective of government, subjects were distributed as a continuum of cognitive conditions requiring various kinds of management. Those with little cognitive ability required containment in long-term care facilities, as did the chronically insane. The recognition of acute cases, that is, treatable insanity, gave birth to the 'mental hospital' in the early twentieth century. Normal people could be governed through the dominant liberal model of self-government. The residual population that came to trouble liberal governments consisted of those who were capable of normal cognitive functioning, were not insane, and yet could not be relied upon to self-govern. The study shows that personality arose as a space for interventions aimed at shaping the capacity to self-regulate in those in whom it was problematic.

The study moves from nineteenth-century separations within institutions of lunacy to the psychological and physiological discourses aimed at developing an understanding of this borderline group, and hopefully a measure as well. The early work concentrated on showing deformities in the architecture of the brain. Disordered personalities were a product, from this perspective, of the absence from some individuals of the structures designed to lengthen the physiological links between stimuli and responses, which formed the space for 'prudence'. This early work was enough to encourage new laws and institutions in the 1920s aimed at identifying and treating disorders from out of populations like school children. The problem with this approach is that it did not yield a ready metric for intervention. A second wave of scientific theory in the 1930s through to the 1950s moved out from the specificity of the subject to look at relations with others. The sociopath was increasingly seen as a problem of relationships rather than the deep internal structure of individuals. The term personality fitted this new imperative to map social relations and the spaces between people rather than internal features of a subject. Within this new space was a class of individuals with 'defective personalities' whose conduct could not be effectively dealt with through standard psychotherapeutic treatment or through penal law. What they required were interventions aimed at the capacity for self-government.

The study concludes that if personality disorder is itself a kind of artefact of a whole history of efforts at governance in liberal societies then perhaps it is the requirements of liberal government itself which need to be debated and studied, rather than the suitability of one or another set of labels.

1   Law, psychiatry and the problem of disorder

> For many, you are the fear that quickens their steps as they walk alone, or that causes a parent to look anxiously at a clock when a child is late. I suspect that you will never fully comprehend why this should be so, as, for reasons which we do not understand, you are not one of us.
> (Mr Justice Vincent, Supreme Court of Victoria, cited in *The Sunday Age*, 28 August 1994, on the sentencing of a man found guilty on three charges of murder in 1993 in Melbourne.)

The prisoner is not known, perhaps even to himself, except in his dangerousness. The newspaper provides a brief report on the psychological and psychiatric evidence that the prisoner has an antisocial personality disorder, and that the precise cause of the disorder is '. . . unknown, beyond a complex, unpredictable cocktail of personal characteristics, early childhood experiences and possible instances of minor brain damage'.

It has now become commonplace to link the psycho-medical concept of antisocial personality disorder with calculations of dangerousness and explanations for the violation of social norms. The language and conceptual terrain of personality disorder has entered into the routines of calculating and administering 'problem' groups in social work, the magistrates' courts, the mental health system, as well as in cases of horrific crime. Justice Vincent may well have reflected a level of community outrage at the crimes for which the individual appearing before him had been found guilty; he may also have reflected a general impression that somehow this person might exist 'outside of society'. But his remarks also point to a number of ways in which this individual is 'not known' within the conventional categories of persons which present in the penal system.

This 'failure to know' the individual is not simply one of the judge's making. In the last few decades, much attention has been given in psychiatric, psychological and legal studies literature to a multitude of problems at the interface between law and psychiatry: the difficulty of predicting dangerousness, the problem of evaluating levels of individual culpability in criminal acts, and the broader interrelations between the criminal justice and mental health systems over the management and treatment of offenders.[1] One underlying premise has perhaps been that law and medicine have a reciprocal role to play in a penal system which increasingly makes judgement on the criminal rather than the crime, in the interests of delivering a better justice system.[2] Or is it, as some would argue, that law and medicine simply have different professional interests to pursue: the doctor concerned with diagnosis and treatment, the courts with the relationship between a person and a particular act?[3] In these domains, a field of 'personhood' arguably remains problematic and many of these difficulties stem in part from basic problems of definition. For example, there is still no authoritative and generally accepted medical definition of what constitutes 'disease of the mind'.[4] Whether or not antisocial personality disorder is a mental illness is a source of ongoing uncertainty in both law and psychiatry.[5] Diagnosis of mental illness is considered to lack reliability, especially in the court system. And finally, psychiatry is not regarded as capable of predicting dangerousness with any great precision.[6] Indeed, while the public, the courts, the legal community and the legislators often see psychiatry as the professional group most rightfully charged with the responsibility to predict the potential dangerousness of individuals, the results of much of the research into predicting dangerousness seriously question the existence of any such special insight and many psychiatrists would themselves shy from any such claims. In Cocozza and Steadman's research, for example, the single factor influencing psychiatrists in their decisions about dangerousness was the seriousness of the charge on which a defendant was arrested – a factor which, they argue, any professional or lay person could employ.[7] A public view equating mental health issues with dangerousness is one which psychiatry has long sought to correct.

The main body of studies on predicting dangerousness offers little support for the validity of clinical predictions, although for various reasons the evidence is regarded as inconclusive. There are consistent findings of over-prediction of dangerousness by psychiatrists and psychologists dating from the 'first generation' studies of the so-called Baxtrom patients.[8] These studies involved a follow-up of a quarter of almost one thousand patients after their transfer from a prison hospital for the criminally insane to civil mental hospitals as a result of a United States Supreme Court finding in 1966 of wrongful detainment. The studies showed that after four years only nine individuals had been convicted, mostly for non-violent offences. These early studies have been criticised for their sampling problems, the failure to distinguish between dangerous disposition and the actual occurrence of a violent act, the tendency to underestimate actual violence, and also the difficulties of generalising findings to a range of settings.[9] However, more recent 'second generation' studies argued more cautiously that little is known about dangerousness predictions, as they tended to focus on predictions within particular settings and over shorter time periods. On these studies it was concluded:

. . . predictive accuracy remains to be demonstrated, even in the short term, but the available research cannot be regarded as definitive because of methodological shortcomings . . . [I]t is also likely that ethical constraints may preclude definitive studies being carried out, since those predicted to be violent are usually subject to interventions which prevent the testing out of the prediction. It therefore remains possible that predictions are valid under some conditions.[10]

Besides their interface at the question of predicting dangerousness, another important formal context in which law and psychiatry enmesh in a legal setting has to do with the rules governing the use of expert evidence about a criminal defendant's mental abnormality, in order for the defendant to sustain a plea of 'diminished responsibility'. The place of psychiatric expertise in these cases varies depending on the jurisdiction. To cite an Australian example, the procedures relating to the defence of diminished responsibility are a consequence of amendments in 1974 to the NSW Crimes Act Section 23a (1), which Gillies summarises as follows:

Where, on a trial of a person for murder, it appears that at the time of the acts or omissions causing the death the charged person was suffering from such abnormality of mind (whether arising from a condition of arrested or retarded development of mind or any inherent causes or induced by disease or injury) as substantially impaired his mental responsibility for the acts or omissions, he shall not be convicted of murder.[11]

The defence would be obliged to lead expert evidence if it wished to elucidate the nature of the defendant's mental abnormality, although it would be for a jury to decide what weight to put on this evidence and whether other sources of evidence should be considered. The English decision in *Byrne* (1960) has been treated by courts in that country as the leading statement of the elements of the defence, and the notion of 'abnormality of mind' contained in that decision is the foundational concept of the amendment in the state of New South Wales and some of the other Australian states.[12] It has been further explained, in a court ruling in *Biess* (1967) in the state of Queensland, that although 'abnormality of mind' is a legal rather than a medical concept, it is nevertheless synonymous with mental illness and must normally be identified and proved by evidence based on medical science generally, or psychiatry in particular; that is, that mere 'loss of control followed by impulsive, aggressive behaviour does not, of itself, indicate such an abnormality since it is a phenomenon of normal behaviour'.[13] Moreover, it was not required in law that the abnormality be identified as an 'inherent' one, although it must be 'virtually permanent' in order to be characterised in terms of the inherent leg of the provision. Subsequent to these rulings, the range of conditions satisfying the concept of abnormality of mind has been broadened, including the condition known as psychopathy (deriving from 'inherent causes') as well as epilepsy and depression. On the other hand, factors designated as 'psycho-social . . . (psychological and social influences resulting from the defendant's environment) would not by themselves be considered as abnormality of mind, but they may be when combined with disease or injury. The English decision of the Court of Criminal Appeal in *Byrne* (1960) was an important point of separation and difference, between the common law defence of insanity and the statutory defence of diminished responsibility. In summary, compared to the insanity defence, diminished responsibility 'may be grounded by reference to a much wider spectrum of disorders or disruptions of the mental process' – the defence could present evidence that while a defendant's cognitive process might be more or less normal, his emotional state at the time of the killing was such that his mental responsibility for the killing was substantially impaired, provided that the emotional state derived from a relevant abnormality of mind.[14]

Finally, a broader question remains whether the criminal justice and mental health systems in tandem provide an effective or reliable way of managing individuals as well as protecting communities from potentially dangerous persons.[15] Bernadette McSherry's review of the rules of law governing a defence on the ground of 'automatism' (the name given in some jurisdictions to 'conduct which is involuntary') showed that the eventual disposition of persons in cases where this defence had been used tended to be fairly arbitrary, and depended on the available medical evidence before the court at the time and on the question of what was to be done with an acquitted person who might be dangerous:

. . . the courts have allowed factors relevant to the question of what to do with an acquitted person who may be dangerous in the future to impinge upon the assessment of who should or should not be excused from criminal responsibility.[16]

In addition, there is criminological evidence in Australia and the United Kingdom that psychiatric diagnoses of the condition known as antisocial personality disorder added a 'spurious scientificity' to court proceedings and an equally spurious promise of rehabilitative treatment in the prison system.[17] The physical conditions of imprisonment made it impossible for prison authorities to act on even the most basic psychiatric diagnosis, added to which conditions in prisons could be shown in fact to cause violent and abnormal behaviour.

In the face of seemingly intractable difficulties in calculating and predicting dangerousness, governments have attempted to find solutions through changed sentencing policies and other means. Across jurisdictions, these attempts by government have displayed varying degrees of sensitivity to establishing a balance between the rights of the dangerous individual to treatment or care, and the rights of the community to protection.[18]

Governing dangerousness: comparative legal perspectives

The sentencing issues and broader questions of the disposition of offenders may be examined by looking at successive attempts by authorities to regulate the dangerous individual by changes to legislation.[19] In the United Kingdom many of these issues can be traced to legislative reform around the treatment of capital offences. Science and expertise generally took on a larger role in English courts after the passage of the Homicide Act 1957, which had opened up the possibility of the plea of diminished responsibility. The new legislation was designed to introduce flexibility in sentencing for murder which previously had been absent. For capital murder the punishment was death, and for simple murder life imprisonment. Capital murder included murder by shooting and murder in the course of theft. In the new legislation, section 2 (1) says 'where a person kills or is party to the killing of another, he shall not be convicted of murder if he was suffering from such abnormality of mind (whether arising from a condition of arrested or retarded development of mind or any inherent causes or induced by disease or injury) as substantially impaired his mental responsibility for his acts and omissions in doing or being a party to the killing'.[20] However, the new legislation also produced its own uncertainties and confusions.[21] An analysis two years following the Act showed that in two-thirds of the cases in which the plea of diminished responsibility had been raised, a verdict of manslaughter rather than murder was returned. In most of the successful cases, there was a record of mental instability prior to the crime for which the accused person was on trial, but other factors distinguishing the successful from the unsuccessful plea were more difficult to find. For example, there appeared to be little recourse to evidence of physical symptoms of disease as a way of defining the kind of mental disorder that might lead to diminished responsibility. There did not appear to be anything significant about the nature of the crime to distinguish between the successful and unsuccessful plea. Nor was there evidence that diminished responsibility was being interpreted by English juries in terms of an intellectual capacity. The most common diagnostic categories used by examining doctors, usually prison medical officers, were depression followed by personality disorder, schizophrenia, brain damage and mental handicap.[22] A common feature of the medical reports in which a diagnosis of diminished responsibility was reached were references to 'emotional immaturity', 'mental instability' or 'psychopathic personality' of the persons concerned, indicating at least some degree of consensus within medical opinion about the type of mentality said to be associated with impaired responsibility. Significantly, however, if it were asked by what kind of evidence the presence of these conditions was established, any consensus immediately started to break down.

So while the 1957 legislation permitted greater flexibility in sentencing for capital offences – to the relief of many, it opened up alternative avenues to the mandatory death penalty – it also raised considerable if not insurmountable problems. It imposed upon juries the burden of having to answer questions which many believed at the time were not only beyond the competence of experts, but by their nature were not answerable by anyone.[23] Ironically, the amendments may even have given encouragement to courts to allow those who are most likely to commit further crimes to be returned to the community more quickly than those whose criminal propensities were less definite or predictable. Applying the McNaghten rules was regarded as child's play compared with the problem of assessing responsibility. Moreover, the logic of the amendments seemed to run directly counter to the requirements of social protection, in that a person considered to be not fully responsible was afforded the opportunity of a lighter sentence.

A more comprehensive inquiry into the effects of introducing the provisions of the diminished responsibility defence was carried out several years later for the Institute of Psychiatry in London.[24] A survey over the ten-year period from 1966 to 1977 showed a steady rise in the number of men convicted of manslaughter by reason of diminished responsibility, mirroring a rise in the number of men convicted of homicide overall. The survey revealed that in 1964 half of the offenders were given hospital orders, and this proportion rose to seventy per cent by the end of the sixties. But then the proportion of hospital orders started to decline, falling to a third in the seventies and then to a quarter of all cases. At the same time the use of imprisonment increased substantially. According to the report, the reason was a reduction in the number of cases in which the reporting doctor recommended a hospital order. Further, a comparison of the medical officers' recommendations and the category of diagnosis showed that while hospital orders were maintained or increased for prisoners diagnosed with schizophrenia, there was a decline of up to a half in the recommendations for prisoners diagnosed with depression or with a personality disorder. Even without the required doctor's recommendation for a hospital order a judge could opt for a non-custodial sentence, yet a clear preference was given for imprisonment. The report argued that judges, faced for example with a psychopathic homicide, would want a secure institutional place, 'and would therefore turn to the one institution which lacks the power to refuse admission'.[25] It concluded that if the mandatory sentence for murder was abolished '. . . there would be an end to the stretchings and manoeuvres which have now to be undertaken in order to give homicides suitable, instead of unsuitable, sentences. Not only the defendant, but judges, doctors, and lawyers would benefit from the change.'[26]

The Butler Report in England in 1975 recommended changes to the provisions originally laid down in the Mental Health Act 1959, where in the United Kingdom the term 'psychopathic disorder' first appeared. Changes were recommended including abandonment of the term psychopath and replacing it with 'personality disorder', and provision for hospital orders in cases where the disorder was believed to be connected to a medical or psychological disorder and where there was an expectation of therapeutic benefit from hospital admission. Psychopaths sent to prison were to be placed in special experimental units for their treatment, and a 'reviewable sentence' would be available for dangerous mentally disturbed offenders who could not be dealt with under the Mental Health Act 1959. But the recommendations came to nought and the problems persisted – or as one legal commentator put it 'the medical model has failed the psychopath'.[27] Academic lawyers in the United Kingdom were critical of the medical profession because of the way in which the treatability issue had been handled in legal trials. Many believed the health service in Britain had abdicated its responsibility by refusing to admit psychopaths on the grounds that they were not amenable to treatment, and that the trend towards the imprisonment of these persons had accelerated. They suggested that if the definition of medical treatment could be extended to include 'nursing . . . and care and training under medical supervision', a legal framework could be set up which would allow a more appropriate and just treatment of severe personality disordered persons. In practice, the alternative was prison, often for fairly short periods of time because of the petty nature of the crime, and in an increasingly overcrowded system which provided limited care and greater control problems. The circumstances were created in which both law and medicine could retreat from overseeing and taking responsibility for the troublesome antisocial personality disordered individual.

From the detailed analysis, it is clear that many inside and outside the legal community who were opposed to capital punishment welcomed the flexibility in sentencing provided for in the amendments to the Homicide Act 1957. But for others, the system also resembled an attempt to 'ride two horses simultaneously in the opposite direction'[28] which could be avoided only by removing the onus on medicine to make judgements on the vexed question of individual will or culpability. If the notion of the responsibility of the defendant could be allowed just to wither away, psychiatrists would no longer need to masquerade as moralists but could adopt their proper role as applied scientists – analysing causes, predicting developments and indicating methods of control. If one could just forget about responsibility, so the argument went, we need not ask whether the offender *should* be punished but only whether he is likely to benefit from punishment.

In the decades following the introduction of diminished responsibility legislation, the old insanity defence became virtually obsolete in the United Kingdom.[29] In jurisdictions within the United States, on the other hand, the McNaghten principle had dominated until the 1960s, but throughout the 1960s and 1970s the insanity defence was expanded considerably to include both cognitive and volitional components of a defendant's actions. The cognitive aspect required that the defendant '. . . could not appreciate the nature or wrongfulness of his act', while the volitional required that the defendant '. . . could not control his conduct so as to conform to the law'.[30] The application of the volitional aspect, as well as the emphasis in the first on the term 'appreciate' rather than simply 'know', were generally understood as an expansion of the grounds of diminished responsibility.[31] These two components were the essence of the American Model Penal Code test for insanity which had developed during the 1950s and gradually came to supplant the McNaghten test. (The test came to be known as ALI because it was a product of the American Law Institute.) Although developed in the 1950s, the ALI came into its own in the 1960s and 1970s based on an increased confidence that psychiatry and psychology had developed to the extent that volition was knowable and testable, both in science and law. The state of Idaho, for example, moved from McNaghten to the ALI in 1967 on the grounds that the McNaghten test was too restrictive, while in 1975 the American Bar Association officially adopted the two prongs of the ALI in the light of a 'wave of clinical optimism' around the scientificity of the concept of volition.[32]

During the 1980s the tide turned against psychiatry and against what it promised, more specifically for its promise of a science of volition. Unquestionably the impetus for this public loss of faith was the successful plea of insanity by John Hinckley, stalker of Jodie Foster and would-be assassin of President Reagan, who was diagnosed as having an antisocial personality disorder. Hinckley relied on the volitional aspect of the ALI for his defence, and his successful plea of insanity caused a public outcry. One academic lawyer noted:

The Hinckley acquittal brought to a head a long-smoldering discontent with the defense based on a widely held perception that particularly within the past two decades the insanity defense has developed serious and counterproductive flaws.[33]

The Hinckley case was the impetus for principal bodies such as the American Bar Association, the National Mental Health Association and the American Psychiatric Association to form working groups to revise and consolidate their position on questions of the insanity defence and diminished responsibility. The Bar Association had an explicit change of policy in which it rejected the volitional element of the ALI.[34] The American Psychiatric Association focused on clearing up psychiatry's relation to the courts and the status of its evidence, in particular about what it could and could not be asked to deliberate upon. In 1983, the APA position was summarised by the *Washington Post*:

Psychiatrists are unable to predict which persons might be dangerous . . . and their testimony in court cases should be limited to the areas of their expertise – the defendant's mental state and motivation . . . but not on whether a defendant is insane or can be held legally responsible.[35]

The APA wanted to defend the insanity defence because it rested on a fundamental tenet of criminal law, '. . . that punishment for wrongful deeds should be predicated upon moral responsibility', and that persons so mentally confused that they do not comprehend what they are doing should not be expected to bear responsibility for something they cannot understand. Nevertheless, against a groundswell of scepticism, they also argued that persons should be acquitted on grounds of insanity only if they were diagnosed as having a 'serious' mental disorder, which usually meant a psychosis rather than the 'less serious antisocial personality disorder'. A person with a psychosis was frequently out of touch with reality, whereas a person with an antisocial personality disorder usually knows he is committing anti-social acts but does not care.

The positions held by both legal and psychiatric bodies found their way into Congressional Hearings, and the legislative changes that followed in 1984 determined that mental health professionals could no longer render an opinion to a jury on the question of the defendant's sanity.[36] These bodies were needing to make concessions as a way of preventing the more radical conservatism of the Reagan administration from having free rein and, if not abolishing the defence altogether, restricting it to the application of the concept of *mens rea*, under which 'the defendant's mental condition would only have been a defense if it prevented the government from proving a required mental element of the offence, such as that the defendant acted willfully'.[37] In the washup, the Comprehensive Crimes Control Act instituted the most profound changes to sentencing guidelines and a narrowing of the insanity defence, which came to be limited to 'persons who could not appreciate the nature or wrongfulness of their conduct' and 'no longer applies to persons who simply claim they could not control their conduct and acted due to an irresistible impulse'.[38]

In Australia, a landmark case in the state of Victoria (*Attorney-General* v. *David*) sharpened dramatically the points of contention between law and psychiatry which had been in evidence in other jurisdictions for some time. In 1989, a Victorian parliamentary committee concluded that antisocial personality disorder could not be classified as a treatable mental illness.[39] The committee tried to address the limitations faced by both the criminal justice and mental health systems to manage persons considered to be dangerous. It reported at a time when the government, with uncertain authority and jurisdiction, could not resolve the problem of the need to confine one particular person who was considered dangerous. Gary Ian Patrick David (alias Webb) was convicted in 1980 of shooting and crippling two people and was sentenced to fourteen years gaol. While in gaol he was hospitalised more than eighty times for a range of self-inflicted injuries, including cutting off his nipples and parts of his penis. On release from gaol, David had threatened to become 'Australia's most brutal mass murderer'. When he had completed a prison sentence and at the time of his release, a Mental Health Review Board, made up of psychiatrists, lawyers and lay-persons, refused to rule that he was mentally ill. They found instead that he suffered from an 'antisocial or borderline personality disorder'. Prior to this, the Victorian Law Reform Commission had recommended that the relevant mental health legislation should be amended so as to allow the involuntary confinement of persons who suffered from an antisocial personality disorder and who were dangerous. Eventually, the government enacted the Community Protection Act, considered by one jurist an 'extraordinary and unprecedented piece of legislation',[40] giving the Supreme Court power to detain this one individual beyond the expiration of his sentence. The prisoner/patient was placed in specially constructed confinement and alternated between prison and hospital until his death in 1993, not because of a crime he had committed or because he was diagnosed as mentally ill, but because of specific legislation enacted to secure him for what he *might* do. One psychiatrist, William Glaser, who was also a member of the Mental Health Review Board, commented that 'society had failed' in the Gary David case, due to a 'fundamental inability to define conceptual boundaries'.[41]

The same parliament in more recent times has passed legislation similar to that in other parts of the world designed to increase the penalties for serious sexual offenders and serious violent offenders, by empowering courts to impose indefinite sentences for persons convicted of such offences, and requiring courts under certain circumstances to consider the 'condition' of the convicted person, including the 'character' of the person. The Sentencing Act 1991 in Victoria applied to a person who 'appears to be suffering from a mental illness that requires treatment', in circumstances where 'the treatment can be obtained by admission to and detention in a psychiatric in-patient service' and where the court has received a report 'from the authorised psychiatrist of the psychiatric in-patient service to which it is proposed to admit the person'.[42] In contrast, the later Sentencing (Amendment) Act 1993 allowed for an indefinite sentence if it was satisfied to a high degree of probability that the offender was a serious danger to the community. Serious danger may exist because of the nature and gravity of the offence, and because of the offender's 'character, past history, age, health or mental condition'.[43] In determining whether an offender is a serious danger, the court must consider questions of risk and whether the serious offence is 'exceptional', but also 'anything relevant to this issue contained in the certified transcript' and 'any medical, psychiatric or other relevant report received by it'.[44] Although the amendment makes reference to assessment, diagnosis and treatment covered in early Acts, these conditions appear to constitute a considerable extension of the provisions of the 1991 Principal Act.

The David case resulted in the enactment of a specific law for a specific individual, in circumstances of an administrative inability to 'know' a person in ways which would permit their proper management – an instance, perhaps, of what we might call a 'failure of government'.[45] The case also prompted the state government to enact changes to the Mental Health Act which would allow involuntary patients who are no longer mentally ill to be detained for a period of a further three months, if in the opinion of the psychiatrist the patients would seriously harm themselves if released. A psychiatrist may apply for this extension to the chief psychiatrist, the application must be approved by a panel of three psychiatrists each of whom interviews the patient, and the Mental Health Review Board needed to approve the application and notify the Public Advocate of the application.[46]

Let us return to Glaser's point about ill-defined conceptual boundaries to try to make sense of these local governmental attempts to manage dangerousness. Much of the debate between law and psychiatry around the Gary David case focused on the work of the Victorian Law Reform Commission, an advisory body to government with a long-term interest in the trial, disposition and release of people who have been found unfit to be tried or not guilty of an offence by reason of mental illness. It has published extensively in the field.[47] In a 1986 interim report, *The Concept of Mental Illness in the Mental Health Act*, the Commission recommended that the Mental Health Act should be amended in order that a person who suffered only from an antisocial personality disorder, and who was dangerous, should not be prevented from being considered mentally ill for the purposes of the Act. The purpose of the proposed amendment at that time was to put beyond doubt the extent of powers under the Act to detain people who were mentally ill, and who also posed a serious threat to the public. The Commission Report was extremely critical of decisions by the Mental Health Review Board on personality disorder. The Board had decided, in an earlier case, that a person suffering from a borderline personality disorder fell within the meaning of 'mental illness'. But in a carefully wrought set of distinctions,[48] the Board indicated that its decision was strictly limited to borderline and not antisocial personality disorder, on the grounds that the existing Mental Health Act explicitly stated that a person could not be considered mentally ill merely because he or she had an 'antisocial *personality*' (the distinction being whether one had a *disorder*). The Mental Health Review Board had also rejected the view that the meaning of 'mental illness' could be determined by reference to 'the views of ordinary sensible people' on the grounds that, since other parts of the Act required consideration of treatment and care, the view of an expert group – psychiatrists – had to be relied upon.

The Law Reform Commission rejected most of the Mental Health Review Board's arguments. It proposed that psychiatrists could still decide what treatment was appropriate for the mentally ill, but '. . . without definitively labelling that condition for the purposes of the application of Section 8 [of the Act]. That is a legal question not a psychiatric one.'[49] Moreover, the Commission pointed out that a majority of psychiatrists was against the classification of antisocial personality disorder as a mental illness, but that this view was formed on the grounds that the disorder was largely untreatable. Treatability, the Commission said, should not be regarded as the defining condition of mental illness any more than it should be regarded as the defining condition of a physical illness such as senility. The Commission found other arguments of the Mental Health Review Board either untenable or irrelevant. These included a concern expressed by the Board about the proportion of mental health resources taken up by personality disorders, and about changes to legislation that would compromise psychiatry in its long-standing battles over the distinction between 'mad and bad'. The Commission pointed out that psychiatry regularly treated people with antisocial personality disorders as voluntary patients, and that the Mental Health Act in Victoria was inconsistent with legislation in other jurisdictions which allowed for the involuntary commitment of people who constituted a serious danger and who suffered only from antisocial personality disorder, such as had operated in Tasmania, South Australia, Western Australia and parts of the United Kingdom.

In its debate with psychiatry, the law reform position was defended in terms of the law's public duty to protect the rights of citizens. It was the province of legal process to determine on the question of a person and an act. While it may be perfectly clear to psychiatry that the criterion of mental illness was the systematic inability to function rationally – that a person had lost his or her reason – the general community nevertheless was entitled to question the professional judgement upon which the civil liberty of citizens depended, particularly in those borderline areas of definition between the mad and bad, the hospital and prison.[50] The role of legislation was to state clearly what mental illness was, and what it was not, and in the case of persons deemed to be dangerous a balance had to be struck to ensure society's protection from dangerousness on the one hand, and the rights of these persons to appropriate treatment and care on the other. For example, one senior penologist opposed what he called 'the humanitarian theory of punishment', a 'tyranny' under which crime and disease became the same thing: 'any state of mind which "we" choose to call "disease" can be treated as crime and compulsorily cured'.[51] In line with this view and in support of the civil liberties argument, the Law Reform Commission recommended amendments to the Mental Health Act to include *all* people who are mentally ill. Explaining the recommendation, it wrote:

The Act should not arbitrarily exclude a particular group of mentally ill people merely because psychiatrists classify their underlying condition as a disorder rather than an illness; or because psychiatrists cannot successfully treat them; or because they create major problems for the mental health system. The Commission's strong view is that mentally ill people should be dealt with in the mental health system. Prison is an inappropriate place for such people. The only people who would be detained as a result of enacting the proposed sub-section 8(4) [of the Act] are people who are considered to be mentally ill because of antisocial personality disorder and are highly dangerous. The provision would be used only rarely. The suggestion that it would result in substantial net-widening and that it is a threat to civil liberties is groundless.[52]

The claim over civil liberties came from members of the psychiatric profession, from some legal expertise, and from civil liberties and health consumer groups. On this side of the scorecard, the psychiatrist Glaser attempted to clarify the conceptual boundaries. The decision to exclude the disorder was in keeping with the definitions of 'key concepts', and 'the development of *psychological* concepts such as "personality" and "personality disorder"' (*emphasis added*):

'Personality' simply refers to a person's characteristic way of functioning psychologically: in the same way that people may be fat, thin or bald, so various individuals may be described as shy, friendly or sensitive. A 'personality disorder' differs from a 'normal' personality only as a matter of degree. Thus, we all do morally and socially 'bad' things some of the time; and a person with an 'anti-social personality disorder' is just somewhat more 'bad' than the rest of the community. She or he lies, cheats, has trouble with the police, is involved in multiple unstable relationships and has a poor work record.[53]

Personality, Glaser argued, referred to a way of functioning psychologically since childhood. In contrast, mental illness resulted in a qualitative change in personality, involving a fairly sudden change in behaviour. Granted that the Mental Health Act did not define what mental illness was, it did set out the conditions to be satisfied before a mentally ill person could be involuntarily admitted to a hospital. On this point, psychiatry established the justification for excluding personality disorder. Section 8(2) of the Act listed antisocial personality disorder alongside instances of 'social and political deviance' which ought not to be used to justify involuntary detention: expressing certain political beliefs, engaging in unusual forms of sexual activity, or being intellectually disabled. In addition, because of their social position some persons were more likely to be defined as having antisocial personality than others. In this view, an attempt to assert that 'persistent badness' was an illness which must be treated against a person's will constituted a danger to civil liberties and was antithetical to a free society.[54] So both sides of the argument were to claim the protection of freedoms as part of their armoury. And importantly for our later arguments, personality was to be designated a psychological concept.

Objections to the Commission's proposed changes to mental health legislation in Victoria also came from mental health consumer groups, who asserted the rights of those suffering from mental illness to be protected from the abusive and disruptive behaviours of persons with a personality disorder.[55] They argued that the inclusion of personality disorder under the Mental Health Act would stigmatise mental illness while not offering any benefit to those suffering from such disorders. From this point of view, doctors already acted within questionable legal frameworks. Dangerousness was difficult to predict and diagnoses of personality disorders changed over time – did not the *Diagnostic and Statistical Manual* at one time classify homosexuality as a disorder?[56] Surely the category of disorder was open to abuse and infringement, simply because it was historically and socially defined? The Council for Civil Liberties in Victoria concluded:

The favoured way would be for the most part, to implement the present *Crimes Act*, and if necessary, extend that, where a person is thought to be dangerous and should be detained. The community should be honest and own a *Dangerous Persons Act*.[57]

Some have described proposed changes to the law as an attempt to change the medical facts of mental illness to conform to theory. What was needed was a more flexible legal theory to accommodate the need to further detention of persons who posed a threat, rather than resorting to 'fictions' about a person's psychiatric condition.[58] Others have argued that a 'detentionist' view was the better alternative to 'retributism' and 'protectionism', and that a genuine alternative to ideas of 'just deserts' and 'public protection' might be found in a new kind of institution of confinement having its justification in neither of these camps, a 'social protection institution' in some ways analogous to a quarantine centre.[59]

The committee looking at this in the Victorian Parliament recommended a staged re-entry into the community for the quite specific category of the dangerous individual, one which should be more supported by post-release programs, and using high security accommodation currently in use for prisoners with intellectual disability and protected witnesses. The committee also suggested looking at the Crimes Act in relation to persons who make generalised or particular threats to kill. In an attempt to skirt around the conundrum set up by law and psychiatry, it stated:

The real issue is the perceived dangerousness of the person, not an argument about what causes them to be dangerous. The Law Reform Commission solution would achieve detention of the dangerous person by defining them as mentally ill. For some reason in our system, it is seen as OK to detain people, so long as it is for a mental illness, rather than to detain preventatively to stop them from manifesting dangerous behaviour. So in a way we thought it was a dishonest way of achieving detention.[60]

The committee went on to look at ways of reducing the dangerousness of a person rather than simply searching for some legal means of detention.

A more recent review in the United Kingdom, published by the Home Office and the Department of Health, has used the term 'dangerous severely personality disordered' (DSPD) to describe a small group of people who pose a high risk to others because of serious antisocial behaviour resulting from their disorder.[61] The review calls for public responses to two main recommendation options focused around this new penal/psychiatric amalgam. The first retains the existing statutory framework but would permit greater use of discretionary life sentences with improved quality of information available to the courts, as well as removing the requirement of 'likely to benefit from hospital treatment' in the case of DSPD individuals detained in civil proceedings. As part of the first option package, specialist facilities in prisons and hospitals would be improved and the links and protocols between the two services would be developed. The second option proposes a period of compulsory assessment in a specialist facility, and a person under this direction would be detained in that facility until such time as they were no longer considered to present a serious risk. Both policy options recommend amending the criminal sections in the Mental Health Act 1983 to remove the power of courts to order admission to hospital in cases where an offender is diagnosed as suffering from 'psychopathic disorder'.

Much of the above discussion about the confusions and uncertainties around personality disorder draws attention to what is claimed to be a failure of language to describe adequately the realities of the two domains of law and psychiatry, beginning with the absence of unambiguous definitions of mental illness itself, as well as the competing claims to the truth of personality disorder.[62] The point about clarity of definition is doubly made in the case of disorders because, as McSherry argued, the terminology of personality disorder often becomes a 'loose label' to describe a broad range of people who have merely exhibited antisocial behaviour.[63] Other studies have pointed to the way language can manipulate the facts of medical science to accommodate the prejudices of lawyers, penologists, civil libertarians and ethical philosophers. For example, a claim of 'misuse of language' is made by the academic lawyer C. R. Williams against the Law Reform Commission, which had argued that involuntary detention of persons with antisocial personality disorder would be legitimate simply if it could be authorised under the 'care' provisions of the existing Mental Health Act.[64]

These approaches tend to focus on the way language fails to grasp the truth of its objects, and that it misrepresents and confuses realities. However, what is lost in this attention to language as an instrument of representation is its productive aspect: the way language carves out new domains of existence, new categories of person, new spaces for the play of power. This is not to say that these approaches have no relevance. On the contrary, the struggles between law and medicine over the definition of persons is a crucial site of contemporary politics – one that reveals more than simply faulty thinking or bad science. Such struggles show that political interests have a bearing directly on the practice of law, and that individual states of being are constructed in terms of these contestations. But the focus on language merely as misrepresentation of a pre-existing reality overlooks the possibility of viewing the language of law and psychiatry as instrumental in producing new forms of thought about persons, and new ways of calculating those very areas of human affairs which need to be managed and governed. It is to suggest that language as an 'intellectual technology' acts over time to produce knowledges of particular types of existence and categories of person, in order to seek to manage individuals and govern populations.[65] It becomes possible to examine the history of the category of disorder precisely in these terms. Indeed, this book develops the argument that the category of antisocial personality disorder came into being, and undergoes change, under definite historical conditions and requirements of penal and mental health systems and the broader demands of governing populations. It is not merely a product of struggles between professional groups but rather an attempt by a range of knowledges to grasp the truth about those needing to be managed. Distinctions and specificities in terminology, such as the invoking of the term 'personality' as a site for locating disorder, came into being in answer to the requirements for persons within these populations to be pinpointed and fixed. In specific intersections of law and psychiatry, and in the context of specific technologies of liberal governance (such as the requirement for individuals to govern themselves), it becomes possible over time to 'think' the problem of dangerousness and violations of social order within the psycho-medical category of antisocial personality disorder. More broadly, these circumstances provided new territories and spaces for the workings of modern power over whole populations.

The David case provoked a number of discussions in the academic literature in Australia, ranging from questions concerning the place of violence in understanding social life,[66] to the interactions between expert knowledges and popular understandings of dangerousness in determining the outcome of a trial.[67] But the aim here has been instead

to survey the way in which these problems of knowledge and government are posed, as evidenced in legislative and governmental decisions
over time and in different jurisdictions, and to demonstrate what
Glaser called the failure in respect of 'conceptual boundaries'. The
governmental arrangements surveyed above have been problematised
historically, and it is to these accounts that we now turn as a way of
clarifying the specific approach to historical investigation contained in
this study.

Towards a genealogical approach

The two characteristics most in evidence in conventional historical work
on psychiatry and madness are what might be termed the 'history-as-
progress' narrative of the advance of psychiatric knowledge, found
mostly in the history of medicine and psychiatry itself; and secondly, the
various applications of social control theory which have sought to
explain the social functioning of medicine and psychiatry over time. The
approach seeks instead to utilise and extend the work on genealogy and
governmentality initiated by Michel Foucault and developed in a now
wide-ranging literature spanning two decades, aspects of which are
taken up at the end of this chapter. For the moment, let us briefly
examine each of the above aspects of historical work in turn.

In 1983, psychiatrist A. S. Ellis published his book *Eloquent Testimony*
on the history of mental health services in Western Australia. The cover
depicts the 'before and after' of psychiatric reform over the past two
centuries: on the one side, a mix of raving, violent and demented bodies
sprawled inside dark and barred cells overseen by callous attendants; on
the other a 1970s photograph of freedom in outdoor games with both
staff and patients enjoying the atmosphere of 'creative expression' in the
modern mental hospital.[68] This is a characteristic historical view of the
project of Western psychiatry. In Australia as in other places, much of
the story is about making visible and making known the 'mentally ill',
who emerge from the half-light of the early asylum thanks to the
dismantling work of psychiatry. Psychiatric histories speak of breaking
down the walls of the old asylum to reveal the existence of the real
mentally ill in the dark recesses of these institutions, awaiting their
discovery by means of the rational, liberatory practices of medicine. It is
back there, in the reform of dingy places of confinement, the lifting of
mechanical constraints on the body of the lunatic, the winning over of
an oppressive bureaucracy and apathetic public, that we are to find the
point of origin of the psychiatrist and modern psychiatric knowledge. As
Ellis tells it

the story reflects the changing attitudes towards the mentally ill, from nuisances who had to be restrained and cared for in custody, to sick individuals who could be treated, and who could maintain or regain their places in an increasingly complex society.[69]

Here the object of psychiatry is made to be the continuous figure of the mentally ill person coming to be discovered by a progressive mental science: 'from the beginning, the mentally ill were there'. These teleological narratives of psychiatry's discovery of mental illness provide a vantage point from which to view the early asylums and their practices, but they assume their object – the mentally ill – to be a pre-existing ahistorical given. An alternative view, not available to these lineal accounts, is to take seriously the marking out of the lunatic as first and foremost an administrative act – an act of separation and management within a bounded population – which then serves as a condition of possibility for the emergence of a specifically psychological medicine, the latter *following rather than preceding* the arrangement of bodies in the asylum.[70] The next chapter advances this argument in some detail, by reassessing conventional accounts of the 'dawn of psychiatry' in a way which no longer assumes the mentally ill as a fixed unchanging entity, but rather focuses on the means of calculating and distinguishing the particular kind of person who will become the object of the newly emerging psychiatric practice. For present purposes, tools of calculation become of particular interest as they are applied to the nineteenth-century separation of the lunatic and the criminal.

Psychiatry's own view of the progressive advance of psychiatry contrasts with accounts of the social and historical functioning of psychiatry which have tended to problematise the operation of medicine and psychiatry within the social theoretical terrain of deviance and social control. Indeed, the contrast points to a basic dichotomy between the promise of liberation and the burden of social control – a grid which frames much contemporary theorising about power, knowledge and social order. Of particular interest are the various accounts of the ways in which the human sciences might serve to control particular problem groups in society, in the sense that terminology is provided in ways which define problems in medical terms, or which justify or legitimate actions to constrain individuals and groups. Analyses focusing on 'deviance' show how the medical model has been used in the social construction of the reality of social problems and how interpretive processes have come to define the deviant as sick.[71] While the dominant conceptual terrain used in these analyses centres on the concept of social control, the kinds of approaches and conclusions reached vary considerably. Psychiatry and psychology have been ripe candidates for analysis of more-or-less overt functions of social control played out by institutional practices in asylums or psychotherapy or psychiatric diagnoses used in the courts. An instance was the socio-logical insight of the British criminologist D. K. Howard, who argued that the inmates of nineteenth-century prisons suffered from such severe physical and mental deterioration because of prison conditions that their appearance on release only confirmed Lombroso's theories on the 'constitutional' causes of criminality.[72] Similarly, *dementia praecox*, a term to be later replaced with schizophrenia, was thought to reflect the sufferers' total degeneration resulting from long-term incarceration in asylums rather than the symptoms of an actual disease, and the change in terminology was considered to be contingent on improved institutional arrangements.

Social historians have tackled the same kinds of problems embraced by the 'psychiatry as progress' school but working from a different set of questions and assumptions. They sought instead to try to explain why the asylum was considered a desirable and necessary institutional development in Western liberal democracies from the late eighteenth century, and also why it persisted as the main social policy approach to madness well beyond the period when reformers had recognised its limitations and failures. According to this view, all kinds of incarceration policies, including the prison, asylum, orphanage and almshouse, appeared on the scene more or less contemporaneously and cast doubt on the claims of psychiatric historians that the asylum was a reform consequent upon breakthroughs in the field of medicine – that is, as simply a logical outcome of medical science. Some have interpreted the rise of the asylum as a coercive response to the disciplinary problems of urban industrial society. Others have located the asylum along with other similar institutions as a response to a broader and more complex set of problems of social organisation and social stability. In the United States for example, the post-Revolutionary period of the 1820s and thirties became preoccupied with the origins of deviant and dependent behaviour and with a concern to produce remedies to 'faulty organisation' of the community.[73] The solution was to withdraw the insane from society and create a model environment. There has been considerable debate over these propositions and variations on them over the past three decades in the writing of history, where there is an attempt to elaborate a structure in sociological terms which links the practices of psychiatry with the problem of explaining social order.

Andrew Scull's *Museums of Madness* is perhaps the foundation text in critical sociological accounts of insanity, the asylum and the medical profession in Britain.[74] Scull accounts for the appearance of a specifically medical conception of lunacy throughout the nineteenth century as an outcome of medicalisation, the process of defining certain phenomena as illness which then require intervention by the medical profession for their treatment. The story of the birth of the asylum and the mental hospital consists of a grasp for medical control by a group of largely self-interested doctors who set about the manufacture of scientific claims about insanity as a way of ensuring their monopoly over the field, both at an intellectual level and financially. The sociological themes of rationalisation, labelling theory and professionalisation dominate the account. As Jeffrey Minson has pointed out, the work suffered from a unitary form of explanation such that important divisions within the profession itself were obscured and major shifts in psychiatric practice, such as the take-up of so-called moral treatment, were not able to be accounted for.[75] Neither was the role of medicine and moral entrepreneurship in the nineteenth-century campaigns in England for the reform of the family, where the private sphere became a privileged site for the emergence of 'individual deviations'. Minson also observed that historians' 'carceral tales' of oppression of individuals and social groups were unlikely to lead to a transformation of institutions like asylums. His critique of Scull's broad brush-stroke approach to the history of psychiatry has implications for the current study:

These 'moral' sciences and techniques indicate that the recasting of thinking on madness partly depended on the construction of definite categories of individual, person, moral responsibility, etc. against which psychopathological categories are defined. The latter are not simply imposed on pre-social moral persons. Here we touch on the . . . decline of conceptions of madness in terms of a rational human essence. What replaced this was an accent on 'individual differences' defined by reference to population norms over a wide range of individual behaviours.[76]

In a later chapter we will take up Minson's arguments against the totalising aspects of these historical accounts of psychiatry and the historical role of moral regulation which many of these accounts presume. In the meantime, it is important to show how social control theory has shaped not only the mainstream histories of psychiatry and madness but also the accounts of the relations between law and psychiatry and the range of 'individual behaviours', mental disorders and pathologies which have come to prominence during the twentieth century.

Relations between psychiatry and the legal system have been of concern to critical sociology in terms of the way psychiatry has become increasingly involved in defining various kinds of criminal behaviour as 'sick' or as indicative of individual pathology. Sociology would, for example, rail against attempts to define antisocial conduct such as aggression as a disorder which has a biological or genetic cause, such as is demonstrated in the work of Ginsburg, Moyer and Hare in the United States from the 1980s. In Australia, Denise Russell has explained the increasing dominance of bio-medical psychiatry in legal and penal matters as due to the absence of good alternative theories of criminality, the increased marketing of psychiatric drugs in the penal system, and the inroads of the bio-medical model into criminology.[77] For Russell, a telling instance of the medicalisation of criminality is to be found by making a comparison of the definition of antisocial personality disorder in *DSM–II* and *DSM–III*. The earlier description is reserved for individuals who are basically unsocialised and whose behaviour patterns 'bring them repeatedly into conflict with society', but with the caveat that '. . . a mere history of repeated legal and social offences is not sufficient to justify this diagnosis'. This contrasts with the *DSM–III* which states that '. . . the essential feature is a Personality Disorder in which there is a history of continuous and chronic anti-social behavior'. The later version also differs in that the outward behaviour offensive to others is stressed, as distinct from an 'inner state' which may or may not be problematic to others. In essence, Russell claims, there is no clear distinction between the antisocial disorder of the *DSM–III* and criminality.[78] Russell's critique shares some of the difficulties pointed to by Minson – an analysis, in terms of power relations, that an 'essential feature' of psychiatric practice must be its insidious and repressive functions.

One current explanation for the confusion between antisocial personality disorder and criminality is that there has never been a clear definition of insanity or mental disorder, and therefore theorists have always confused undesirable behaviours with mental aberration. The Sydney psychiatrist John Ellard, in his provocatively titled *Some Rules for Killing People* (1989), has traced the history of personality disorder to early attempts to formulate a taxonomy of psychiatric illness in the writings of Thomas Sydenham and Thomas Arnold at the end of the eighteenth century. Ellard saw in the modern term antisocial personality disorder a confusion of medicine and morals, the insane and the vicious, whose origins lay in a fundamental confusion in these founding texts about the meaning of insanity.[79] He cited Arnold's *Observations on the Nature, Kinds, Causes and Prevention of Insanity*, published in 1806, in which the definition of insanity was supposed to exclude 'all but the really insane'. So merely because certain persons were '. . . under the influence of strong, or even habitual passions . . . I reckon such persons vicious, but not insane', wrote Arnold. One had to be insane first, on definite criteria, and only then could certain vice-ridden behaviour be considered in assigning persons to a particular classification of insanity. Ellard's point is that whereas Arnold wanted to make a clear and unambiguous distinction between insanity and viciousness, the term 'morally insane' adopted by Arnold only perpetuated the confusion.

Ellard claims that Prichard's schema of 1837 contained a similar confusion, moral insanity becoming

a form of mental derangement, in which the intellectual faculties appear to have sustained little or no injury while the disorder is manifested principally alone, in the state of the feelings, tempers or habits.[80]

In 1844, Woodward had argued that moral insanity could be distinguished from mere depravity because it was always preceded or accompanied by 'some diseased function of organs' so subtle it could be detected by a psychiatrist, but not by a court or jury. But Ellard claims that this form of insanity '. . . existed only in the psychiatrist's imagination'.[81] For him, the distinction between insanity and wickedness had been lost in the successive confusion of medicine and morals: Issac Ray's 'moral mania' (1871), Spitzka's 'moral imbecility' (1887), Koch's 'psychopathic personality' (1891), Cleckley's 'psychopath' (1941), Bowlby's 'moral defective' (1949) and finally the *Diagnostic and Statistic Manual's* 'sociopathic personality disturbance' (1952):

The wheel has turned full circle; we are back with Prichard, but not exactly. Whereas Prichard's disorder was a derangement of the moral faculty, an entity in one's head, the *DSM–III* disorder is of the traits. Traits are not entirely in one's head; they are 'enduring patterns of perceiving, relating to and thinking about the environment and oneself'. They are processes and not entities, factors rather than faculties. But only just.[82]

For Ellard, the psychopath has become a household word because it retained the status of both explanation and cause, its function that of maintaining a class-based social order. Why has a man done such terrible things? Because he is a psychopath. How do you know he is a psychopath? Because he has done these terrible things. In the end, the description of an antisocial personality disorder is essentially that of a 'hoodlum from a poor and disadvantaged family', a judgement arising from the customs and prejudices of a particular group from which psychiatrists are themselves drawn and who therefore fail to see this incongruity.

Ellard's account attempts to explain the current weaknesses of psychiatry as a weakness in scientific activity – by its failure to separate medicine from morals. He traces uncertainties of meaning and breaches of scientific convention to fundamental confusions reproduced over time in psychiatric texts, as science struggled to know its object independently of social and political strictures. In addition, for Ellard the particular category of disorder remains constant over time, changing only as the terminology changed to reflect the progress (or confusions) in psychiatric knowledge. His contemporary use of the term 'moral insanity' becomes a starting point from which to venture back into the history of what for him was a pseudo-science, inasmuch as it merely paralleled the narrowed outlook and social position of psychiatric practitioners and theorists. His work assumes the continuous but confused figure of the 'morally insane' through to the modern period, as psychiatry sought to clarify its categories. Ellard is not alone in this view about the contingent nature of psychiatric categories. We recall that his argument would support that strand of legal and psychiatric opinion opposed to changing mental health legislation simply by changing the definitions of persons. The jurist C. R. Williams, for example, argued that to advance a case for legal reform, on the basis that 'medical facts' will have to be altered to conform to the will of legislators, amounted to a perversion of scientific validation techniques and knowledge.[83] And Glaser declared that changing the Mental Health Act to incarcerate the dangerous was an attempt by the state to 'massively shift the power/ knowledge balance in its favour' by attempting to redefine the boundaries of scientific knowledge for 'purely political purposes'.[84] Importantly, all these three accounts assign a prior existence to different categories of mental illness and disorder independent of their historically specific means of calculation. The account developed in this book seeks to problematise precisely those modes of calculation and the conditions of possibility for knowing these different categories of person, rather than assume their continuous (even though unrecognised or confused) existence over time.

More recent work by Kurt Danziger in fact takes this very direction, by showing historically how the concept of personality emerged from experimental psychology in the early part of the twentieth century.[85] Danziger argues that the concept of personality grew out of the limits of intelligence testing to grasp onto and measure a broader range of qualities in individuals, such as leadership and assertiveness. He points to the realisation among research psychologists in the United States during the 1920s that the factor of intelligence was only one of the determinants of real life performance, to which could be added character, personality, will, attitude and so on. He further illustrates how personality as a psychological and administrative category came into existence alongside the invention of the personality test itself. According to Danziger, personality as an object of research relied on an 'additive' model of the person, and that this numerical structure referred to something which existed in measurable quantities across situations and persons, such as 'ascendance' or 'introversion'. Performances on personality tests were then taken to reflect inherent properties of the task:

. . . the fundamental psychological meanings and reference of the empirical data were constituted by an interpretive construction that was not derived from those data but preceded their collection.[86]

Danziger claims that personality tests transformed a set of language terms such as 'dependence' into unambiguous properties of the natural world which could be investigated in the same way a physicist might investigate electrical resistance. What this amounted to, for Danziger, was '. . . a masquerade in which categories generated by a very specific social order were held to represent an ahistorical natural order'. He then goes on to explore the cultural preconceptions and interests of the groups, such as psychologists, who were responsible for developing the tests. The main strength of his analysis, however, is his account of the contribution by psychology to the production of personality as a space for the calculation of individuality, and to the new tools of calculation and the raft of statistical laws which emerged from the tests.

This last point – that personality was formed as a means of calculation and management – provides the clearest linkages to the present study of genealogies of disorder. It asks us to take seriously the appearance of the category of personality within the context of successive attempts to know and manage certain population groups. It suggests that conceptions of individuality framed around personality and its calculable properties may not be merely the result of the evolution of psychological concepts (Glaser) or the residue of fundamental historical confusions of knowledge (Ellard), or the effect of the limits of language to represent the empirical realities of the natural world (Danziger). These perspectives on knowledge and power do seem to imply that it is possible to conceive of psychiatric and psychological knowledges as potentially free of and unsullied by the effects of power. The approach here suggests instead that the problematising of personality might better be understood as part of a 'history of political technologies of individuality' – a history of what Nikolas Rose has described as the shifting ways in which 'political power has come to bear upon subjects, and has sought to understand them and govern them'.[87] In contrast to the accounts outlined above, the emphasis in this study is on the positive and productive effects of power in the way it carves out new locations for rule, rather than power being conceived as camouflaging and mystifying existing realities, or as the crushing of truths and repression of rights. The aim is to show how personality emerges as a new 'internal' space for

the play of public powers, and how the history of this emergence is co-
terminous with the history of antisocial personality disorder disentan-
gling itself from other categories and ways of being. Specifically, this
account diverges from that of Danziger by suggesting that, rather than
the category of personality emerging from an inquiry into the constitution of normal personalities, the conditions of possibility for the formation of a space called personality derives from governmental attempts to
know and manage disorder, unruliness and dangerousness.

Indeed, the argument advanced in this book is that the modern
concept of personality comes into existence as an index of risk management. As a complement to recent studies in theoretical criminology,
most notably John Pratt's exhaustive examination of the connections
between legislation and concepts of dangerousness,[88] it proposes that
governing populations and individuals in the context of late twentieth-
century advanced liberalism presupposes that individuals will govern
themselves through the deployment of techniques of the self which are
historically contingent, as distinct from naturally and spontaneously
endowed.[89] The book attempts to mark out the terrain upon which, in
the context of governing problem groups and individuals in the twenty-
first century, a new kind of bio-politics is emerging that constructs
problems of crime control and sentencing issues around categories of
the monstrous and evil, the grossly disordered, the genetically pro-
grammed and constitutionally wicked.[90]

It should be obvious already that the objectives of this present study
could not be achieved by advancing separate historical accounts of
psychiatry and psychology on the one hand, or of law and the criminal
justice system on the other. This brings us to the final point about
approaches to historical investigation, and in particular to our interest in
the kind of work initiated by Foucault. Much of the conventional
historical work on criminality and madness consists of discrete works
charting the internal dynamics of institutional development of these two
domains. In contrast, Foucault's interventions into law and psychiatry
have provided a theoretical warrant to problematise such fields in ways
which emphasise their convergences and interrelations. He has shown
that complex interdependencies in the operation of law and psychiatry
followed from the transformation of criminal responsibility in early
nineteenth-century European penal law where, he has argued, increasingly the intelligibility of a criminal act came to be referenced against the
character and antecedents of the individual. Foucault writes:

The more psychologically determined an act is found to be, the more its author
can be considered legally responsible. The more the act is, so to speak,
gratuitous and undetermined, the more it will tend to be excused. A paradox,

then: the legal freedom of a subject is proven by the fact that his act is seen to be necessary, determined; his lack of responsibility proven by the fact that his act is seen to be unnecessary.[91]

The reciprocal functionality of law and psychiatry made it possible, later in the century, to establish the determination of not just the great and monstrous crime but also everyday minor infractions and common delinquency, along an increasingly diverse psychological and psychiatric register. As conceptions of insanity and mental illness shifted, the psychiatric and criminological continuum could allow for an almost infinite proliferation of psycho-medical conditions and categories of person. The historical collaboration of law and psychiatry, and the 'psychiatrisation of criminal danger',[92] is critical in the evolution of psychological and psychiatric categories and their social functioning in the present. By themselves, neither conventional psychiatric histories nor the more dispersed histories of penal law and criminality are helpful in formulating a perspective on these conditions and categories. Categories of person do not emerge into the present by means of a continuous line of development traceable within the histories of either psychiatry or criminality, but rather are constituted at the intersection of both domains.

Foucault's writings have been a source of irritation for historians, often because his work has raised difficult questions about the politics of history-writing and the role of the intellectual. His *Madness and Civilisation* still provokes debate among historians.[93] A survey of the book's reception claimed that there had been no real test of the fruitfulness of Foucault's 'complex interpretive framework', and so for some his status as a historian of madness must remain an open question.[94] Here is not the place to offer a defence against these claims, even if this were needed. Foucault answered some criticisms in 'Questions of Method' and other writings where he attempted to answer the claim that his work provided no encompassing explanatory framework. He said that his critics complained of no structure in his work: '. . . no infra- or superstructure, no Malthusian cycle, no opposition between state and civil society: none of these schemas which have bolstered historians' operations, explicitly or implicitly, for the past hundred or hundred and fifty years'.[95] The debates on his history of madness continue, despite the fact that the abridged English translation still makes Foucault's original *Histoire de la folie* something of an 'unknown book' to English readers.[96]

While for some the jury might be still out on 'Foucault the historian', there ought to be less reluctance to acknowledge the contribution which Foucault, and those influenced by his work, have made to the method of inquiry he described as 'histories of the present' – the use of historical investigation for the purposes of diagnosing problems in the here-and-now. A major field of interest to Foucault concerned the contemporary functioning of the penal system, the mental health system and another whole dispersed set of institutional mechanisms of governing, as a way of seeking to problematise the forms in which freedom is exercised in modern liberal societies.[97] In this sense, Foucault's work has encouraged new approaches to old questions largely as a consequence of the conceptual 'toolbox' he developed through his own historical inquiries. So rather than providing 'schemas' and closures, the implied intellectual invitation is to take up his methods of inquiry as a way of charting new territories and formulating questions in different sorts of ways. His works on the asylum and the prison, posed in terms of disciplinary techniques, ought to stand as exemplary points of departure on methodological grounds, as well as on the grounds of the sheer weight of historiography. His use of historical investigation is as a philosopher seeking to elucidate questions of the present rather than the professional historian providing an empirically sound record of the past. Foucault sought to make more limited claims about the role of the intellectual by providing the 'instruments of analysis . . . a topological and geological survey of the battlefield',[98] and to use history as a mapmaker into new territories of human affairs.[99]

Foucault has argued that psychiatry came into its own during the nineteenth century through its undertaking to provide an explanation for the inexplicable monstrous crime. The notion of homicidal mania allowed psychiatry to intervene in the justice system by suggesting that the basis of dangerousness lay in the social body, conceived of as having a biological reality which required the intervention of medicine. Once the focus of the penal system had tilted away from the crime and more towards the criminal, and the problem was to reveal the antecedents of dangerousness in the body of the individual, questions of causality came to be applied across a range of infractions which demanded psychiatric intervention. The 'psychiatrisation of criminal danger' meant that any criminal could be treated as potentially pathological, any minor infraction as suspect, any variation an antecedent.

The concern here is to examine the synergism of the psycho-medical concept of antisocial personality disorder and calculations of dangerousness. But the language and conceptual terrain of disorder has entered into the routines of calculation and administration applied across whole populations, in social work, the magistrates' courts, the mental health system, and not simply in the case of the horrific crime. Other versions of the concept, such as conduct disorder, have entered the language of primary and elementary school. It is difficult to find any zone of exclusion in the grid of calculability spread by psycho-medical language and expertise. In the political rationalities associated with neo-liberalism over the past two decades this language has permitted a range of criminological approaches, but most recently has allowed the assertion of notions of an 'essential evil' residing in individuals and an emphasis on permanent incapacitation and indefinite sentencing policies.[100]

In concluding, it is worth recalling two elements of the previous discussion. First, it is necessary to take seriously the contemporary problem of knowledge and government articulated at the beginning of this chapter – the problem of knowing and managing dangerousness, and the 'fundamental inability to define conceptual boundaries' – this failure properly to know and administer. Second, there is reason to examine in some detail the historical specificity of the means of calculating different categories and types of persons. Categories of person are the product of the available tools and techniques for knowing the person. On these grounds, it is proposed that rather than antisocial personality disorder appearing as a problem which must be administered *by* government, disorder comes to be understood as an *effect of* techniques which seek to calculate, understand and govern individuals. Personality itself may be understood as an artefact of government. This suggests that knowledge of particular types of persons is made possible by means of a complexity of interrelations between law and psychiatry and the institutional spaces in which they operate, rather than the happen-chance discoveries of the human sciences or essential properties of persons described in law or medicine. The 'psychiatrisation of criminal danger' involved a collaboration over new techniques of management focusing on the instincts, motivations and will of individuals needing to be transformed. Historically, the dangerous individual produced a reciprocal functionality for law and psychiatry at a time of changing mechanisms for governing the social body.

2   Histories of psychiatry and the asylum

As an alternative to the teleological narrative of psychiatry's discovery of mental illness in the early nineteenth century, it is possible to take seriously the separation of the 'lunatic' population, and classifications within it, as first and foremost an administrative act – as an act of population management. These separating practices can then be understood to serve as conditions of possibility for the emergence of a specifically psychological medicine, which follows rather than precedes the fixing of bodies in the asylum.[1] A study of the government of lunatics entails also the recognition of a more complex set of relations between the juridical and the medical than is implied in either psychiatric histories or in the more recent social histories of the functioning of modern psychiatry. Rather than presupposing the continuous figure of the mentally ill person, or the criminal, or the historically inevitable tension between these two in the dualism of 'bad or mad', it is suggested that the study of particular problem populations must account for the way in which categories of person are 'made up' and become known in order to be governed.

Psychiatric histories

A long-standing common law distinction between 'ideots and lunaticks' (*a navitate* and *non compos mentis*) was brought to Australia in 1788 in the outline of government inscribed in Governor Phillip's letter of commission.[2] Alongside powers to grant land, mobilise a navy and an army, erect fortifications, control ports, markets and places of trade, and oversee public finance, Phillip was given specific powers in respect of two types of persons; first, to pardon and reprieve offenders in criminal matters, and second, to take charge of 'ideots and lunaticks and their estates':

And whereas it belongeth to us in right of our Royal Prerogative to have custody of ideots and their estates and to take the profits thereof to our own use finding them necessaries and also to provide for the custody of lunaticks and their estates without taking profits thereof to our own use.[3]

36

The Governor was entrusted with the 'care and commitment of the custody' of lunatics and idiots and gave to judges of a civil court the responsibility over such persons and their estates. How is it that lunatics and idiots appear on a short list of authorisations granted to the Governor-in-Chief of a new penal colony? The problem of governing lunatics was an important element in establishing the *principle* of sovereignty and guardianship that was to form the basis of a particular mode of governing whole states.[4] The individual was to be an autonomous entity carrying out rational exchanges as a free citizen, or else the individual's inability to operate within the contractual arrangements of liberal government rendered a person irresponsible and needing assistance. The solution to the problem of madness was important to the legitimacy of government on a much larger scale, from an older order of royal sovereignty to the idea of a social contract among citizens,[5] and laws regulating madness came well in advance of other kinds of social legislation. The medical remit over incarceration becomes significant in these terms. Once the obligations, duties and status of the citizen are formally conferred on all subjects and there is a requirement that constraints on freedom be guaranteed in law, medicine provides a solution to the need to preserve social order while at the same time responding to the demands of constitutionality.[6] Phillip's instructions provide a blueprint of what constitutes good government, but the specifics relating to lunatics and idiots are an historical marker of a broader reformulation of the problem of government whose techniques would extend over the whole population.

The late eighteenth-century model of government reaffirmed long-standing distinctions between criminals, lunatics and idiots and the legal protocols surrounding the writ of *de lunatico inquirendo*,[7] even though we know that these categories of person will routinely share the same institutional space for another one hundred years at least. The distinction in law between lunatics and idiots existed in old English common law. A jury of twelve might find a person to be *purus idiota* in which case 'the profits of his lands, and the custody of this person' may be granted by the King to a person 'who has interest enough to obtain them'.[8] Similarly, the method of proving a person to be *non compos mentis* was undertaken by the Lord Chancellor by special authority of the King, who would grant a commission of inquiry into a party's state of mind and if found *non compos* would 'commit' the care of the person along with an allowance to some friend who would then be called his 'committee'. These procedures followed historically from the repeal of the Witchcraft Acts of 1736, as well as various certification processes brought into being to protect the citizen from wrongful detention. The safeguards against misuses of detention of the wealthy were later extended to paupers. They were a development of an older royal prerogative to act as guardian of idiots and warden of their estates in return for maintaining the idiot, which was formalised in early English statutes in the fourteenth century and later delegated to the Lord Chancellor and the Court of Chancery. These same powers were entrusted to Governor Phillip in his second commission. For persons of substance, the process of *de lunatico inquirendo* continued until the Lunacy Act of 1878 created the Office of Master of Lunacy to manage the estates of insane persons.

It was a matter for a *civil* court to determine whether or not one is a lunatic and what use was to be made of that person's estate. It will also be within the jurisdiction of the courts that doctors seek to lay claim to special knowledges and techniques relating to the lunatic.[9] As between criminals and lunatics, Phillip's commission was one which required a rationalisation of constraints on freedom within a contractual society. The right to punish the criminal had from the outset a juridical basis, founded on the contractual obligation of the state to respect the liberty of the citizen, and conversely, the right of the state to punish any transgressions of this order. To incarcerate the lunatic required another set of rationalisations not provided by the purely juridical. Medical techniques would come to occupy a field of problems set for it by the requirement to provide justification for incarceration. The warrant for different practices on the idiot and the lunatic related to temporal distinctions dependent on the permanency and the degree of a person's infirmity. The estates of idiots were to be appropriated indefinitely and used for an individual's 'necessities' during life-long confinement, care and protection. The estates of lunatics on the other hand were to be managed on behalf of the lunatic until such time as he or she recovered. But in the earliest legislation medical distinctions were not privileged, and any distinctions between lunatic and idiot which might carry through to specific placement of such persons were subsumed under the category of 'dangerousness', and were simply not relevant. For example, the New South Wales Dangerous Lunatics Act of 1843 gave a court the power to commit a person to a gaol *or* a public hospital 'upon proof on oath by the said two medical practitioners to the effect that in their opinion such person is a dangerous lunatic or a dangerous idiot'.[10] The temporal aspects of the reclaiming and restoration of the lunatic were apparent in the late eighteenth century separation of the lunatic and the idiot, but only later would medicine begin to form its object of inquiry by attempting to draw boundaries and typologies, with a critical gaze on the aspect of temporality and restoration. At that point, medical knowledges and techniques would have specific effects quite apart from the burden of constitutionality. With increasing evidence that the English authorities were deliberately emptying their institutions of 'disordered and helpless' individuals by means of transportation to Australia, the practical requirement to sort and distribute became all the more urgent.[11]

For the Australian psychiatric historians, the asylum begins a story of the colony's unique social experiment. For Eric Cunningham Dax, it is a history dotted with progressive developments of all sorts, by international standards. He cites the compulsory admittance and detention of inebriates introduced at the Retreat in Melbourne. Later in the century the Kew Cottages for Idiots were built, described as one of the first and best of its kind in the world.[12] An electric treatment machine dating from the 1850s was discovered at Lachlan Park in Tasmania and used on 'catatonics' for half an hour each day. More regular treatments from the 1860s are reflected in Rudall's work, which included bleeding, scarification, cupping and setons, as well as hydrotherapy and isolation. Rudall's belief was that the focus of treatment needed to relate to the flow of blood to different parts of the brain. With Dax, the modern is pitted against Rudall's conviction that religious mania had its origins in sexual misbehaviour which also affected the colon, so that as a treatment he had great faith in leeches applied to the anus!

An early distinction between idiots and lunatics also allowed psychiatric historians such as Dax to discover retrospectively the 'mentally retarded' and the 'mentally ill' and to relate the administrative separation of these categories to the plea, from as early as 1848, for the removal of 'the imbeciles' from the asylum.[13] But the term 'taking profits', for the upkeep of an individual, reinforced the point that the issue of the estate was inseparable from the problem of the lunatic, and that the problem of managing the lunatic was primarily an administrative problem of managing the lunatic-and-his-estate, rather than a medical one. The estate was not a side issue, although the psychiatric historian John Bostock interprets the emphasis in Governor Phillip's instructions as merely a sign of an overly materialist society.[14] The matter to be decided, before a jury rather than a doctor, was whether one could manage one's own affairs. In 1805 Governor King directed the Provost-Marshall to summon twelve good and lawful men to '. . . make enquiry upon view of examination of Charles Bishop, to say on their oaths whether the said Charles Bishop is a lunatick'. The inquest found him to be 'incapable of governing himself, his chattels, lands and tenements'. Whereas Bostock has suggested that the natural path would be to call a doctor, why would one call a doctor when the issue to be decided – whether Bishop was a lunatic or not – was a question of whether or not he can manage his affairs? The Governor committed Bishop to the safe custody of John McArthur and the Reverend Samuel Marsden to manage his affairs. They then called on persons of the colony, in the *Sydney Gazette*, to establish any claims on Bishop's estate, in a civil court to be convened after the harvest had been declared.[15]

In 1810, the jury of twelve was replaced by a board of three surgeons, suggesting to Bostock that '. . . thought had been given to the growing problems of mental illness'.[16] There is, however, little evidence for this claim. Rather, there is evidence that the authority of the doctor in the court and later over the asylum was drawn not from science but from the moral authority of a 'wise man'.[17] The scrutiny of the medical men remained fixed on the issue of whether or not the individual could manage their affairs and perform duties. Take the case of Alex Bodie, master of ship, found to be in a state of mental derangement '. . . which disqualified him for the duties of the Master of the ship and required personal care and attention to be paid to him'. Governor Macquarie responded to the case by appointing a non-medical committee of management – Marsden, Jenkins and William Bodie – as 'Curators and Committee of the person and property of the said Alex Bodie and to perform such acts as may be most conducive to the restoration and right exercise of his mental faculties'.[18] The role of the surgeons was to testify about an ability to manage and the response was to take over the management of the person's affairs, not the management of a disease. The first asylum opened at Castle Hill outside Sydney in 1811, under the reign of Governor Macquarie, and four years later Reverend Marsden was again placed in charge of overseeing the affairs of lunatics. But now a medical board would sit on behalf of the court to determine the mental state of individuals and their ability to manage. In 1825, in the case of one Dan'l MacDonnell, a board of surgeons found the only remains of complaint to be 'some general debility and a degree of mental despondency, not amounting to disease'.[19] So while it appears that by this stage the medical board was expected to determine whether the patient's condition constituted 'disease', there was no clear medical function to act upon the disease but rather to determine – in the fashion of a jury – whether or not he could manage his affairs. The evidence drawn from these accounts suggests that the management of lunatics derived from a set of calculations on a grid of 'self-management', rather than from medicine.

On the question of treatment, the presence of a medical officer in the early asylums related to the need of any given population (an army, a ship, a prison) for medical services ministering to the physical body, rather than to the particular 'mental ills' of the lunatic population, and the term 'surgeon' as applied in navy and military contexts extended also to the asylum. The historical account uses the present tense when describing the close relations between 'physical and mental ills' of the patients, as though these relations are universal and ahistorical:

Gradually, the necessity for a permanent hospital for the insane became imperative and a system of administration had to be elaborated. It was early realized that a medical man as well as a superintendent was needed in an asylum where the physical and the mental needs of the patients are so closely related, and steps were taken towards this end.[20]

However, in the documents presented there is scant evidence of this relation. There is little indication that medical need was particularly privileged in the asylum at this time, or that the surgeon was called upon to attend to the mental ills of the lunatics. William Bland, the first to serve in a medical capacity at Castle Hill (while also serving a seven-year sentence for murder by duelling) gave evidence to Bigge that all bar one of the inmates were prisoners, that there were no medicines on hand in the asylum, and that he reported directly to the Governor and not the Principal Surgeon.[21] Bland's list of the causes of insanity in 1821 included two or three from the stresses of transportation, two who had been sent to the colony because of their political opinions, one woman who had been involved in the Irish insurrection, a few affected by inebriety, and two as a consequence of religious fanaticism. In his first medical report in 1814, Bland indicated he held little hope for recovery of most of the patients.[22]

Landholding rather than the opportunity to advance psychiatric medicine was the major incentive to attract suitable candidates to work in the asylum. The letter appointing Bland as the first medical officer granted him permission to cultivate some government land at Castle Hill '. . . for your mutual use and benefit, so long as you shall continue to act as surgeon to the lunatic asylum'.[23] George Suttor was offered the superintendence '. . . by the government and Mr Marsden. I thankfully accepted it, with the use of all the Government cleared land there.'[24] Only much later in the century would superintendents of lunatic asylums come as persons experienced as 'keepers' and doctors be required to be experienced in the field, but in the early period the employment of asylum personnel was clearly not oriented towards mental medicine. When Macquarie issued instructions to the lay super-intendent, Mr Suttor, he made it clear that day-to-day treatment of the inmates was in the hands of non-medical attendants, and was to deal with regularity, cleanliness, dress, exercise and diet, and only after all that with their medical treatment. Suttor gave out tea and tobacco because 'it seems to allay and calm the state of their minds'.[25] The instructions to the superintendent regarding his role in relation to the surgeon suggest the latter's concern was with general health and capacity to perform work:

... you are to follow and comply with such directions and advice as you may receive from time to time from the Surgeon appointed to attend to the Lunatic Asylum at Castle Hill; and you are on no account to make any of the Lunatics work in the garden or elsewhere, without the approbation and sanction of the Surgeon, as he alone is capable of judging whether such labour be good for their health or not.[26]

For his part, the Surgeon was instructed to assume medical duties, cooperating with the superintendent 'in the care, management and proper humane treatment of the unhappy persons placed under your charge, with a view to render their situation altogether as comfortable as their unfortunate circumstances will admit of'. Medicines would be supplied on written application to the Chief Surgeon, D'Arcy Wentworth, and the surgeon would write monthly reports to the Governor on the inmates' state of health. The role of the non-medical superintendent had a great deal to do with health, in the sense that his responsibilities in providing cleanliness and comfort, kindness and humanity, productive amusement and exercise, were understood as major preconditions for any rehabilitation and 'restoration of dignity'. This domain needs to be compared with that of the medical officer, who had the much narrower role of administering to physical ills. Similar institutional arrangements were eventually laid down in Victoria, the Colonial Surgeon acting as medical officer to both the gaol and the new Yarra Bend asylum. The contemporary rationale for getting lunatics out of the watchhouse, which they still shared with criminal offenders, was not specifically medical but rather the result of complaints from neighbours about 'maniacal yells and laughter'.[27] So there appeared to be at least two conceptions of 'health' or 'care' in evidence at this time, one to do with the management and general well-being of the inmates, and the specifically medical one to do with physical ailments.

As the asylum developed, a distinction between 'moral' and 'physical' treatment became more apparent, and was used at first to articulate a clear demarcation between the terrain of the superintendent and that of the doctor. From at least 1817, medicine argued that the whole asylum should be under the authority of a medical officer. Doctors complained that the superintendent countermanded orders and made it impossible for the doctor to 'try the effect of Medicine'. In practice, the effect of medicine at this time amounted to a concern with physical ills, as well as a new demand from medicine to separate and classify the inmates. Dr

Parmeter in 1818 gives an account of 37 patients, nine of whom were women, with the complaints classified as 'mania, epilepsia, amentia, melancholia, nostalgia and debilitas'. Treatment of one male patient with 'opthalmia [was] somewhat relieved by purgatives, blisters to the Temples and opening an Artery and supplying a Seton'.[28] In 1838, classifications included 'confirmed insanity (paralytic, quiet or dumb)', 'deranged (slightly or much)', 'idiot', 'fatuous' and 'fatuous epileptic'. By 1846 'dementia', 'paralysis', 'homicidal insanity', 'imbecility' and 'puerperal insanity' had been added.[29] By the 1850s there were four groups – maniac, melancholic, epilepsia and 'the women', and a paramount concern was to provide separate accommodation for the latter. At Parramatta in the 1860s, however, there were still no means of separating criminals from other patients or of isolating curable from incurable:

> I could say shortly, with respect to the men . . . that the paralytic, imbecile, and idiots are kept separate from the rest; the noisy, and those under any active delusion are kept in what we call the refractory yard; and the quiet are put in the green yard.[30]

Separation was also a step to improving the physical condition of the wards and preventing abuses by both patients and attendants. In an inquiry following the death of a 'Portuguese maniac' at the hands of an idiot named Griffiths, Parmeter complained that his instructions preventing wood-chopping by certain classes of inmate had been ignored, and,

> . . . in consideration of the late melancholy catastrophe, do, Mr Coroner and Gentlemen of the Jury, [I] strongly advise that proper cells should be made for the various patients of the Asylum, according to a proper Classification that I should make for the purpose in question.[31]

The commentary on lunacy made much of the propensity to violence and mischief within the convict/lunatic population and the thoroughly disruptive effects of the small minority of 'utterly depraved' men who could not control themselves and could not be controlled. A new category was applied to this kind of inmate by the surgeon of the convict establishment in Western Australia, George Attfield. He arrived in the colony in 1857 well acquainted with modern British thinking on lunacy, and concluded that many of these men were 'morally insane': 'they would not submit to any discipline, they will not control their ungovernable tempers, and are utterly reckless of consequence'.[32] Often within this population, doubtful cases were classified as moral insanity, with the judgement that if the person was in control of his actions then his insanity was of a 'moral' nature. The term imbecility in the nineteenth century often referred to a general state of 'personal weakness', both mental and physical, and idiocy was distinguished by 'lack of energy'.[33]

When the first specially built asylum at Tarban Creek was designed, the architect Mortimer Lewis drew upon the plans of Dundee Asylum in Scotland. It consisted of a central two-storeyed building with two single-storeyed blocks of cells on either side, enclosing airing yards. The main building was to accommodate the staff and 'upper class' patients upstairs, while pauper and convict patients occupied the cells.[34] During this period the doctor's role in the institution remained subordinate to that of the 'head keeper', except for the treatment of physical ills. A case in point is Joseph Digby and his wife. The superintendent and matron arrived in 1838 to take up their appointments at the new asylum and 'bring the requirements of modern treatment' imported from St Luke's Hospital in London.[35] The reign of Digby, whose care of lunatics is claimed to be 'primitive and harsh',[36] began full of incident and finished with the doctor, for the first time in Australia, taking complete charge of asylums. Digby was reported to be a specialist in superintendency and an expert in the latest techniques of 'moral treatment'. He ordered specially designed locks for different parts of the body, and strong furniture which could be screwed to the floor. Innovations included elaborate fireplace safety grills and window sashes which swung on pivots to prevent escapes, based on a design brought from the famous Retreat at York under Tuke.[37] Leather, wooden and iron restraints of all types and sizes were ordered, including 'thirty yards of strong linin ticking' for making strait waistcoats. He issued sets of orders governing the conduct of the institution in minute detail: disciplining the times of waking and sleeping, proper conduct at mealtimes, maintaining personal hygiene and care of clothing and appearance, and strict controls on the movement of patients. Rules for the attendants were rigorous, and it was the lay superintendent who specified the tasks of attendants *vis à vis* the medical officer:

In every case of illness, a report [is] to be made immediately to the Surgeon and likewise to the Superintendent. All medicines to be duly and regularly administered, and particular attention to be paid to all orders from the Surgeon respecting the Medical treatment of the Patients, to report the state of their bowels, or any sudden change that may take place in their health, and that the slightest appearance of any sore to be reported both to the Surgeon and the Superintendent.[38]

The doctor was given the charge of persons 'actually sick' but would have nothing to do with the general duties of the establishment, which would remain under Digby. The orders concerning the admission of patients would be addressed to Digby, and since 'the Lunatic Asylum is not a hospital',[39] the role of the Inspector-General of Hospitals was also very limited. In 1846, in his testimony to a Committee of Inquiry into Tarban Creek, Digby spelt out the distinction between the medical and the moral and the protocols to be observed:

> Every morning at ten, when the bell rings, the doctor and myself go around together, when we consult upon the treatment of the various cases. I do not pretend to make any suggestions as to the medical treatment of the patients, of course: but if he suggests any alterations to their moral treatment, and it appears to me an improvement, I act upon it. If, however, I do not approve of it, I do not yield to him. For instance, he might recommend that restraint should be taken off a patient, but I from my better knowledge of the party, might not deem it advisable to do so. I would therefore refuse unless he chose to incur the responsibility.[40]

This inquiry finished up with a recommendation which would place a doctor in charge of the asylum in New South Wales, and Bostock argues that the main reasons were the inadequacy of asylum records, and the fact that moral treatment and physical restraint were in the hands of a lay officer.[41] There is little or no evidence to suggest that medical control was achieved as a response to advances in psychiatry. To understand this move fully and its significance, however, it is important to clarify the exact nature of moral treatment and how the doctors related to it.

Moral treatment

The history of psychiatry claims it is with the appointment of a doctor, Francis Campbell, as superintendent of the asylum at Tarban Creek in 1848 that 'Australian psychiatry began'.[42] The installation of the 'medical model' of mental illness was supposed to have accompanied this move, and so importantly did the first moves to separate the incurable cases – 'serious mental retardation or general paralysis of the insane' – in order that Tarban Creek might be used solely as 'a curative asylum – well adapted for the treatment of acute and recent mania'.[43] And there is considerable evidence that the authority of doctors was seen as an important source of improved management, so as to stem the continuing scandals and accusations of abuse which plagued this 'model' institution of colonial administration. But rather than seeing this as the triumph of the medical model, the evidence points to the important implications of the doctor taking charge of what was called moral treatment. The conditions of possibility for the practice of moral treatment lay in a more individualised gaze on the lunatic, involving a set of techniques for calculating and knowing the various types or

classifications of lunatic. These techniques of classification and transformed modes of address to the lunatic – referred to by one contemporary observer as the 'soothing system'[44] – were administrative and
political in the sense that they involved the elaboration of new sites of
administration and separated treatment which would allow new forms
of knowledge of the individual lunatic.

Thus, hand in glove with these changed lines of authority, spatial
adjustments and new modes of address, came changes in the way the
lunatic came to be known. Different kinds of persons came into being as
their classifications became inscribed.[45] That the basis of moral treatment was administrative rather than medical can be seen in accounts of
the conduct of relations between doctor and superintendent, showing
that moral treatment was a 'system' applied in the institution overall, in
ways which affected both attendants and lunatics, even the doctor.
Observe the nature of the authority contained in Dr Campbell's acerbic
remonstrations to Digby, who was being criticised for withholding
rations from an attendant because he was late for the bell:

If I were Steward, knowing this as you ought to have done, I would not have
ventured upon so despotic a mode of acting, but would cheerfully, at all personal
inconvenience, have performed that most necessary part of my duty . . . You
might expect that degree of mechanical regularity which led you into error in the
attendant when you could screw up the patients in rack-chairs, bolts and stocks
and thus exempt them altogether from the necessity of an attendant; but under
the present system you should have remembered that the care is now altered.[46]

The relations between these two particular men was far from cordial –
one of Digby's many dogs once attacked Campbell's infant child in the
face[47] – but the point of historical significance centres not on differences
between doctor and lay keeper on questions of medical techniques on
the lunatic, or on the personal animosities between them, or by reference to the perennial squabbles between medical and administrative
personnel, but rather on the nature of the communicative order between
'keeper' and 'kept' which was made exemplary in the newly changed
relations between doctor and head keeper. The marking out of the era of
medical dominance in asylum affairs is inadequate if it does not take
into account medicine's appropriation of moral treatment as a specific
form of ministration to persons, which served as a condition of possibility for formulating new knowledge of the lunatic.

In some accounts, moral treatment is heralded as the turning point
for humanistic psychiatry, inspired by the humanitarian efforts of practitioners such as Pinel and Esquirol in France and William and Daniel
Tuke in England, and taken up with enthusiasm by Conolly at Hanwell
Asylum in England and Benjamin Rush in the United States.[48] The aim

was to alleviate suffering through the abolition of mechanical constraint and seclusion, and to secure this by treating inmates with gentleness, patience and respect, by encouraging different modes of employment and recreation, and by establishing rudimentary classification for different mental disorders. However, the approach was augmented by a rigorous case study of each individual, given a lead in research from the 1880s by Kraepelin, Krafft-Ebing and Bleuler, who had begun to evolve more complex systems of classification based upon detailed historical and clinical studies of each patient. For example, Adolf Meyer's 'distribution analysis' involved a meticulous study of every aspect of the life and development of the patient, including heredity, physical and emotional stress, and the intricate details of day-to-day existence.[49] A further differentiation can be made between physical and moral treatments.[50] Physical treatments included the use of drugs, cold water baths and leeching, all of which were a matter of trial and error. Moral treatment was supposed to provide an environment conducive to recovery and directed towards restoring the patient's self-control by means of strict discipline, regular routines, profitable employment and pleasant surrounds. The notion of a medical cure was commonly criticised throughout the 1800s, and Baldwin for example, who had been superintendent at both Sunbury and Ballarat asylums in Victoria, gave evidence at the Zox Inquiry towards the end of the century that medical treatments of the insane were 'one of the greatest humbugs of this present age'.[51]

At about this time, curative treatments of the insane were being surveyed by a private practitioner G. A. Tucker as part of a massive study he conducted of practices in European, North American and Australasian institutions.[52] Cages, iron chains, handcuffs, hobbles, straps, crib beds and fixed chairs were basic instruments in most asylums. Baths, either shower or immersion, were becoming the favoured means of tranquillising excited patients. In better managed places, curative treatment 'consists in supplying nourishing food, tonics, exercise, occupation, etc.' Superintendents reported that they chiefly depended on 'moral and hygienic treatment', but that the more modern idea of 'purely hospital or infirmary treatment' was beginning to catch on,

. . . commencing, on the admission of the patient, with placing him at once in bed as a sick person, instead of turning him loose amongst the other patients . . . and the soothing influence of the prone position, a comfortable bed and pleasant surroundings, tend to rapidly allaying the excitement and to producing quietude.[53]

Though these seem to imply a medical model at work, they clearly reflected an orientation on the moral. Tucker in fact differentiated between medical and moral treatment, and the medical was understood to be authorising the methods of restraint of the past. In contrast, moral treatment was to develop techniques of self-restraint:

Moral treatment is considered even more important than medical treatment, as being more universally applicable, and more likely to be successful in any given number of cases. It is a great and reprehensible mistake to deem it necessary to commence an acquaintance with a patient by a display of physical strength. Esteem is a more powerful and more beneficial agent of control than fear, and the best form of restraint is self-restraint. Gentleness should take the place of violence, and every effort should be made to divert and improve the 'mind diseased', by conversation, amusement, cheerful surroundings, bodily exercise, etc. In short, as far as possible, patients should be treated as rational and responsible beings, and made to feel that they are being so treated. In this way their confidence is gained, and the enfeebled powers of their mind exercised and invigorated. There is no more well-founded observation in lunacy management than that the increase or decrease of physical restraint is dependent on the extent to which judicious moral treatment is carried out.[54]

There are claims that moral management took hold of professionals in charge of institutions in Western Australia from the early twentieth century,[55] and was a term used for the belief that a staple diet, exercise, religious instruction and the instillation of values and morals, combined with lack of punishment and restraint, was the treatment most likely to lead to recovery. The caveat, however, is that such treatment remained an ideal rather than a practice.[56]

The variations in the historical accounts of moral treatment are an obstacle to evaluating its significance. In some of the histories of psychiatry, much store is placed on how the error of 'moral causation' was replaced with new theories of scientific medicine. The distinction is a critical one in the account of the birth of psychiatry. William Isdale, for example, draws on Aubrey Lewis's influential book *The State of Psychiatry* to introduce the history of psychiatry in Queensland in the following terms:

Psychiatry emerged as a distinct discipline around about the last decade of the *eighteenth* century. By that time those suffering from mental illness were treated 'on medical rather than moral lines'.[57]

Another describes the nineteenth-century view of madness as 'moral depravity'[58] or 'moral disease',[59] and characterises changes to the internal architecture of the asylums later in the century as a means towards promoting the effectiveness of 'moral reconstruction . . . [m]edical therapies were a secondary consideration',[60] with the former understood as an ideological prelude to the latter, scientific outlook. Milton Lewis, on the other hand, interprets 'moral' as '. . . more or less the same as the modern term "psychological", except with some ethical overtones':

> moral treatment or management was based on the doctor's involvement with his patient's 'moral capacities'. The doctor appealed to the patient's conscience and will instead of imposing restraint on him . . . moral factors such as habit, perseverance, will and character were seen as forces in the patient that could be strengthened to counteract insanity.[61]

Lewis's account gives a different treatment, in that it treats the move to moral management as a sign of broader philosophical changes in the early and mid-nineteenth century towards individualism and policies of *laissez faire*, whereby lunatics, like children and the poor, were increasingly understood to be amenable to self-improvement by drawing on their inner resources.[62] This same spirit of reform is represented by Virtue in his account of the 'maturing' of the colony of Western Australia, aided by the dominance of progressive 'liberal' political forces in the late nineteenth century. During this period a major shift from 'custodial management' to 'curative treatment' occurred, a move which Virtue claims derived from the relative success medicine had achieved at curing the mad and providing plausible explanations for how this was accomplished.[63] However, rather than seeking explanations for these events in terms of the march of science, or as an effect of a broader sea-change in social philosophies, it is possible to make sense of these changes in management in rather more local and mundane terms: as the effect of new techniques of measurement and calculation deployed in the asylums to focus a more intense scrutiny on the individual body of the lunatic, and in particular, the calculation of recovery.

It is quite clear, in the early period, that both the superintendent and the surgeon acted upon persons rather than diseases, and that the domain of the moral was disputed territory between the two. The Dangerous Lunatics Act 1843, requiring medical certification for admission to the asylum, followed a successful legal case of wrongful confinement brought against Digby and a police magistrate,[64] and this event certainly acted as a catalyst for the doctors to establish themselves at the centre of asylum affairs. Similar legislative moves in Britain were also a factor influencing developments in Australia. But rather than throwing over the 'moral' in favour of the 'medical', the doctors took charge by adopting the terrain of the moral as their own. It is not as though medicine is brought in from the position of a marginalised discipline relative to moral treatment, but rather that there occurs a transmutation of 'moral' concerns into the medical domain, within the bounded space of the asylum. The point was emphasised in the Principal Medical Officer's insistence in 1848 that the new superintendent of Tarban

Creek be addressed not as 'Medical Superintendent', as this would infer that he was 'only the Medical and not the Moral Superintendent of the Asylum'.[65] The transmutation is accomplished in part by the doctor exerting authority and control over the practices of keepers and attendants. But these practices in fact lie at the core of what was described as 'moral treatment', applied to both patient and keeper. The fact that the doctor was practising upon an insane population was not a consequence of specific medical calculations upon insanity as such, but on a bounded population in incarceration.

'Making up' the mental patient

A primary site of the medical man's intervention in lunacy affairs occurred at the point of entry to the asylum. It was here that medicine established its jurisdiction over the problem of the justification of incarceration. This was the point of deciding insanity/sanity, where, initially sitting as a member of a jury, the medical man would exercise authority. In the period from 1805–1810 his role remained almost entirely juridical, in that he listened to testimony and decided whether or not it made sense. The role of the visiting asylum doctor was not particularly privileged. In 1815, a Major West gave evidence that '. . . I never knew an instance in which Surgeons at Castle Hill have decided upon the sanity or otherwise of persons sent there'.[66] Similarly, Digby was asked at the 1846 Enquiry how he would classify a patient if he did not consult with a medical man, to which Digby answered '. . . as there were only two yards the difficulty was not great after seventeen years experience . . . [T]he medical man was not as a general rule called to see a patient unless he had some appearance of disease'.[67] He practised upon a physical disease rather than a medical problem relating to insanity.

But by the end of the century the site of medical intervention was also to occur at the point of exit, and at the level of calculations to be made about 'the effects of medicine'. The recognised reforming doctor in the later period was Francis Manning, who in 1881 pointed to the increasing disenchantment of difference in society, along with an expanding requirement of the system for careful counting: 'a growing disinclination to tolerate irregularities of conduct, and those whose insanity was not in former times detected, stand but scant chance of escaping numeration'.[68] When Manning's superintendence at Tarban Creek (Gladesville) was completed, he embarked on a thorough listing of the causes of insanity derived from the records of the hospital from 1869 until 1878, a total of over 3,000 patients. The causes were broadly distributed into moral and physical causes. Well over a half were counted as physical, a quarter were not able to be ascertained, leaving about a fifth described as moral, including domestic trouble, mental anxiety, religious excitement, disappointment in love, fright and shock, isolation and nostalgia. The major physical causes were intemperance, sunstroke, epilepsy and 'hereditary taint'. The latter became an underlying pre-disposing factor, especially following the works of Darwin and Morel. It was Darwin's view that 'the weak in body and mind' were soon eliminated in primitive societies and that it was only with the intervention of civilisation that these basic laws were modified. Manning's interest in Morel's ideas of degeneracy led to his second major inquiry into the genealogy of imbecile and idiot patients who appeared on the 1884 register of the hospital for the insane at Newcastle in New South Wales. Another long-term conviction of Manning was that the production of insanity was due to the influence of modern civilisation itself, confirmed to some extent by his recognition that insanity was a very rare affliction among Australian Aborigines 'whilst in their primitive and uncivilised condition'. The specific adverse factors of modern civilisation were high pressure and mental excess: 'life under the stress of modern competition and hurry, the haste to get rich, the habit of overwork and the abominable practice of keeping up steam by stimulants'.[69]

The statistics collected by Manning in 1877, of the operation of all the colonial asylums, shows the steps taken to separate different classes of patients. In New South Wales imbeciles and idiots were housed in a separate institution at Newcastle where they were trained in the habits of order and cleanliness, although Manning mentions that no attempt had yet been made to provide scholastic teaching. Ordinary lunatic patients were housed in five separate establishments and the chronics were kept in Parramatta, which also contained the only criminal asylum existing at that time in Australia. In Tasmania, South Australia and Western Australia no such separate accommodation existed, with the idiots distributed throughout the lunatic wards in South Australia and kept in a detached house at New Norfolk in Tasmania. Victoria had the largest number and the highest proportion of lunatics, with only male imbeciles and idiots contained at Ballarat and the criminal lunatics distributed throughout the wards. Queensland separated the 'chronic and demented' classes at Ipswich and the rest at Woogaroo. Manning noted that because of the vastness of the colony and difficulties of communication, five 'reception houses' had been established in remote areas where by law lunatics could be kept for three months, and from which a number had been discharged as sane. Of considerable satisfaction to Manning was his charting of the overall numbers recorded as discharged 'recovered' or 'relieved'. The tables presented in 1879 give percentage figures on those who had recovered, ranging from 35 per cent in 1872 to 55 per cent the following year, despite an increase in admissions during the preceding decade. Manning gives credit to the Victorian establishments especially, for their high rates of recovery.[70]

By the turn of the century the term mental disease was used as a catch-all grouping which would also come to include a new kind of person called the moral imbecile, according to Barker's *Mental Diseases: A Manual for Students,* published in 1902 in North America, Europe and Australia by Cassell. Barker had been medical officer at Hampshire County Asylum in England, before coming to Australia to take up the appointment as medical superintendent at Ballarat and later at Ararat. Within the disease classification then available, mental deficiency was firmly positioned as a mental disease and was described as congenital insanity of two kinds, idiocy and imbecility. Acquired epilepsy was also classified as a mental disease. Then followed general paralysis of the insane, mania, melancholia, dementia, delusional insanity and moral insanity. Within the group of congenital insanity are children who degenerate at a particular period of infantile development and are thus referred to by the term developmental idiocy, and another type whose appearance has already been noted by the School Board in London but had been noticed too by the psychiatrist McCreery in Victoria, founder of the New Idiot Asylum. These were defined as a distinct form of mental deficiency, although not sufficiently intellectually deficient to be classed as idiots or to require restraint, or even to be classified as insane, but differed from the average as to be of inferior mental calibre. Their defective nerve and muscular vigour was such as to manifest sluggish performance. Too often there was an 'imperfect moral development' as well, leading Barker to term these children 'moral imbeciles':

. . . these children may exhibit decided propensities towards petty criminal acts, such as lying and thieving, and so become an intolerable burden to their friends. No social grade is exempt from this affliction, although such cases are, for obvious reasons, more numerous among the lower classes.[71]

The obviousness of the class connection was not spelt out by Barker, although clearly it related to a notion of 'inherited constitutional defect' and any other 'agency likely to promote a degenerate or immature development' which could immediately be linked to the more frequent appearance of these characteristics in the parents of these children. Suggested causes included transmitted neurotic taint, inherited constitutional defect, and illness in infancy. In none of these forms of mental deficiency was there necessarily abnormal shape or size of the cranium,

except perhaps some slight inclination to be microcephalic from retarded development, and the sexual instinct was commonly feeble and
immature. Heredity could be found to be the single most important
cause: 'the insane, the epileptic, the paralysed, the drunken, the syphi-
litic, and the depraved will, as a rule, beget degenerate offspring'. Little
further was said on the subject of the moral imbecile at this time, but the
prognosis and treatment for the broad category of idiot was generally
positive. By judicious and painstaking moral training, Barker noted,
such as was in force 'in that admirably organised and philanthropically
conducted institution at Kew', the results that could be obtained were
nothing less than astonishing.[72]

Accounts of the 'dawn of Australian psychiatry'[73] give a description of
'moralisation' of both keepers and the kept, as doctors sought to impose
order and civility on the administration of a more-or-less undifferentiated group of inmates. The doctors argued for medical control partly
to 'try the effect of Medicine' and also to stem the unacceptable
behaviour and unruliness of the attendants. In this sense, moralisation
was an important governing activity in relation to both the lunatic and
the keeper. The issue is not one of a medicalisation of lunacy by means
of superior claims to truth about the lunatic and the replacement of
moribund ideas about moral treatment with 'medicine', but rather the
selective carving out of an object amenable to governing by means of the
techniques of moralisation. The take-up of moral treatment as a set of
techniques suggests that medical ascendancy was premised on the
possibility of addressing the lunatic as a particular kind of 'citizen',
determining in new ways how this person will come to be governed.
This process of *subjectification* is revealed in the detailed descriptions of
the routine of the asylum under the new regime, where a particular
subjectivity of the patient amenable to the psychiatric gaze emerges; a
certain type of lunatic becomes known in terms which render him or her
capable of being acted upon and redeemed. Andrew Tolson's analysis of
Henry Mayhew's discovery of the 'little watercress girl' amongst the
mid-nineteenth-century London poor makes a similar kind of point.[74]
Techniques of calculation through moral treatment were one of the
means by which particular populations became visible and able to be
categorised. So, for example, a visitor to the Yarra Bend Asylum in
Melbourne in 1853 observed how useful work given to the lunatics
revealed their true selves behind the sometimes miserable and violent
exterior:

. . . the house-keeper's assistant maids, the laundresses, and the cook's assistants
are insane patients, yet they rarely destroy things beyond other servants
elsewhere, who are supposed to know better. The outdoor labourers on the

improvements to the grounds are insane, yet they seldom do any damage. The man in charge of the cow is insane, yet not the less careful and proud too of his charge . . . and if they now and then make a blunder, or spoil something, Dr Bowie smiles, and says inwardly never mind, it is not lost – it is a part of the medicine, and the means of the cure. I need not say after all this, that the method adopted of late years by the best practitioners, viz, the 'soothing system' is the principle now in operation in this asylum. No such thing as ill usage of any kind is for a moment countenanced under the present management.[75]

Once the doctor takes charge of moral treatment, which includes the classification of patients, their physical arrangement into separate institutions and different parts of the asylum, and decisions about their individual confinement, the doctor is in effect taking over the means of curative treatment of lunacy. Whereas previously the doctor's role in the institution is as a medical officer attending to physical ills that might afflict any population, the doctor in charge of moral treatment is taking over the dominant paradigm of lunacy treatment. The means of classification, the individualising of the lunatic, the intense scrutiny and 'full insight into the character and mental condition of the patients' – these are the conditions of possibility for a strictly psychological medicine. In these terms, the design of asylums to include exercise yards which will allow 'without constant or ostentatious supervision . . . the close observation of each patient' makes possible the study and recording of different cases of lunacy and different stages of progress to recovery.[76] Similarly, establishing the 'cottage system' of care for chronic lunatics, which was recommended by a Select Committee in Victoria as early as 1858,[77] was a means of combining close scrutiny and family-style governance common to a range of institutional sites from this period.[78]

A major part of the historical work on early lunacy administration entails a kind of marking out of the insane as a separate group within a more-or-less undifferentiated problem population, a move which is held to be significant in terms of a specifically medical intervention. As we have seen, an early distinction was made between the lunatic and the idiot. A second distinction was made between the criminal and the lunatic, which in the colony of New South Wales was built around the segregation of lunatics in the Town Gaol at Parramatta, then in the new Castle Hill Asylum in 1811, and later in 1838 at Tarban Creek (Gladesville). In 1839 a new block of seventy-two cells for refractory inmates was built at Parramatta in three tiers, the lowest level having no natural light in order that it could be used as punishment. During the 1860s a small prison was built inside the grounds of Parramatta, containing sixty cells for the criminally insane, but which also included ordinary patients who proved to be violent.[79] In the 1860s the divisions in a newly built asylum planned to be attached to the Fremantle convict establishment involved the separation of maniacal and dangerous, quiet and chronic, melancholic and suicidal, and the idiotic, paralytic and epileptic, but when it was finally completed in 1869 it immediately became overcrowded and the classificatory system devised earlier became unworkable.[80]

In the late 1840s, convict lunatics were separated from non-convicts.[81] But, through medicine's incorporation of moral management and its transmutation of such forms of management into new techniques of *medicine*, we can begin to discern an important separation within the asylum population along the lines of amenability to *treatment*. From the beginnings of the establishment of the asylum in Australia, the 'quiet and harmless' had been partitioned, as means lent themselves, from the noisy and troublesome, the refractory and the violent. For instance, at Castle Hill there existed 'two or three cells or separate compartments . . . divided off from the principal rooms', for separating the dangerous from those regarded as safe.[82] (And, of course, Digby's 'two yards' divided the population according to broad criteria of manageability.) Dax locates the historical turning point with the appointment of Dr Campbell, who 'first introduced maximum freedom, minimum restraint and short periods of solitary confinement'.[83] The point to be made here is that within the old asylum there were legitimate techniques for managing the more or less troublesome, dangerous and violent lunatics. But with the centralising of the medical gaze upon the patient who could be managed according to the principles of 'soothing' treatment, a shift takes place in the conceptualising of inmates in terms of their manageability. The more or less troublesome become transmuted into the more or less amenable to treatment. It becomes possible to separate inmates in terms of who is, and who is not, the proper subject of psychological medicine.

The different types of patients are written up in these terms in the Campbell's 1848 case notes. A difficult case was Edwin Withers – 'this spiteful unquiet and remorseless little man' – dispatched to the 'Ward of the Imbeciles' as beyond treatment. He can be compared with Myles Sheehy, who provided an excellent vehicle for the soothing method:

All those passions of the soul which have the power to strew according to their motive influences the path of life with sunshine and roses or encumber it with cares and disquietudes and difficulties are completely obliterated in him.[84]

One can speculate that formerly a patient like Withers, known as violent, would have been subject to restraint and seclusion, as part of the practice of asylum management. Now under the gaze of the doctor, the first principles of moral management – reasoning, rather than restraint and seclusion – have been hoisted to the terrain of proper medical treatment. Known under the medical gaze as violent and troublesome, he is subject to restraint and seclusion as an indication that he is beyond the limits of the practice of psychological medicine. That is to say, in his dangerousness he is placed to the edge of psychological medicine's governability.

The forms of calculation deployed by practitioners in the mundane evolution of different kinds of asylum had effects in fabricating what eventually was to become the 'mental patient'. These were not discoveries of mental science, nor were they merely changes of terminology reflecting a newly found humanistic outlook. And neither again were they simply the effect of social control mechanisms aimed at establishing a more general social order. They have significance historically, however, for how population groups and different kinds of persons will come to be defined within a more evolved matrix of legal and medical knowledges.

Traditional reformist psychiatric histories frequently recollect the early nineteenth-century assertion that 'the asylum is not a hospital' as a means of indicating how far psychiatry has come in its enlightened replacement of 'asylum' with 'mental hospital', and later, indeed, just 'hospital'. For example, when the psychiatric historian C. J. Cummins observes that the administration of Castle Hill was more an extension of the principle of benevolence than medicine, and that the Colonial Medical Service played a minor role, this is only to underscore his argument that psychiatry had to really force its project of lunacy reform on a tardy and unenlightened bureaucracy;[85] similarly, Ellis's use of the colonial surgeon's statement, implying that 'the lunatic asylum is not a hospital', is made to bear witness to the problems early psychiatry had to overcome.[86] Such accounts often figure the psychiatrist as wall-breacher in a tale of the release of the mentally ill from their confinements and restraints, and the de-mythologising of their dangerousness – that is, the making safe of the mentally ill – which corresponds to their movement historically from asylum to community.[87] A new catch-cry of an enlightened and enlightening psychiatry emerged – 'the hospital is not a prison'. And yet the marking out of this terrain of the proper concerns of psychiatry, central to which is a 'safe' patient amenable to treatment and belonging to the 'community', necessitates some kind of boundary or limit. Psychiatry, after all, can only go so far. Can we see something of the beginnings of the production of the limits and the consolidation of the terrain of modern psychiatry in the figure of the patient who is named as not amenable to a newly medicalised moral treatment – and hence incarcerated? The figure of the dangerous patient named by psychological medicine as unable to be treated, and consequently sent to the cells, functions to produce a border which helps both to consolidate and define psychiatry. The figure serves as an occupier of a liminal zone, serving to negotiate and mark out the ongoing definitions of increasingly distinct territories of medicine and incarceration.

3   The borderland patient

That the borderland between normal and abnormal is hard to define is
a truism which needs no repetition. It is a territory disputed both by
psychology and psychiatry and raises many mutual problems.
(W. S. Dawson MD, Professor of Psychiatry, University of Sydney, 1927)[1]

We have seen from the accounts of the psychiatric historians a fundamental change in the calculation of the lunatic which has been driven by
a spirit of reform and which recognises an underlying humanity in the
lunatic. The lunatic became a different humanised kind of person and
there is an administrative response to this in terms of the lifting of
restraint. So this is an account which posits changes in the administration of the lunatic as an effect of changes in the recognition of the
lunatic. However, it is also possible to argue that the administrative shift
from non-mechanical restraint itself helps to produce the categories of
person in the institution – the mental patient, and at the same time the
dangerous or refractory patient, in a way that places the latter at the
periphery of proper, modern asylum practice.

In the mid nineteenth century, the Chief Medical Officer reported
diseases on an annual basis using a classification system similar to one
operated by the statistician Archer, which included zymotic, constitutional, local and developmental diseases, and violence. Under local
diseases were included diseases of the nervous system and they varied
depending on the particular institution, but included mania, convul-
sions, hysteria, epilepsy, insanity, softening of the brain, and hypo-
chondriasis. *Delirium tremens* and intemperance were classes under
zymotic diseases. A further breakdown was made of the curable and
incurable, of which for 1873 only 200 were considered curable and
448 were harmless, imbecile and idiotic, out of a total asylum population of 2346 patients. It was estimated that imbeciles could be
maintained at a cost of 9 shillings each per week by removing them
from the asylum where the rate of maintaining inmates was 15
shillings.

By the turn of the century there were concerns that the number of certified lunatics in most countries was increasing at a rather rapid rate. These were answered in part by the claim that the meaning of the term 'lunacy' had been extended to include many more conditions of an abnormal state, and that there was less inclination to allow harmless lunatics to wander at large. So while there was a large accumulation of incurables moving into the asylums this should not be viewed as proof of an increase in the disease. The death rate of lunatics had decreased as well. The institutional moves from this period into the twentieth century set the context for a more fully conceptualised product of the penal and mental health systems to emerge. These moves reflect complex shifts involving the shaping of the more-or-less amenable to treatment by organised medicine, the removal of the dangerously disordered to the outskirts of medicine, the shifting role of restraint in asylum practice and extensions of the space and time available to decide the question of sane/insane. These moves are best demonstrated by examining the main reformist developments of the second half of the nineteenth century – the reception house and the refractory ward.

Reception house

The 1869 Joint Committee established in Queensland, and the follow-up Royal Commission of Inquiry into the Woogaroo Lunatic Asylum and Reception Houses, provide a focus for understanding these institutional changes and the way in which the question of restraint in treatment is conceptualised.[2] By the time of the Royal Commission in 1877 a settlement had been reached within asylum authorities that mechanical restraint was generally unacceptable as a standard treatment. At the Commission hearings, when witnesses were asked to describe what means of restraint are employed, a certain hierarchy of acceptability emerged. Witnesses admitted to the need for the single cell as a resort in the first instance and only rarely was it stated that mechanical restraint was used. In evidence to the Commission there were calls from medical personnel for more cells. The cell was seen as a replacement for the camisole and other forms of mechanical restraint as a more legitimate means of managing the refractory patient, such that non-mechanical restraint became productive of the physical and conceptual partitioning off into cells of a class of 'refractory' patients. The cell came about as a new technique of management and was repositioned conceptually as belonging to the outer limits of asylum practice. The Commission's concerns were articulated in terms of how these cells were incorporated into management techniques and to ensure that the cell did not become central to asylum practice – that they were not used 'in the ordinary course', 'habitually' or as 'bedrooms' or 'dormitories'.[3] The cell has its proper place at the extreme edge of asylum practice. This positioning contributes to defining the boundaries of an emergent psychiatry. It is possible to discern a hierarchy in which the patient becomes capable of being differentiated along the lines of being amenable to accepted practice.

The invention of the Reception House allowed a temporal and spacial expansion of the act of judging whether someone is insane or not. The line between sanity and insanity opens out into a space with its own institution and its own practices. It is clear from the Commission's report that there were different kinds of reception houses. The outposts away from Brisbane, at Toowoomba for example, seem to have been little more than an alternative to watchhouses for holding lunatics before sending them on to either Brisbane Reception House or Woogaroo Asylum, and reflected a consensus of opinion that lunatics should not be held in prison cells. One problematic group which strained the legitimacy of the distinction between the asylum and watchhouse, and where the reception house came into its own, was the group affected by alcohol. By extending the holding period in this not-quite-asylum, it was supposed that distinctions could be more easily drawn between different kinds of drunkards, especially between those suffering from *delirium tremens* and those with dipsomania.[4] Mention is made of other kinds of temporary insanity, including sunstroke and puerperal insanity. The reception house thus came to be a place for deferring any permanent and decisive classification, in recognition that there will be cases which, if left more-or-less alone in an appropriately ameliorative environment, will take care of themselves. This was the purpose of the reception house even though many became places to dump drunks of one sort or another to see if they would recover sobriety. A further unease surrounded the location of the reception house, how firmly it should remain within the precinct of medicine, and how it should be placed geographically and conceptually in connection with the General Hospital or the asylum proper.

Much to the consternation of the medical superintendents, the Commission heard evidence suggesting that, as a smaller quieter institution separated from the 'seething mass of insanity', the reception house actually worked better than the asylum because of its curative potential. Certainly the testimony of O'Doherty, Fellow of the Royal College of Surgeons, speaks of the reception house as a place ahead of its time and one which would drive the separation of functions to achieve better rates of cure:

I believe, if a skilled medical man were appointed there [the Reception House], it would tend to lessen the general expenditure of the colony upon lunacy; that a skilled medical man there would have a large number of patients – a larger number than probably now go in – and day by day use of Woogaroo would become more defined, as merely an institution for the chronic cases and the permanently and incurably insane, whilst here in this temporary institution you could have every appliance that could possibly be desired. It can be enlarged to any extent you like . . .[5]

So the space provided by the reception house allowed for the possibility of concentrating on the line between sanity and insanity, and expanding that line into a set of institutional practices liminal to the asylum proper. As a corollary it allows for a rethinking of the 'seething mass of insanity' and for the possibility of thinking the 'acute' as separate from the 'chronic' which became one of the first large disaggregations of the asylum proper. As will become clear, it is via the slow shapings of the 'chronic' that the psychopathic personality was eventually fashioned. But despite O'Doherty's visionary rhetoric, these are not the grand beginnings of a reformist psychiatry. Rather, the possibility for O'Doherty's vision rested on an everyday attempt to solve the problem of what to do with the serious drunkard.

In Victoria, on 23 July 1862, Surgeon Superintendent Bowie of Yarra Bend Asylum wrote to the Chief Secretary requesting 'that a Receiving House be provided in Melbourne for cases sent, according to the present custom to Gaol, so that they could at once be placed under Medical Treatment until they could be removed to this – as a proper Lunatic Asylum'. Bowie requested that two detached buildings or cottages be added to the Melbourne Hospital each containing from fourteen to eighteen patients. The Inspector's reports in this period make mention of a receiving house in Carlton, probably the old Collingwood Stockade (now part of the Lee Street Primary School) which had subsequently become an asylum for incurable and imbecile cases, and afterwards in 1873 was transferred to the Education Department after the inmates were moved to the new building in Kew.[6] From its conception, the function of the receiving house was to be taken from the gaol and yet would lie only on the outskirts of the hospital, on the borderline of medicine proper. The plan in Victoria in the late 1890s was to send those who were 'clearly insane' directly to the asylum and those whose mental condition might be considered 'doubtful' to the receiving house.[7] McCreery reported in 1899 that building the receiving house would be very expensive, but he was more concerned about the fact that repeated examinations would do injury to the patients and wanted the clauses in the Lunacy Act changed so that the 'clearly insane' could be sent at once to the asylum. This move would make room for those still kept in gaols to be remanded for 'safety and observation' to the receiving house. The Vosper Committee in Western Australia (1902) originally recommended a place for 'patients of doubtful insanity' to be attached to a central police station, but plans drawn up in 1906 located it instead in the grounds of Perth Hospital. Ellis claims it was the first hospital in Australia to open a ward for the 'suspected insane'.[8]

The receiving house at Royal Park in Melbourne opened in 1907, located less than half a mile from the acute mental hospital, and at this stage it was clear that it was to act as an adjunct to the mental hospital or even as a ward of the mental hospital. Note the definition of this institution as 'for the early treatment of recent and recoverable mental disorders'.[9] The receiving house was an institutional expression of the line between sanity and insanity: it sits on the borderline, it is installed to receive borderline cases, and because it provides the time for scrutinising the line between sanity and insanity it also opens up a space wherein would reside the 'suspected case'. Chisholm Ross speaks of the 'borderland patient' in 1909 when he refers to the recent opening of an 'annex' to the Sydney Reception House for non-certified cases.[10] Correspondence from the Crown Solicitor's office in the same year made the judgement on the relevant statutes that the receiving house was 'something separate and distinct from the hospital for the insane' which provided 'machinery for resolving that doubt . . . to decide whether the person is or is not sane'. Subsequent amendments to legislation limited the reach of the Master-in-Equity over receiving house patients and voluntary boarders. By 1910 the Kew and Yarra Bend asylums were almost entirely for chronics and the majority of the curable cases were treated 'with apparently the happiest results' at the 'Receiving House' and the 'Acute Mental Hospital'.[11] Other localities were not so provided for, such as Ballarat where acute cases were still being admitted to either the district hospital or the Ballarat Gaol 'pending certification'.[12] Limits were placed on the length of time a person could be detained in a receiving house, from two months in 1928 to three months in an amendment to the Victorian Lunacy Act 1941.[13] With the opening of the receiving house we see a new category of the suspected insane, a person of disputed status, but also we see increasingly the replacement of the insane with the mentally ill. In the returns for the receiving house at Royal Park in 1907 the category of idiocy and imbecility were classified into two types – intellectual and moral.[14] In the statistical returns for 1911, causes of mental disorder were summarised as follows: worry, trouble, adversity and the like (90 cases);

heredity, including psychopathic and alcoholic ancestry (117); excessive alcoholism (74); syphilis (32) and senile changes (72 cases).[15]

The Reception (or Receiving) House, later to become Home, was the first of several new sites opened up in the early part of the century for practising upon the mentally ill rather than simply holding and certifying them. The documentation accompanying their development makes clear the purpose is about acting upon the patient, that the hospital is a workplace rather than a holding place or a gaol. The plans included first the receiving house, but then the Out-Door Clinic, mental wards in general hospitals, observation wards, day psychiatric clinics and so on.[16] The category of habitual inebriates received separate accommodation in 1889 when a retreat was opened at Beaconsfield and another the following year at Northcote (on the current secondary school site), to try to respond to the claims that drunkenness was the 'one great cause of insanity in the country'.[17] There is a widening of the architectural, bricks and mortar space for different kinds of work to be done on the mentally ill but in addition a widening of the conceptual space in which to think them. The temporal aspects which underpinned the centuries-old basic distinction between lunatics and idiots were elaborated further as a way of classifying and separating out the insane population. The receiving house is a site for early cases as well as doubtful; there are also the acute and the chronic, the transient and incipient, the curable. Forms of insanity map onto different kinds of workplaces which begin to open up. Psychiatrists like Springthorpe, Downey and Ernest Jones in the early twentieth century wanted to change the focus of insanity from a legal one to a modern scientific one, and thus to move the core activity of the asylum from holding to treating. The receiving house, often with a small hospital added alongside,[18] answered their need for a place for early treatment of incipient insanity. And early treatment, to borrow the analogy from physical disease, gives greater possibility of cure.[19] It would obviate the need for certification of the incipient and remedial, and the stigma which certification brings.[20] The receiving house is the site of the first major bureaucratic disaggregation of the old asylum population, where the 'doubtful' separates from the 'not so doubtful', and the chronic separates from the acute. Disaggregation reinforces the focus on possibilities of treatment, and moves away from earlier pre-occupations with certification, incarceration and penality.

With the receiving house now in place, there are two ways of entering a mental institution. The first is to be certified insane and go straight to the hospital; the second is to be certified apparently insane and go to the receiving house. After one has been in the receiving house for up to two months, one is insane and goes somewhere else, or one is discharged.

However, to avoid the bother and risk of difficult relatives and possible legal action, medical practitioners preferred to certify their patients as 'apparently insane'. It quickly became obvious that the receiving house had turned into a mental hospital in its own right, with its clients attracting the stigma of insanity which the receiving house had been designed to repel. Its purpose of more intensely scrutinising the patients was also compromised. When this problem arose, as it often did, the solution was to recast the physical location of the receiving house in relation to the main asylum in terms of its intended function. The receiving house at Royal Park in Victoria for example was taken over by the Army during the 1914–18 war for shell-shock victims, and its inmates were decanted to the mental hospital, where they remained. A committee of inquiry in 1949 recommended it be re-established in its original location, in a separate building on the periphery of the main institution, and next door to the railway station.[21] In a further modification to the Act in 1955, the words 'apparently insane' are replaced by 'suffering from some mental disorder'.[22]

By retrieving the receiving house government was reaffirming a medical rather than penal superintendency of insanity, but not by incorporating its activities wholly into the mainstream mental hospital. There was to be a single intermediary site holding a disputed population, which was devoted to the decision 'insane or not' with an expanded time-frame for this decision to be taken. The invention of extended time and discrete space located at a distance from the main hospital allowed for two developments: the first was the burgeoning of new practices concerned with the decision 'sane/not insane'; the second was to set up the possibilities of new types of disorders which amounted to alternatives to the 'sane/not insane' decision which were never fully incorporated into older classifications of insanity, but which nevertheless came out of and remained under the superintendence of psychiatry. We can look to the receiving house for the psychiatrised categories of disorder which otherwise appeared in penal contexts as categories of disorderly conduct and disorderly character.

Legislation in 1903 in Victoria allowed for the erection of reception houses and wards for the observation of the doubtful, and also for early treatment facilities. This became a place of treatment and the acute hospital or the 'mental hospital', as distinct from the 'hospital for the insane' (the old asylum), was spoken of as its adjunct or natural predicate. The receiving house and the acute mental hospital were increasingly thought of in the same way: as a means of separating acute cases into places of intense medical treatment, while places for the chronic seemed to be repositioned conceptually and geographically on the periphery of medical practice. The hospital for the curable – the mental hospital – is envisaged as having a larger medical staff than the older hospital for the insane, and soon, as an outcome of systematic transfers of patients, a number of these established institutions became *de facto* asylums for chronics. From 1910 onwards, these institutions complained about the number of 'chronic', 'hopeless', 'hopeless and troublesome' patients sent out to them. At the same time, the receiving house/mental hospital duo complained about the danger of its losing its distinction as a special place for the curable, acute and borderline group as doctors continued to send the obviously incurable to them. In summary then, the modern mental hospital with its emphasis on treatment and cure grew out of the space provided by the reception house, which itself emerged out of an expansion of the space on the border between sanity and insanity.

Refractory ward

A further physical displacement of individuals from within the main walls of the old asylum needs mentioning here. These are individuals who, after the medicalised asylum, were not able to be accommodated within its main walls but nonetheless remained 'on the books'. The dangerously disordered patient was less of a problem prior to the period when non-coercion became the officially accepted treatment. If there was a 'spill' in the governing of the dangerously disordered, it was contemporaneous with the instalment of the doctor as practitioner of a non-coercive treatment. Not that of course, with the lifting of physical constraints, the dangerous began to run wild. On the contrary, there is considerable doubt whether there was much actual lifting of constraint, as can be seen from Campbell's case notes in the 1860s right through to the mental hospital inquiries in the 1950s. Rather, the dangerously disordered was a group displaced to the margins of thinking the doctor-insane relationship framed around the new normalised model of non-coercion. Any relationship based on restraint cannot be thought of as central to this frame. The coerced patient was displaced away from the central model for acting upon the insane. The patient who continues to be managed by coercive means comes to be the 'impossible patient'.[23] It is no longer possible to think of him or her as central to the frame of the asylum concept. One such patient, Murphy, is recorded in Dr Campbell's case notes as a person so unmanageable that he is 'not mad'. Withers, another of Campbell's 'difficult cases' and described by Bostock as displaying 'studied and consistent anti-social conduct', was ordered by Campbell to be sent to the refractory ward .

The earlier inquiry into Woogaroo (1868–9) heard evidence about the position of the refractory patient at a critical time in the transition towards moral treatment and non-coercive approaches to asylum management.[24] At the time of this report the asylum was not completed according to original plans, and what was intended as an administrative block had become the main quarters for inmates. According to architect Charles Tiffin, it was in the haste to remove the lunatics from the gaol that the building was occupied before completion. At first there was a yard for females and another for males, which was known as the 'refractory yard' or just 'the yard'. In the 1868–9 evidence, the meaning of the term refractory floats around according to the context. Brosnan, for example, gives evidence that the patients 'were confined in the refractory yard by day and slept upstairs at night', unless refractory, in which case they were confined to the cells.[25] By the time evidence was taken, there was more than one yard for males, the females having been removed to a building originally intended for paying patients but which had stood empty for a number of years, so that by the 1870s one of the three male yards became a refractory yard. Sometimes a refractory patient was defined as dirty and destructive and was put in the refractory cells on the perimeter of the refractory yard. So there appears to be a number of little pockets of confining places for putting various noisy, destructive, dirty, refractory, infirm and generally troublesome patients. Although the Surgeon Superintendent Callan, whose competence is in question during the inquiry, indicates fairly clear-cut categorisation processes, this is contradicted by a wealth of insights into the day-to-day administration by warders and patients which appears in the evidence of this inquiry.

Throughout the testimonies there is a nervousness involved in talking about the practised forms of physical restraint. The Reverend William Draper describes the moral control which the matron exerts over the female patients in order to make them perform their allotted work, and John McDonnell, the visiting justice, was 'particularly glad to see that the system of non-constraint seemed to be the system of the place'.[26] But this kind of testimony is later contradicted by Manning's observation, which suggests that physical restraint in handcuffs was widespread throughout the asylum.[27] Physical restraint, involving handcuffs, straitjackets and tying the patient down was generally considered unacceptable except in instances of very last resort, but opinion over the use of seclusion is much more ambiguous. The superintendent on the cells in the refractory yard notes: '. . . the patients mentioned could not have been treated in a milder or more suitable manner anywhere . . . there was no other place where these patients could have been placed'. And the chief warder comments: '. . . refractory cells are the only available cells for the seclusion of refractory patients'. It is worth noting also that before the women could be moved into the building originally intended for paying patients, the two additions deemed necessary by the Surgeon Superintendent were eight refractory cells and a lavatory. Even the lavatory was taken over as a sleeping place for the 'not quite so bad'.[28]

At Woogaroo in the 1860s the asylum was an institution where physical restraint and outright abuse was fairly widespread, but was covered up or denied as best as can be. Also, the word 'refractory' was a broad and inclusive category, and principally involved various means of confinement in one of the many pockets of complete or limited isolation distributed throughout the building. The administrative importance of such seclusion was fairly openly and frankly discussed, but in a way which differentiated the practice from outright physical cruelty and neglect. Whereas in the early twentieth century annual reports of the asylum or mental hospital the issues of seclusion and restraint were discussed under the same rubric, the place of seclusion as it was enmeshed within the principle of moral management in the 1860s was ambiguous and ill-defined. By then the principle of moral management had become a kind of 'motherhood' issue in asylum management, and the practice of moral management took the form of a more 'humane' approach to the more 'reasonable' lunatic. Also, we have noted already that the practice of moral management allowed for the invention of a group within the asylum population who were responsive to the more reasonable and humane treatment. The more reasonable lunatic required moral treatment for its emergence. In this way, it has been possible to conceptualise moral treatment and the reasonable lunatic as having 'invented each other'. There is further evidence for this in the principles of management in the Adelaide Lunatic Asylum, which are cited with approval by the witness Hobbs, before the Woogaroo inquiry:

In dealing with the insane, it is erroneous to suppose that any special line of conduct is necessary; it may be laid down as a broad principle that the more nearly they are treated as sane and reasonable beings, the more easily they are managed; and success will follow in proportion, as approximation is made to this standard.[29]

The cottage system was one of the emergent architectures of reasonableness. This is the architect Tiffin spelling out the principles of the cottage system based on his research on Manning's ideas, in response to questions put to him in the inquiry:

Do you think the plan of putting a large number of patients in one building is better than the cottage system? I think it as necessary to carry out all systems, both the associated and the cottage systems. I think it is not a good plan to put very mad people in the same place as quieter patients . . .

You spoke just now of wood for cottages – that you would recommend wood. Do you think that is a safe material? Yes; for the kind of patients it is proposed to put into those buildings.

The inference is that the new plan based on the principles of the cottage system had as its ideal subject, and as its central focus, the reasonable lunatic. The corollary is that the 'very mad' are written out of this equation of reasonableness.

The architect's 'very mad' who are displaced from the cottages would correspond to many of the 'most confirmed', 'violent', 'very bad', 'dirty and destructive' cases that had fallen under the inclusive category of refractory. There is a more explicit reference to the writing out of refractory in the evidence of Dr Waugh:

Do you think it is desirable to confine the patients in one building, or in a number of buildings: the objects in view being their safe detention and perfect cure? Detached buildings would necessitate more superintendence and more means of detention than would be required where the patients were more confined; but as I have already said, whatever form the institution may take, there must be a large amount of room detached for separating patients in certain cases from the mass of other patients . . .

What would you rely upon as the principal means of curing patients? . . . Strict surveillance, great kindness, and the education of their power of self-control . . . Moral treatment is as much medical treatment as is the administering of drugs . . . In all hospitals there are some cases which are incurable; but we always act on the principle that they are curable.

Would you consider it sufficient to divide an asylum into a refractory yard, and a place to which the other patients could have access? No, I do not believe in a refractory yard.

Do you think it would be possible to dispense with the use of physical restraint? Altogether, except the temporary restraint necessary in fits of mania, where, for instance, there is a tendency to suicide while the fit lasts . . .

I would recommend no punishment whatever; the patients are sick and require to be cured.

. . . as to the additional space required for the classification of patients, you consider it essential that there should be different departments, that the more violent patients should not be mixed up with the others? Undoubtedly . . . that is why I would recommend a number of small wards for separating the patients.

. . . No doubt, restraint is necessary . . . what I mean is, that a man should not be confined to his chamber, because he has, on the previous day, shown homicidal mania. Coercion must not be carried out from day to day; it should only be employed to keep the patient from hurting himself, or others . . .

When you object to the use of a refractory yard, is it not merely the term 'refractory' to which you take objection, rather than the use of such as place? If it were merely a yard of separation, I should not object to it.

Waugh, another witness, is an advocate of moral management. Under his principles, there is no room for punishment or something called refractory. But in the set-up of detached buildings, a separation 'from the mass' of patients is a necessity. But there is no attempt to name a class that is to be separated; the intention is to refuse to so name, and certainly to refuse to name as refractory. There are also no cells in Waugh's ideal establishment.

In the 1868 body of evidence from doctors, warders, patients and the like, the antonym of refractory seems to be 'convalescent'. Patients could be removed from refractory arrangements into various convalescent arrangements. For example, they could have their meals in the 'convalescent room', or, on being convalescent could take their meals with the working men, a 'privilege', or apply for work outside the asylum. Convalescence denotes a deal of self-management. Thus, the refractory and the grossly sick were thrown together in various ways and the convalescent were removed from them. Refractoriness was assumed inasmuch as it denoted the 'main bunch' of lunatics from which later a separation could be earned: '. . . when patients are first admitted to the Asylum they are generally put in the refractory yard, and on their becoming convalescent they are removed; if they misbehave themselves they are sent back again'.[30] Inmates had to work hard to disengage themselves and to keep themselves disengaged from the refractory. The refractory patients – the dirty and destructive – could be put into cells on the perimeter of the asylum, but the noisy and most refractory were likely to be locked up in the main building with the sick. If any group had a less than central position in the asylum it was the convalescent, which denoted a certain reasonableness, an ability to abide by the asylum rules and not to cause trouble. It is convalescence that signals the possibility of removal from the main body, a shift of asylum location more approaching the exit. With the demise of the ordinariness or taken-for-grantedness of the refractory, a newly centralised 'associated mass of ordinary patients', governed by the principles of curability, and responding to the principles of the exercise of reason and self-control, emerged. It is a group that will eventually transmute into the 'acutes' as the privileged subject of psychiatry, and to cause the set of transformations and diffentiations which brings about the 'mental hospital' and a residue of problematic groups.

Over the next half century then, a reversal takes place in the relative positions of the refractory and convalescent. The categories which eventually emerge from the convalescent group become the central focus of asylum practice, while the refractory and sick are moved to the periphery. The Woogaroo inquiry results in legislation to set up reception houses – institutions from which hospitals specifically for the acute will eventually take shape. The reception house became important for a decentralising and recentralising process whereby it became possible to reshape the convalescents into a class amenable to treatment. Hobbs, the Government Medical Officer, gave evidence as follows:

Do you think detention in the asylum after they are sane has any tendency to cause them to relapse into insanity? Certainly, nothing can be so bad as to detain a man in the asylum after he is in a state of consciousness. That is the reason I recommended some additional buildings, where convalescents might be placed, and not only for convalescents, but for the reception of patients who are sent there for the first time, on their admission.[31]

Hobbs plainly sees that those who fall into the category of refractory have no place in these new arrangements:

My reason for recommending a ward of that description [convalescent asylum] was a twofold one – first to receive lunatics on their arrival, and to let them be treated there for a few days until the surgeon-superintendent should make up his mind how to classify them, and in the next place, to provide the necessary accommodation for convalescents and the quiet patients.

But then you would have all sorts of cases mixed up together – those who were perfectly sane with others who were raving maniacs? It would not be necessary to keep a raving maniac there five minutes. The surgeon-superintendent would soon send him to his proper place.[32]

All the legislation in the colonies at this time make reference to the New South Wales Dangerous Lunatics Act 1843 in order to define the categories of person for whom the reception houses will be established – that is, for 'dangerous lunatics' and 'dangerous idiots' inscribed in this earlier legislation: 'An act to make provision for the safe custody of and prevention of offences by persons dangerously insane and for the care and maintenance of person "of unsound mind"'.[33] The dangerous lunatic is one defined in the legislation as needing safe custody and especially needing custody for the sake of prevention of crime, including suicide. The legislation did not prohibit such people being kept under the care and protection of friends if they could guarantee 'peaceable behaviour and safe custody'. Nor did it mean that those 'who are insane but not dangerously so' could not be kept in an asylum or sent to one of its collection points. The word dangerous has a quite specific meaning and function in the Act. It indicates anyone who needs institutional care and control for the sake of themselves or others. In addition, it functions to limit the application of the Act, in the sense that it prohibits constables from dragging every idiot son out of the farmhouse kitchen.

It is clearly not referring to those who, within the asylum, would come to be marked out as violent and troublesome, as the candidate for the refractory, or as Hobbs' raving maniac. Legislation was passed in many states to pick up on those who previously would be defined as dangerous in this sense, and who would have first appeared in the gaol or hospital on their way to the asylum, but who now could go to the reception house.

The refractory ward appears as another constituent of the peripheral zone. In the plans for the Sunbury asylum in Victoria, a substantial building was added on to the site to situate the criminally insane, although it was never actually used for this purpose. It was built after the main asylum, at the edge of the main institution on a site carved out of the hillside, and it was used as a confined space for those who did not conform in the main asylum. It is the opening up of the borderline of the asylum, where the line becomes a space in which types of person more complex, more problematic than the insane, can be produced. Dance, Funstan and Rubbo make the point in their discussion of the Sunbury asylum that the reception house and the refractory ward make their appearance on the grounds of the asylum at about the same time.[34] It was as though they were complementing each other. As we trace through the inauguration of the refractory ward, in just one small part of the country, it is possible to see how it acts as a surface upon which a kind of 'making up' of persons takes place. In the shift of architectural forms and in the naming of persons, we see the early signs of the beginnings of a displacement of the refractory and the replacement of a group which may be seen as the precursor to the modern mental patient and the eventual proper subject of psychiatry.

As a corollary, other kinds of persons come to occupy a peripheral place both geographically and as objects of the medical gaze. But peripheral only to medicine. The gradual removal of the class of imbeciles from the broader lunatic population brought these groups under an educational rather than medical gaze, although medicine continued to have carriage of the whole field in government reporting and administration. To take the example of Victoria, the Zox Commission which met during 1884–6 was specifically asked to report on how classification of imbeciles and the insane could be improved, and in its recommendations wanted to have a clear distinction made between the imbeciles, criminal lunatics and inebriates. In 1887, the first three children's cottages for child imbeciles were opened, known as Kew Cottages, where the children received basic instruction, gymnastics and singing, and training in regularity and habits. Later, in the mid 1890s, an enthusiast by the name of John Fishbourne established a day-school for young imbeciles which was to become the model for developments initiated by the Department of Public Instruction well into the next century. A report of the 'school for afflicted children' appearing in a daily newspaper reported that the pupils 'vary between actual idiots and children in whom it is almost impossible for an outsider to detect any sign of mental disturbance . . . Without proper training such children would necessarily merge either into hopeless idiots or criminals of the most depraved type.'[35] The school, St Aiden's in Puckle Street Moonee Ponds, ceased to function after the death of Fishbourne in 1913, but by that time public education authorities had opened a special school for feeble-minded children in Bell Street Fitzroy and began a new set of calculations centred on measuring the performance of pupils as a gauge of 'intelligence'.[36] So these other kinds of persons became distinguished in the changed context in which they found themselves and the manner in which they were examined and calculated. It became possible to think the separation of these groups as outside of the lunatic population.

Tools of calculation

There have recently been claims that deinstitutionalisation has increased the number of dangerous people let loose in community settings, on the assumption that these were the persons at some stage held behind walls, who are now 'released'. A related concern in the move from asylum to community is the progressive decline in public psychiatry and the consequent diminution of services to persons with severe psychotic illness, especially those with 'behavioural disfunction', who may be too difficult to treat in any other setting than a public psychiatric unit. In Australia, the in-patient population of psychiatric hospitals has fallen by about seventy per cent in the past thirty years, while the proportional exodus of psychiatrists from these hospitals has occurred at an even greater rate. This is despite the fact that the number of psychiatrists has increased five-fold during the same period. Similar movements have occurred elsewhere. In a rather nostalgic piece, James presents this as psychiatry's desertion of its 'heartland', upon which it built its long history of clinical responsibility, and which it now needed to rebuild in the public sector.[37] After all, the asylum had been the setting for the discovery of manic-depressive illnesses by Falret and Baillarger, the distinguishing of *dementia praecox* by Kraepelin in Germany and later schizophrenia by Bleuler in Zurich, the discovery of ECT by Cerletti and Bini in Rome and of lithium by Cade at the Royal Park Hospital in Melbourne. As mainstream medicine developed in the general hospital and particularly the teaching hospital, psychiatry despite its successes was lodged behind the asylum walls and to some extent segregated from medical confreres in other fields. The patients were kept at some distance from other health settings and often from their families as well. On the other hand, the conditions in the asylums reinforced mental health as a domain unlike any other field of medicine. Henry Handel Richardson's *The Fortunes of Richard Mahoney* graphically depicts the violence which could be inflicted on an educated middle-class professional person in late nineteenth-century asylum in Melbourne:

Richard, forced by this burly brute to grope on the floor for his spilt food, to scrape it together and either eat it or have it thrust down his throat . . . she had to hear from Richard about the means used to quell and break the spirits of refractory lunatics . . . There was not only feeding by force, the strait-jacket, the padded cell. There were drugs and injections, given to keep a patient quiet and ensure his warder's freedom: doses of castor oil so powerful that the unhappy wretch into whom they were poured was rendered bedridden, griped, thoroughly ill.[38]

Our discussion in the last two chapters picks up on a number of key points of interest in the historiography of psychiatry and psychology in Europe, North America and Australia. These relate to what are regarded as pivotal events in the history of psychiatry: the doctors taking charge of the asylums in what Robert Castel has referred to as 'the golden age of psychiatry' – the removal of constraint and repression over the inmate and its replacement with a rational mental science;[39] the adoption of 'moral treatment', discussed in Scull's history of madness in England as an alternative technique of management of inmates based on 'psychological control';[40] the separation and differentiation of the asylum population which served to separate the chronic from the acute, the mentally ill from the mentally defective, the imbecile from the moral imbecile. For the purposes of the present study, these become important fields of historical investigation as a means of addressing the contemporary question of how it has become possible to think and act upon the problem of dangerousness in terms of the conceptual framework of personality disorder.

The way in which problems 'of the present' are to be diagnosed brings on a concern to problematise certain events and changes 'in the past',[41] involving a number of historical sites besides those which formally belong to the past of psychiatry. A history of contemporary problems is not able to be understood through a single continuous line of descent into the present.[42] A genealogy of personality disorder involves histories of psychiatry and psychology, but also law, penality and criminology, social work and education. In addition, each of these is implicated in what we might call histories of subjectification, or accounts of how individuals have come to understand themselves and 'the self' as an object to be managed.[43] The present study draws attention to the possibilities entailed in the *mode of calculation* of persons and how persons are 'made up' and become objects of knowledge in relation to changes in the functioning of institutions. As an alternative to current histories of psychiatry, it is possible to consider these events in terms which, borrowing from Ian Hacking's *The Taming of Chance*,[44] suggest that the paradigm of human nature is linked to modes of calculation, that increasing acceptance of new ways of acting upon persons such as the criminal and the lunatic arose from particular kinds of calculations made upon the body of the criminal and lunatic as a consequence of particular ways of managing these persons; that the possibility of 'chance' – the chance of recovery or reformability, the chance co-relation of factors which make up types of persons, the chance co-existence of behaviour and personality traits – arose from the production of statistical probability and the very fact of collecting information by means of an ever more intense scrutiny of the population.

The initial focus on the nineteenth-century asylum prepares the way for understanding an important break, which is the invention of person-ality. This move is accompanied by a shift of interest of psychiatry during the first half of the twentieth century away from madness and towards a range of behavioural disorders and personal distress. Cate-gories of persons are formed by means of techniques of calculation which problematise the individual in terms of their distance or relation to other individuals, a calculation of the spaces between people as epitomised in the *Diagnostic and Statistical Manual*, rather than, as previously, of the spaces within individuals such as those provided by means of laboratory techniques and appearing in the anatomy and physiology manuals. The distance on the reflex arc, or the composition of neuronic structure, makes way for a statistical co-relation between conduct and life circumstances. But this governmental activity around attempting to know and act upon the disordered and unruly in turn sets boundaries within which individuals will themselves freely work upon the production of ordered selves. Personality, under liberal forms of government, is the space in which one regulates one's own selfhood.

In this half-century, the workings of the asylum served to begin to make as separate objects of knowledge the chronic from the acute, the mentally ill from the mentally defective, and later the imbecile from the moral imbecile. From the middle of the nineteenth century it became possible to calculate a rate of reformability of patients, and asylum statistics showing rates of recovery started to appear in annual reports and in the popular press. In a crude form, the calculation was on the basis of the proportion of inmates discharged in any particular year. The concept of reformability was an artefact of the particular *modes of calculation*, bringing these types of persons into existence through techniques of calculating within the specific confines of institutional spaces. It became possible to conceive of variation and malleability of human kind within this population from the numbers derived from their governing. The possibility of chance appeared almost automatically from the tables and measures produced of this population.

Separations within the asylum saw a transformation of a person previously known as the 'troublesome' into a person 'not amenable to treatment' or the 'impossible patient'. New geographical and conceptual spaces will allow the consolidation of a group within the population of the asylum who would constitute the true object of psychiatric knowledge; and a residual group – the borderland patient – while remaining within the broad oversight of the asylum and psychiatry would become the object of different modes of calculation.

4 Counting, eugenics, mental hygiene

> Mr Darwin wrote to me that he had long thought that habitual
> criminals should be confined for life, but that he had not, until reading
> my views, recognized the importance of extinguishing the breed . . .
> the lives of criminals, lunatics, and idiots are not only useless, but
> painful to them, a mischief to society and far worse to posterity. The
> humane course is to narcotise them on their first conviction. Ten years
> of this system would go far to abolish crime, if not lunacy, and would
> rapidly raise the average of morality and intelligence of the human
> race.[1]

From its 1893 conference, the Australian Association for the Advancement of Science presented scientific opinion on questions of population
improvement and public health under a new section titled 'Mental
Science and Education', replacing an earlier chapter of the association
with the incongruous title of 'Literature'. The new category consoli-
dated a scientific approach to the population question which would,
with certain exceptions, find its solution not in programs of selective
breeding and 'narcotism' favoured by the Melbourne doctor cited
above, but rather in programs of classification, segregation and a
diversification of mental fitness strategies including special schools. The
'final solution' methods appeared to lose support or went underground
in many countries by the late 1930s, when they attracted comparison
with Germany's attempts at 'racial purification'.[2] In the last decades of
the nineteenth century in countries like Australia with compulsory
school attendance laws, doctors and educators shared an interest in
producing a more stable, healthy and productive citizenry, an outcome
now demonstrable in health and school statistics and the various
categories of 'redeemable' or 'restorable' person which had been revealed in the exercise of separating and counting. In this strategic
alliance, it became possible to carve out a terrain of enquiry and
practical intervention that allowed the population to be differentiated
according to the laws of measurement.

The links between public medicine and public education staked out the ground which the discipline of psychology would occupy. The crucial discovery was that of borderline mental defect, referred to in a 1912 Australia-wide survey of feeblemindedness among school pupils as 'mental dullness'.[3] The diagnosis of amentia (absence of mind) in children had been a jealously guarded medical concern, and doctors had initially opposed the use of psychological tests, such as the Binet-Simon, by laying down a strict distribution of roles between psychiatrist, social worker and psychologist. However, with the discovery of mental dullness and 'high grade amentia', the doctors marked out a field which psychology would come to occupy, and which would also become the province mainly of public schooling rather than medicine.

The links between education and the emergence of psychological knowledge and techniques have been documented in a number of studies on population improvement and the growth of mental testing, in Europe, the United States and Australia.[4] Social historians have tended to explain the links between schooling and the appearance of the psychology of individual differences by appealing to theories of social control. Throughout the century, beginning with Malthus, the spectre of 'racial degeneration' had become a major issue in scientific thinking, stimulated by the observation that the 'less fit' were producing children in relatively larger numbers than the 'best available stock'. At the end of the century these views were bolstered by evidence of the poor physical quality of recruits for military service in the Boer War. The measurement of bodies for war service turned out to be an important tool for assessing the general health of populations. Some of psychology's inheritance in ideas about racial degeneration, population control and eugenics is generally understood in terms of a functionalist analysis of ideology, whereby psychological techniques of measuring and ranking the population are understood to support class and cultural reproduction in order, ultimately, to maintain rule. As one author points out of these studies, they serve as critiques of ideology which seek to demonstrate the falsity of psychological ideas and practices. By revealing the function of the ideas, ideological critique simply explains the falsity in terms of the function it serves.[5]

These histories also problematised the population controllers in terms of a body of scientific thought associated with broader economic and political changes from the mid nineteenth century, when notions of 'innate' human inequality appeared to gain greater prominence, serving in particular to rationalise inequalities in the labour market. These developments have been understood as attempts to repress individuals and groups in the interests of establishing one sort or another of social regulation, involving segregation, surveillance and control. Gaynor and

Fox's account of the establishment of the psychological clinic in Western Australia under Ethel Stoneman is a case in point.[6] Stoneman's single-handed struggle to win acceptance for a clinic which would identify mentally defective or deficient children and place them in special educational institutions is understood by Gaynor and Fox to be a covert attempt by the state to intervene in the labour market and to regulate the supply of labour by means of state policies in welfare, education and training. Underpinning the activities of the psychological clinic was the view that the identification of the mental defective was essential to prevent these groups from reproducing themselves. The element of segregation for social control, particularly over women, was understood as fundamental to the role of the psychological clinic. This kind of account made tests for deficiency and defectiveness a part of the armoury of the eugenicist, in that the testing legitimated the provision of specialist segregated schooling and a limited participation in the labour market:

. . . those deemed 'mentally deficient' to the extent of being unemployable were basically imprisoned in Claremont or other institutions, with consideration given to the possibility of their sterilisation (which would in the long term reduce the total number of such 'unemployables'). In those with a lesser degree of disability, special schooling emphasised very specific vocational instruction from an early age, by which the child would eventually be prepared for entry into a particular segment of the workforce.[7]

Ethel Stoneman was taken to be a 'soft' eugenicist in that she opposed sterilisation on the grounds that the procedure was said to promote promiscuity among the intellectually disabled. Nevertheless, the main contours of the social control argument can be gleaned from the history of her work with the psychological clinic.

The inadequacies of this kind of analysis as applied to psychology and psychiatry have been well canvassed elsewhere. Firstly, the various parts of the psychiatric system, like other practices of governing individuals and populations, do not speak and act in concert and cannot be reduced to a single origin or inspiration.[8] Notions of social control emanating from unitary points of origin such as 'the state' tend to underestimate the diversity of practices and knowledges which intersect, compete or contradict each other. This is a particularly salient point in relation to the practice of psychiatry, since it was critique of outdated and irrational practices towards the mad that advanced psychiatry's claims over the field.[9] Secondly, much critique of psychiatry and psychology as social control begins from an alternative account of the 'truth of madness', and critique becomes a means of developing an analysis of the *function* of psychiatry based on its epistemological inadequacies. Psychiatry's failure properly to 'know' the mad becomes the starting point for an analysis of the ideological and political effects of this systematic mis-recognition. The problem here is that these approaches tend to displace issues of power in everyday social management onto supposedly more fundamental domains such as class struggle or patriarchal domination. Individual and institutional practices are conceived as ideological in the sense that they act 'for something else', and newly carved out terrains within which power operates in modern societies are left under-theorised or ignored.[10]

A further inadequacy of conventional social control approaches is the tendency to ignore the extent to which the regulation and governing of persons presupposes active techniques of self-government on the part of individuals. To pick up on Graham Burchell's discussion of 'governmen-tality',[11] the domain of subjectivity and the 'microphysical' in modern forms of governing is understood not simply as an extension of the 'macropolitical', but rather '. . . technologies of domination of indi-viduals over one another have recourse to processes by which the individual acts upon himself and, conversely . . . where techniques of the self are integrated into structures of coercion'.[12] For Burchell, the term 'government' is used as a synonym or alternative for power, as a way of identifying a field of power analysis; government might be under-stood as a 'contact point' where techniques of domination, and techni-ques of the self, interact. Subjectivity is not the simple outcome of government. Rather, government in general is understood as a way of acting to affect the way in which individuals conduct themselves. On a similar line of argument, Jeffrey Minson takes to task the functionalism of what he calls 'sociological–structural critique', and the ethos of 'political romanticism' which invariably drives it, by pointing to its failure to take seriously the forms of consciousness and subjectivity produced as an effect of government. Minson writes:

> . . . this incapacity or unwillingness to acknowledge the ethical weight of government stems from the self-imposed obligation to go to the causal roots of oppressive social conditions, track the full extent of their pervasive presence in the social and individual body and thereby register the need for radical social change . . . It is 'society' in general and 'social subjects' (human individuals conceptualised in terms of their subjectivity) which form the main, dialectically-related, objects of analysis. The supposition that social relations form compre-hensive ensembles generates the requirement to explain what enables them to continually function as wholes.[13]

So the contact point between the domains of 'self' and 'society' is not merely a functional one achieved through socialisation. It can be analysed directly by means of an investigation of the development of particular forms of social administration and modes of governing, and the existence of certain kinds of subjects and subjectivity which act as correlates of these forms.

In the existing work utilising these insights, the power of psychiatry lies not in a monolithic crushing of individuality implied in social control theories, but rather in what psychiatry makes thinkable and possible and the new types of problems, objectives and solutions it allows us to conceive.[14] Psychiatry and psychology in this view are understood as productive rather than repressive, in that they are constitutive of new power relations which, during the early twentieth century, enabled mental health to be seen as a national objective and a personal desire. New sites for the operation of power are carved out in the way persons are incited to regulate themselves and others according to norms of mental health inscribed in the disciplines of psychiatry and psychology, but imbricated as well in a range of institutional practices which extend a grid of normalcy throughout the social body. This is now the place to extend these alternative approaches to social control theory, to show how the population improvers and eugenicist strategies shaped institutional developments and forms of personhood, and to examine, in the final section of this chapter, the links between these historical movements and the emergence of mental hygiene as a national objective and a means of forging a particular kind of personhood.

Knowledge and government

We have already seen the counting, surveying and charting of the lunatic and deviant population in Australia beginning during the nineteenth century and the significance of statistics for the way in which categories of persons are 'made up' and become objects of knowledge. Recent accounts of statistical movement in nineteenth-century Europe emphasise the development of new modes of governing based on knowledges of territories, populations and the capacities of the individuals to be governed.[15] Knowledges and categories of persons brought into existence by the new 'science of state' form a part of what Foucault called bio-politics, '. . . an entire micro-power concerned with the body' matching up with 'comprehensive measures, statistical assessments and interventions' aimed at the body politic, the social body.[16] The transformation of the population into numbers and types has been conceptualised as a 'moral science', a topography in which suicide, crime, insanity, delinquency and pauperism are mapped, named, ordered and classified. Ian Hacking argues that many of the modern categories by which we think about people and their activities are put in place by an attempt to collect numerical data:

it was not that there was a kind of person who came increasingly to be recognised as such, by bureaucrats or students of human nature, but rather that a kind of person came into being at the same time as the kind itself was being invented. In some cases, that is, our classifications and our classes conspire to emerge hand in hand, each egging the other on.[17]

The enumeration of types of persons within problem populations produces classifications '. . . within which people must think of themselves and of their actions that are open to them'. As an alternative to notions of power as something possessed by individuals and exercised in a repressive way on individual wills, the concept of disciplinary power focuses instead on the complex, multifarious, capillary nature of modern power and the way in which power is productive of particular types of subjectivity.

In short, the governing of persons in this view entails of necessity a certain dynamic nominalism.[18] Particular domains of existence and numerous kinds of human beings and human acts come into being hand in hand with our invention of the categories used to describe them. Our spheres of possibility, and hence our selves, are to some extent 'made up' by our naming and what that entails.

Throughout the nineteenth century, it is possible to discern the new language of governing – a governing over life itself – in a range of sites concerned with the condition of the population. Vocabulary, including charts and tables, come to be deployed in ways which help to construct new sectors of existence, such as separate biological and social domains, as objects of government. This points to the mutually constitutive aspects of language and politics.[19] Language is understood as an 'intellectual technology' through which new forms of thought are invented. On the premise that an object must be known in order to be governed, language renders certain domains of existence amenable to intervention by administrators and rulers. In an exercise of power which is both totalising and individualising, population and individuals are constituted by means of certain forms of calculation and documentation in order to make a particular field of human affairs governable.[20] Population becomes an object of thought and a target of government in virtue of 'life' itself, the life of the species, becoming a key object of political rule.

Population became known through this 'avalanche of printed numbers',[21] beginning in the countries and territories of Europe from the end of the eighteenth century, amassing huge collections of data which brought 'life and its mechanisms into the realm of explicit calculation and made knowledge-power an agent of transformation of human life'.[22] Hacking calls *subversive* the kinds of things and people that are counted. For him, it is not the actual categories of persons that are important, but rather the very idea of categorising them. For example, the class structure by which we view society was designed by early nineteenth-century counting bureaucracies, and prescriptions for how people could die were inherited from William Farr's nosology. The subversive aspects of biopolitics set the stage of categorisation in which we still live. We have already seen the emerging standardised ways of becoming sick and going mad which form over time, and which were written down in medical texts, the psychiatric manuals and later, in the *Diagnostic and Statistical Manuals*.[23]

In Australia, categories of population emerge from the earliest musters designed to estimate food and other requirements of the colony at Port Jackson.[24] The problem of population in Australia in the nineteenth century began as an episode of quite vigorous activity by medical, educational, religious and governmental authorities concerned to map certain characteristics of unruliness and disorder, and to arrest the unstable and nomadic existence in many parts of the Australian colonies. However, the reality which becomes the object of government does not merely await its discovery by the mechanisms of language and statistics. A kind of person comes into being at the same time as the kind itself was being invented.[25] Official statistics and surveys are not simply a collection of existing facts awaiting codification, but rather are a series of events in which critical and contestable decisions are made about categories of persons and separate spheres of living. Governor Phillip recorded the number of children in the colony of New South Wales in 1790, which was possibly the first statistical survey in Australia, coinciding with the first census in Britain.[26] For the next fifty years the church was responsible for registering births, deaths and marriages, and those children who escaped the rites of the church might also have escaped the statistician's gaze. Enthusiasts such as John Dunmore Lang began to collect information on production and related fiscal matters, and used the evidence to make predictions about the colony's power to be productive.[27] Between 1839 and 1856, all the colonies had developed a vital statistics system.

Various committees of inquiry by colonial authorities had begun the mapping of deviance within sections of the population by the middle of the century, such as the 1859 survey undertaken by Henry Parkes in Sydney. The survey problematised the welfare of working-class children in terms of their potential dangerousness, their idleness and threat.[28] The mapping of deviance and the moralisation of the poor through the notion of a normal family were parallel events, bringing about a more intense individualising gaze on the problem of disorder and unruliness, and promoting a private domesticated unit which would automatically produce in its members the responsibility to care for themselves, rather than placing the burden on public authorities.[29] The conditions of possibility for the production of individuals as particular types of family members are not located merely as effects of more fundamental sources of power resting in class and gender relations, but depend for their mechanisms of representation on the mundane, administrative features of person-formation. Statistical treatment of the population left no domain of human inquiry untouched. Many of the modern categories by which we think about people and their activities are put in place by an attempt to collect numerical data.[30]

The statistical sciences are an important field of activity in which the domain of the social and the individual become marked out in terms amenable to political calculation and intervention. The surveys and analyses of the nineteenth-century philanthropists, charity and medical workers show the ways in which categories of persons emerge from early social scientific attempts to study the population.[31] Workers such as the Hill sisters on their visits to Australia mirrored the activities of figures like Mary Carpenter in England in their work with children and the poor.[32] Early medical workers in Australia employed techniques of inquiry from which emerged a 'social individual' constructed with a character and identity, linked to the provision of health care for the poor. Institutions such as industrial schools made efforts to distinguish properly between children of the perishing and dangerous classes, by providing a physical space and administrative framework for intensifying the gaze on bodies and the differences between them.[33]

The effects of a bio-politics – a power which focuses both on individual bodies and on whole populations – thus involves the production of particular categories of person. Data on averages and dispersions of people engendered the idea of the normal, with the counting of human behaviour such as crime and suicide revealing astonishing regularities.[34] Statistical laws seemed to spring from official tables of deviancy, suggesting opportunities for new kinds of social engineering and new ways to modify undesirable classes. New possibilities for action come into being as a consequence of new modes of description.[35] Bio-politics is also part of the history of the modes by which human beings are made into subjects. The modes of objectification in philology, and the dividing practices of the mad, the sick and the criminal, provide the conditions of possibility for the ways in which humans turn themselves in subjects.[36] As a part of the 'science of State', counting and statistics produced the classifications of patients in the asylum and the possibility of recovery according to category of patient. Moreover, early twentieth-century statistics allowed for the possibility of co-relating the attributes of persons, and of measuring present and prior forms of personhood to offer causes of phenomena. The existence of a whole set of concerns and activities grouped together under the rubric of the sciences of population, such as eugenics, was only made possible by the kinds of counting of the population which began in Europe, North America and Australia during the nineteenth century.

Following from these general remarks, it should be clear that the population improvers and specific programs such as eugenics entailed a much more open-ended set of concerns and strategies than might be anticipated from a reading of these events from the perspective of social control. Formally speaking, eugenics in the nineteenth century was the study of population and race with a view to improving its efficiency and purity. Selective breeding to improve the quality of the population was one response to concerns about declining birth rates, low levels of physical health and various measures of degeneracy which had begun to accumulate in Australia and in other places in the previous decades. A characteristic eugenicist line of argument was that persistent degradation led by unwise and unregulated breeding would eventually lead to the 'extinction of the race'. The name of Charles Darwin was used to lend authority to explanations on the scientific causes of social decay, as the earlier quotation from the Adelaide conference of the Australasian Association for the Advancement of Science in 1893 indicates. One view of the role of medicine and science was to improve human life that was useful to society rather than nursing and cultivating those whom nature would otherwise exterminate. Doctors even suggested that these steps would be preferred by the 'less fit' themselves, 'the criminal, the lunatic, the defective and even the incompetent and unthrifty', whose lives were painful to them and for whom a long period of confinement was far too barbarous.[37]

This *negative* eugenic strategy coexisted with a *positive* one of encouraging the propagation of the best stock through financial incentives and social policy measures designed to improve the overall quality of the population. As a political strategy, eugenics was a very diverse set of ideas and proposals which could be linked to a broad cross-section of interests. The problem of population provided the conditions for a complexity of cause and effect relations, which allowed more than simply one strategy to be elaborated in social policy.[38] It permitted the view that as the progeny of domestic animals could be improved, so the same mechanisms could be applied to the improvement of citizens. But the political strategy of eugenics provided a conceptual terminology – a language, a calculation of bodies – that also permitted an opposing political program to be elaborated, focusing on *environmental* reform as a calculated means of population improvement. An important feature of this complexity, as Nikolas Rose has observed in the British context, was a statistical dispute over the significance of the inheritance of acquired characteristics.[39] In Britain, eugenics sat alongside a social hygiene strategy in what Rose describes as 'the unravelling of the confused play of causes and effects which had characterised the nineteenth-century writings on degeneracy'.[40] Moreover, the particular 'environmental' inflection of Australian scientists pointed to by authors like Bacchi for example,[41] may relate more to the specific circumstances of the population problem in Australia than to any peculiar 'liberal mind set' of the Australian political scene.

The positive, environmentalist strategies focused particularly on schooling as the site for managing problems of population quality, coinciding with reforming moves from within the ranks of educationists themselves. Central to this reform was the emergence of the child study movement and the 'scientific educationists'.[42] Childhood was discovered as a special and unique period of life subject to regular and quantifiable developmental stages.[43] A child study association was formed in New South Wales in 1901 to encourage more careful observation of how children learn, and to foster respect and confidence between parents, teachers and pupils. Similar movements spread in the other states. Froebel's theories in particular affirmed childhood as a 'natural' stage of life, but requiring specific types of treatment and cultivation:

Nature requires children to be children before they are men. If we prevent this order we produce forward fruit, neither having ripeness or taste, but sure soon to become rotten. Childhood has its own peculiar manner of seeing, perceiving and thinking, and nothing is more absurd than our being anxious to substitute our own in its stead.[44]

These moves to improve the way that children occupied a proper childhood were progressive attempts to assist children to learn. Education took up science to study ways in which pupils having learning difficulties could be helped.[45] Members of the medical profession gave lectures to teachers on the anatomical makeup of the brain and its various functions, showing how 'brain power could be developed through education and other environmental stimulation'.[46] Dr Stawell's lectures on feeble-mindedness especially pointed to the need for good teaching:

It is shocking to think of a fellow creature locked up in the darkness of stunted growth when early intelligent treatment such as a good teacher can follow out might have opened his prison house and let in the sun.[47]

Frank Tate, the first Director of Education in Victoria, used the language of phrenology as a metaphor to advance his ideas about a liberal education for national prosperity:

. . . the nation will gain school-power which sees clearly that it is long heads and broad foreheads which win in the long run, and which, therefore, spends money wisely in lengthening heads and broadening foreheads.[48]

It was indeed the motivation to help children learn that inspired the first 'intelligence' test in Australia in 1910, administered to pupils in Newtown in Sydney by their headteacher, Margaret Miller.[49] The test, like others given around the same period, replicated the test which Binet devised in 1905 to discover children who were falling behind in class, with a view to remedying the underlying causes. Miller found the major cause of 'retardation' to be a combination of physical illness, poor teaching and irregular attendance. On investigation she found that most pupils were working when not attending school, sometimes running messages or looking after other children at home.

In the following three decades the problem of the mental defective became a major object of concern within public medicine and public education. By the 1920s psychiatry advocated a strict policy of diagnosis and segregation of 'feebleminded' persons, a general category of defectives of all types who were thought to demonstrate 'social inefficiency' in everyday living. A Royal Commission in England in 1904, followed by the Mental Deficiency Act of 1914, provided Australian doctors with a good model of the way the state should ensure that proper institutional care and education be provided for defectives, and that parents be compelled to hand their children to institutions for their own good and to prevent procreation. Defectives were given manual work like bootmaking or handiwork, and new Special Schools opened in the various states from 1914, some using Montessori methods. Psychiatrists took note of research abroad indicating that feebleminded persons possessed animal instincts without the intellectual capacity for control, with one doctor observing that '. . . mere withholding of the marriage certificate will not prevent them when the opportunity is available from indulging their sexual desires'.[50] As well, Melbourne University anatomist R.J.A. Berry had conducted large-scale investigations of feeblemindedness among state school pupils, state wards and prisoners in Pentridge Gaol, attempting to show how these groups displayed lower than average brain capacity. To be precise, the 355 criminals studied had a brain capacity of 1,438 cubic centimetres or five per cent below average, and a further breakdown revealed that 'the cubic capacity of the brain of criminals convicted of the unskilled crimes of petty theft was much smaller than those convicted of the skilled forms of crime'.[51] The scientists of population were embarked on an ever intense scrutiny of individual bodies.

Eugenics was one of the major protagonists in a field of early twentieth-century interests and struggles that set out the terrain of social policy discussion and inquiry. Eugenicist thinking provided a language through which the problem of differences within the population could be posed and acted upon. In the context of an individualised science of population, for example, it contributed to the way in which psychology defined its objects of inquiry.[52] Its effects were also historically specific in terms of a 'will to know' the individual and to confer a particular subjectivity on individuals. However, the productive effects of power in the way in which a population is named and counted suggests that subjectivity is contingent and is not a captive of any one strategy. There is a good case to be made that during the late nineteenth and earlier twentieth century, relations between government and its objects, in particular the concerns with various categories of children, were constituted around the problem of population health measures, and that various kinds of schooling were constituted as a solution to emerging problems of social hygiene.

When confronted with the alternatives, scientific opinion and institutional health and welfare developments sided with policies of segregation and removal of non-Indigenous children from their families based on a calculation of these groups according to specific ability or health needs, or on criteria of need for care and protection – a calculation, that is, premised on a demand for intervention in order to bring social benefit and an improvement in 'the race', often spoken of as the 'imperial race'. On the other hand, and in stark contrast, the strategy for the removal of Indigenous Australian children relied on no such account of personhood or forms of calculation. Its objectives were not the sustenance but rather the removal of 'race' by the breeding out of 'colour' and habits. As Fiona Paisley has noted, the outcome of the strategy for Indigenous Australians was summarised by the chief protector Neville in 1937, against a background of considerable local concern and international protest: 'Are we going to have a population of 1,000,000 blacks in the Commonwealth, or are we going to merge them into our white community and eventually forget that there were any Aborigines in Australia?'[53] A proper comparative view is more fully available in the report of the 'stolen children' inquiry.[54] But a comparison of policies, both those proposed and those actually implemented, serves to highlight the specifically racial elements of programs to improve on the 'imperial race', but which on the other hand were vigorously pursued to attempt to destroy Aboriginal communities. Rather than simply a reflection of generally accepted scientific views of the time, the eugenic strategy against Indigenous peoples was consciously targeted, government authorised, and racist.

The point of arrival: mental hygiene

Within this context, a new chapter was opened in the history of the category of the mental patient. Dr Baker, President of the National Committee for Mental Hygiene in the United States described the mental hygiene movement as 'an effort to conserve and improve the minds of the people, to secure brains so naturally endowed and so nurtured that people will feel better, think better and act better than they do now.[55] Ralph Noble, in charge of the psychiatric clinic at Prince Alfred Hospital in Sydney and in the front line of the mental hygiene movement, drew attention to the formation of mental hygiene organisations throughout Europe and North America, and formed a provisional committee in Australia in 1924. The activities would be involved with education and the removal of the stigma attached to mental illness, promoting aftercare, the establishment of more psychiatric clinics, more study of 'nervous manifestations in childhood', the care and treatment of the congenitally defective, the study of social maladjustments such as dependency and criminality in relation to congenital and acquired mental disorders, and the coordination of community resources for mental hygiene. Noble mentions the Child Welfare Department, the Children's Court, the After Care Association, the Racial Hygiene Association, the National Council of Women, the Board of Social Studies, the Workers' Education Association and the Australian Institute of Industrial Psychology as all relevant to the pursuit of mental hygiene. A young psychiatrist John Bostock, at the same meeting, drew attention to the need for parents' education to remove many of the sources of infant and childhood trauma, especially concerning sexual matters. There was a celebration of the entrance of the psychologist into life's ordinary business, whether this be in family life, education, or adjustment of 'the ordinary man in the street and industry'. The insane and mentally defective would undergo, yet again, a reformation of their conditions. No more 'Bedlams', instead the siting of psychiatric units in public hospitals and the renaming of asylums as hospitals: 'as in every branch of medicine, prophylaxis and early treatment are the desiderata'.[56] Judge Lindsey was reported favourably as presiding over a family and children's court in the city of Denver, Colorado, which dealt with the 'morally ill' where half of the children, mostly girls, came to him of their own accord. Maudsley, honorary psychiatrist at the Melbourne Hospital, wanted the main focus of mental hygiene directed at 'the early stages of development of personality'.[57]

Much of the personality studies literature in psychology was virtually synonomous with mental hygiene strategies in its characteristic fields of intervention in home and family, education, work and social life more generally. In the United States, the books and research output on personality, especially from the 1940s, was quite phenomenal. Some of the key texts have been mentioned already. Figures like Allport, Cattell, Healy and Terman produced key conceptual works on the psychological study of personality, while others such as Bowlby, McCall and Sorokin developed more specific studies on mental illness, measurement, or cultural differences in relation to personality. Some of the texts laid out the criteria for developing balanced personalities for the benefit of the psychologists, teachers and counsellors for whom they were written, and in ways that made them appear almost as manuals for training in civic education. Writing about the concept of mental health, Wallin headed his section with the words – 'the well adjusted life is buttressed upon a secure foundation of good habits acquired early in life'. After this appears definitions of a 'wholesome personality' and the means to achieve it: orderly physical habits, social response and adjustment, emotional control and poise, free of intellectual schisms and inconsistencies. The development of a wholesome personality was the key to mental health.

Inconsistency of thinking, feeling, and doing is an outstanding characteristic of the disordered mind. The wholesome personality will be characterised by optimism; confidence, cooperativeness, frankness, sincerity, intellectual and emotional poise; balanced judgement; wisdom.[58]

The way to avoid mental disease and personality disorders was to devise effective methods of prophylaxis, which could be applied in the home, school, church, factory and playground. Discussing this explicitly in terms of a 'positive eugenics', Wallin argued that it was simply impossible to determine the hereditary limitations of an individual. And a negative eugenics was relevant only in the case of 'grave nervous disorders' such as feeblemindedness and some types of epilepsy and mental disorder. Wallin reported on numerous case studies showing that personality maladjustments of all kinds developed in people who have sound nervous systems and who were relatively free from hereditary taint. Indeed, the best soil for developing a whole variety of mental disturbances was to be found in those whose nervous systems were responsive and highly sensitised.[59]

Certainly, medical and psychiatric training in Australia had become alerted early to the changing object of psychiatric practice and the need for pre-clinical instruction to include topics on the normal and abnormal behaviour, or the 'anatomy of personality'. Australian doctors in particular were aware that the interests of North American and Canadian psychiatry had progressed beyond the abnormal to include 'the average man, his interpersonal relationships and his relation to his environment'.[60] This was a dimension of medical training that had been ignored in the past and required a new appreciation to be given to 'man as a totality':

> To do this adequately, sufficient instruction in psychology, in the mechanisms which govern the development of both normal and abnormal human behaviour – in short, the anatomy of personality – must be included early in the preclinical course, along with teaching given in other basic sciences. Furthermore, attempts should be made, where possible, to integrate the various basic sciences, in order that a holistic viewpoint may be firmly engendered and maintained in the student's mind.[61]

Reflecting on the burgeoning field of psychology, Trethowan, who was now the professor of psychiatry at Sydney University, warned that the medical profession was in danger of being outstripped by lay and nonmedical professions in the advocacy of reforms to mental health, and the loss of respect relative to other professions was already being felt in medical circles.

There is some evidence that psychiatry saw itself under threat from psychology for its moves into the boundaries of medicine. The Director of Mental Hygiene in Victoria, Catarinich, claimed in his report in 1950 that the role of psychology 'in the integration of personality' had been exaggerated, and that the kind of 'brass instrument psychology' used to dissect all kinds of abnormalities in people had led psychology into disrepute in some eyes.[62] In this his last report as Director, Catarinich also criticised psychiatrists about their role in the court system as advocates for the accused rather than as impartial witnesses for the court. In particular, he criticised the tendency to regard any departure from normal conduct as indicative of mental illness with a consequent lessening degree of legal responsibility – 'one has seen such things as variability of moods, a few foolish remarks or some eccentric actions stretched to their utmost possible limits in their endeavour to prove the irresponsibility of the individual'.[63] Here, the psychologist was seen to be in charge of 'eccentric actions' and similar foibles outside of legitimate mental illness. But despite occasional tensions and ambivalence towards psychology expressed by individual psychiatrists, it was still the case that psychiatry gave over significant precincts of inquiry to psychology, while still managing to remain formally in charge of the territory.

Note, however, that the interest of researchers was much more with *dis*order, *mal*-adjustment and *un*balance of personality than with the study of the normal individual. By the late 1920s there was a string of personality tests and inventories available for discovering the factors and traits of individuals: introversion, extraversion, ascendance, submission, dominance, aggressiveness, fears, worries, self-reliance, emotional instability, emotional maturity or immaturity, mood, neurotic makeup, submerged complexes, racial prejudices, social skills and so on. The devices for measuring included Strong's Vocational Interest Bank, Woodworth's Personal Data Sheet, Thurstone's Personality Schedules, Roger's Adjustment Inventory, Fred Brown's Personality Inventory of Children, McKinley's Minnesota Multiphasic Personality Schedule, the Humm-Wadsworth Temperament Scale and Doll's Vineland Social Maturity Scale.[64] In the context of diagnosing, preventing and correcting 'personality blemishes', Wallin reiterates the cooperative aspects of mental hygiene and importance of the team approach to problem areas: the physician, psychologist, social worker, educationist and guidance counsellor underpinned a successful program. Of most interest to the mental hygienist was that group of children who were socially maladjusted and criminally inclined. Wallin referred to 'genetic studies' showing that most delinquents and criminals are recruited from 'behavioristically abnormal children and juvenile social nonconformists'. For example, Kirchwey in 1934 had shown that 92 per cent of 3,000 first offenders appearing before the New York Court of General Sessions on felony charges had previously been in the children's court. On another tack, Kraines undertook a study of the 'personalities' of nations to show how they could be characterised by standard categories of mental disorder: the United States might be compared with a person with manic depressive psychosis, Germany with the depressive-paranoid, Italy with the feebleminded, Japan with the psychopath; China was lazy and philosophical, France tended towards excessive emotionalism and apprehension, and England was too set in its ways; Sweden, Norway, Denmark, Holland and Switzerland, on the other hand, were declared 'normal'.[65]

The changes in the means of calculation were accompanied by administrative and legislative changes. In Australia, what occurred in legislation was the demise, once and for all, of the lunatic, and the arrival of the mental health patient. In Victoria, the new Act in 1933 was called the Mental Hygiene Act, where the Lunacy Department became the Department of Mental Hygiene, the Inspector General of the Insane became the Director of Mental Hygiene, Hospital for the Insane became Mental Hospital, and a Licensed House becomes a Private

Mental Home. There was also a shift in person-formation reflected in how the patients were addressed. From 1951, gratuities were paid to patients who worked at the Ararat Mental Hospital in Victoria. Smaller shifts recognised the patient in a different light, such as the opening of kiosks where patients could make purchases, or a staff and patient magazine such as the one at Beechworth founded in 1952 by the then superintendent G. A. Goding. These developments say something about a new psychiatrised subject of mental hygiene. In Western Australia, a charter for mental health services establishes the principle that the mentally ill should not be discriminated against *vis-à-vis* the physically ill, nor should they be deprived of aged or invalid pensions. In 1971, the department of social security agreed that patients in specified 'open' wards, with a reasonable hope of recovery and free access to the community, could receive an invalid pension; in 1980, pensions were granted to all eligible patients in mental hospitals. The mental patient had now become a person endowed with rights, a person who could claim to be a citizen.

As a marker of the blocks of historical evidence which make up this book, the 1950s should be considered the end point of a long process, beginning at the turn of the century, of the disaggregation of the asylum population into two main groups, the disordered and the defective. By the 1950s a distilling of these groups is paralleled by the two sets of medical practices to which each group has a distinct relation. Broadly speaking, the disordered belong to the precinct of curative medicine with its emphasis on pathology and disease. The defective, on the other hand, becomes bound up with the extended program of mental hygiene with its attachment to public health, education, sanitation and prevention. The end of the period is marked by the solidification of the 'psychopathic' and its formal registration as a psychiatric classification for inclusion in the first edition of the American *Diagnostic and Statistical Manual.*

Before this, we see a category of person emerge from the Receiving House, an institution which carves out a space on the borderline between sanity and insanity, from the separation of the mentally defective who themselves had been gradually shunted out of the emergent Receiving House and Mental Hospital duo, and from the institutions of mental hygiene in child welfare. Once the shift of enquiry takes place, from the internal structure of individuals to a relative position of an individual to others in an external field, one of the important conditions of a mental hygienist approach to mental health is met. This is not simply a public health response nor simply preventative and psychiatrised – it is a governmental attempt to bring the whole population onto a grid of calculability. Mental hygiene accomplished this by accommodating the concept of personality as part of a technology for individuals to act upon themselves and be incited to develop a healthy mental balance.

5   The space for personality

In the period of colonisation, medicine became involved as part of a jury to determine on the question of 'an ability to manage one's affairs', and medical advice added to that of other 'wise men' in determining whether there was justification for incarceration. The temporal aspects of the reclaiming and restoration of the lunatic were apparent in the late eighteenth-century formal separation of lunatic and idiot, but only later would medicine begin to form its object of inquiry by attempting to draw boundaries and typologies, with a critical gaze on this aspect of restoration. Moreover there was discipline. This was increasingly possible, beginning with the placement of the doctor in charge of the asylum from 1848 in New South Wales, then in other states; the building of substantial new asylums during the 1850s and 1860s providing new spaces for the classification and distribution of different cases; the adoption of 'moral treatment' in some of the more enlightened establishments, involving the procedures of doctor–patient engagement designed to give 'full insight into the character and mental condition of the patients'; and the study and recording of different cases of lunacy and different stages of progress to recovery with their respective institutional elaborations. Later, from the 1890s the 'cottage system' of care for chronic lunatics, which was recommended in Victoria as early as the 1850s, was a system of family style governance and responsibilisation common in a range of institutional sites from this period – orphanages and boarding out policies, asylums, industrial schools and so on. Perhaps this is to announce the beginnings of a welfare approach to population management, in the particular matrix of ideas, psychological theories, institutional methods and practices, scientific findings and so on, emerging during the early 1900s. A bio-pathology of life itself was being drawn up by the architects of more differentiated and fixed categories of persons and personhood, artifacts of a more intense study of groups of problem persons located among different institutions on the one hand, and the 'looping' effect of the dynamics between the person and the category of person on the other: how do people 'make themselves up, as they act to conform to, or stay away from, powerful classifications?[1]

In this kind of setting, much of the interest of government in the bio-politics of managing problem populations can be demonstrated in the early twentieth-century inquiry in the biological and human sciences into the problem of mental defect. It became possible to think and act upon disordered and dangerous persons partly as a consequence of the development of specific techniques of calculating mental defectiveness. Let us take up the narrative by making the case for a modern connection between defect and dangerousness.

Mental defect, disorder and dangerousness

Observe the primary separation, beginning in the latter half of the nineteenth century of acute from chronic inmates, who previously shared space within the old lunatic asylum but who now found them-selves in separate, rather more specialised accommodation. The acute patients occupied the newly named 'mental hospitals' while the chronic and hopeless cases were farmed out to peripheral institutions. The chronic and hopeless were described in 1915 as a loose aggregate of 'epileptics, congenital imbeciles, general paralytics, paranoiacs, and senile dements'.[2] They attracted less interest from medicine, perhaps because little could be done in terms of treatment compared with the more interesting and prestigious acute patients. The chronics were also less 'valuable' in a strict economic sense too, because many could not perform work in the asylum. Further, their administrative separation from the mental hospital and from a strict medical gaze was under-pinned by the increasing attention afforded them as suitable objects of education and training, as distinct from treatment. This separation occurs hand in hand with new tools which psychology and psychiatry either inherited, transformed or invented to bring persons into the field of the calculable.

One important historical moment was the formal status awarded to several new categories of person as a result of specific legislation to improve the administration of mental defectives. In England, the classi-fication of whole classes of what was previously called lunacy was carried out by a Royal Commission in 1908, which recommended that the term 'mentally defective' be used as a general term to cover the entire range of lunacy, and that making clear sub-divisions within the overall class of defective would enhance their administration.[3] The interest here was to classify in order to administer. Rather than 'high grade' and 'low grade' idiots and imbeciles, the Commission recommended a sequence of words already in use but needing clearer definition: idiot, imbecile, feebleminded, moral imbecile, epileptic and inebriate. Better classification meant that institutions and homes could become more specialised and better suited. What was the point of sending feebleminded children certified as lunatics or idiots to institutions quite inappropriate to their needs, or of sending imbeciles to expensive establishments when instead they could be provided for economically, '. . . requiring little beyond employment, maintenance, shelter and control'.[4] Another reason for wanting better classification was so that the old asylums could be transformed into proper hospitals, with the implication that people could be treated in them. The Commission also considered some of the legal implications of its recommendations; for example, it borrowed from the 1843 statutes following the McNaghten case the term 'of unsound mind' to refer to the class previously known as 'insane'. As a rule it distinguished its task from the activity of scientific inquiry: it had nothing to say, for example, on the causes of insanity or mental defectiveness, or whether it was mainly inherited or acquired. However, it did receive advice from physicians which sought to clarify those classifications which did not display obvious defect or insanity. One such type which attracted attention was the moral imbecile.

As with the temporal distinction between insane and imbecile, the moral imbecile was distinguishable from the morally insane in that insanity was something acquired later in life: '. . . a person who, after many years of reputable life, all at once unaccountably exhibits vicious propensities, or takes to criminal courses'. In contrast, imbecility including moral imbecility by definition manifested at birth or in early years of life. The Commission recommended a remodelled statute which would deal with people who were 'not lunatics or idiots' and who would require very different administration from either. After the First World War a Mental Deficiency Act was passed in England, providing for the segregation, training and education of defectives. The continuum of imbecility and moral imbecility as enshrined in the English Royal Commission was used for the next two decades or more in both England and Australia as an authoritative set of classifications which would separate them from both the idiot, the insane and also the criminal. In Australia, these administrative and legislative moves were reproduced in the 1929 Report of Mental Deficiency in the Commonwealth of Australia,[5] placing 'moral defectives' into a fourth class of defectives much the same as in the 1908 English report. The definition of moral defective was almost identical: '. . . persons in whose case there exists mental defectiveness coupled with vicious or criminal propensities and who require care, supervision, and control for their own protection and the protection of others'.[6] Ernest Jones told the Australasian Medical Congress in 1929 that the subject of mental defectiveness seemed to be 'slipping beyond the grasp of the medical profession . . . the educationalist and lay psychologist have come into the picture and an attempt is being made to regard this question as being an educational problem rather than a medical one'.[7]

The point to emphasise here is that the development of specific tools of measurement, which would both form and be formed by psychology and its immediate predecessors, was premised on the prior set of administrative distinctions, a group of 'not lunatics or idiots', whose administrative separation from the asylum and from medical institutions was well under way. The administrative separation and relocation established the pre-conditions for developing knowledge of this group. As it became possible through the development of these tools of calculation to identify the higher grades of defective, it also became possible to know this group as distinct from the insane and to know them by means of techniques distinct from medicine. The bureaucratic physical separation of a group which comes to be known as the defective-deficient, their removal to special schools and institutions under the gaze of the psychologist/educator, goes hand in hand with the growth in the availability of tools by which to articulate their identity. There was no simple cause and effect relationship here.

The Royal Commission distinguishes between the imbecile and the idiot on the criterion of 'danger', in this case to oneself rather than others. The imbecile was incapable of earning his own living but was 'capable of guarding himself against physical dangers', while the idiot was one so deeply defective in mind from birth or from an early age that he was 'unable to guard himself against common physical dangers'. The third group, the feebleminded, was marked off according to another distinctive criterion:

. . . capable of earning a living under favourable circumstances, but is incapable . . . (a) of competing on equal terms with his normal fellows (b) of managing himself and his affairs with ordinary prudence.[8]

Prudence was open to several interpretations, which certainly in Australia marked out connections between the feebleminded and their dangerousness. Dr Sanderson Yule at the 1914 Australian Medical Congress drew attention to the fact that the feebleminded were more prolific than normal stock (which constituted a 'danger' to the race), but he could not say whether this was due to a genetic quality or merely lack of control.[9] In 1918, Richard Berry and Stanley Porteus published a practical guide for recognising feeblemindedness – 'having the intelligence of a normal boy of 12 or less and unable to manage himself or his affairs with ordinary prudence, for example, incapable of holding any responsible position where judgement and commonsense are requisites'.[10] Berry enlarged on this later, pointing to 'partially weakened reasoning faculties', 'slow or unsteady in mental operations', and 'falls short of ordinary standards of prudence, independence and self control', as well as making the general observation that mental deficiency was a 'danger threatening the social fabric'.[11] In this he was reinforcing Clause 1 of the English *Mental Deficiency Act* defining feeblemindedness:

Persons in whose case there exists from birth, or from an early age, mental defectiveness not amounting to imbecility, yet so pronounced that they require care, supervision, and control for their own protection or others.[12]

By 1921, Berry and Porteus claimed that diagnosis could be assisted in the form of the Porteus Maze Test, which could 'disclose capacities not tested by the Binet method, such as prudence, forethought, planning capacity, ability to improve with practice and adaptability to a new situation'.[13] Was this a test of capacity for prudence?

So while the idiot and the imbecile are marked off from one another according to the criteria of safety and danger, especially to themselves, the feebleminded – the group in closest proximity to the normal – is marked off according to a lack of prudence. And all these categories are defined according to degrees of ability to self govern, the ability to manage oneself and one's own affairs. However, the point to notice here is that the closer the category approaches the norm in terms of ability to self-govern, the more dangerous the person in this category becomes. They are more difficult to detect, require finer and more sophisticated tools and more specialist expertise to read the stigmata, which become increasingly more subtle and more deeply buried. The point was recognised quite early by the doctors. Stawell, the physician at Melbourne's Children's Hospital, used the term 'mentally feeble' to pin-point that group which was neither imbecile nor normal:

They are practically ignored by the educational authorities, and allowed to drift downwards to the gutter and the gaol, for though they are intellectually feeble, their passions are often strong, and always uncontrolled. Indeed, the fact that they are a danger to society has formed the basis of classification, idiots and low grade imbeciles are classed by M. Sollier as 'extra-social', and the mentally feeble are classed as 'anti-social'.[14]

Similarly, Dr Fishbourne talked of 'a race at once more helpless and more aggressive [than the Aborigine] and fast becoming a standard peril to the nation';[15] Dr Steven considered this group as 'likely to prove a menace to the progress and prosperity of the greatest number';[16] Dr Wood used the American term 'moron' for the highest type of defective, who would yet become 'a criminal of the lowest type'.[17] Another doctor complained to the Medical Journal that the definition of mental deficiency in the British law was 'so wide that it could be applied to the majority of the people'.[18] Berry and Porteus quoted H. H. Goddard on the hidden danger of the feebleminded: 'The most dangerous group of mental defectives are those who are in no way different from the intelligent man; and not only in outward appearance, but in conversation and bearing, these people often pass for normal';[19] and finally the pathologist Dr Lind, whose career was devoted to showing that insanity was caused by syphilis, showed how the great danger of the mentally deficient lay in their hidden role in spreading venereal disease.[20] Certainly the language used was that of hidden danger, elusiveness, of drifting and roaming in our midst, of 'the danger hanging over our Commonwealth'. The higher the grade of feeblemindedness, the greater their indefinability and their dangerousness.

In this situation, what arrived to save the situation was the brain cell, the new unit of primary meaningfulness. It is through the work of Richard Berry that the cell comes fully into its own in the study of defect, linking to existing approaches from the other disciplines. Berry himself wrote in a paper titled 'The organic factor in mental disease': '. . . the neuron is really the one important item and it is very small and very elusive'.[21] Following Bolton, Watson, Mott and Cajel, in order to know the feebleminded it is first necessary to know the brain cell:

. . . unwillingly . . . modern psychologists have been forced to accept the biological basis of mind . . . The absolute dependability of mind upon neurons stares us in the face at every turn . . . the 'unwillingness' can, therefore, only arise from ignorance and ignorance of cerebral cortical histology.[22]

The standards and procedures of the medical pathologist now come to be relegated to the surface, to the superficial, and histology becomes a new surface of emergence for the truth of feeblemindedness. Berry's work indicated how a precise network must be put in place in order to catch the elusive signs of feeblemindedness, and here Berry wanted to highlight not only the structure of neurons but also the structure of linking apparatuses – 'the physical, psychological and social diagnostic approaches' – which were to fix and arrest the defective. Berry, professor of anatomy and histology at Melbourne University, had harsh words to say about that messy association of philanthropists and amateurs who had previously devoted themselves to child study, and presumably he included amongst these the schoolteachers who had participated in the 1912 national survey of feeblemindedness, and who had contributed to the 'ridiculous' results of the survey: Berry noted, for example, that a school in one of Sydney's finest residential areas reported to the survey that one in seven of its pupils was 'mentally dull'. Under Berry, the association between teacher and medical practitioner, as personified in the working relationship between Berry and Porteus, had the semblance of an institutional structure all of its own. *The Medical Journal* described Berry's work on cranial capacity as leading the response:

It co-ordinated the services of the neurologist and the psychologist, and showed how these two, with the assistance of the educationist and the medical man, might pick out from the abnormal types of school life the future inefficients of adult life.[23]

At this stage in his work the pivotal indicator was brain or cranial capacity, though Berry was at pains to show that he was not about suggesting a direct correlation between size of head and intelligence. What counted for mentality was what could be counted. The numerical calculation of a relation between the number of neurons and intelligence was a high point for measurement rather than for the ideology sustained by the results themselves. Later, the number of neurons became secondary to questions of their structure. What physiology and the study of reflexology gave was a quantitative measure, a 'clinical thermometer or measuring rod' with which to recognise defect – something severely lacking in the 1912 survey which had relied on a qualitative assessment of the defective by schoolteachers ill-equipped for the task.[24] Berry anticipated the need for a science to guide the direction he knew would be hazardous, the outcome unknown.

A number of authors have suggested that the basis for conceptualising the reflex model of human behaviour after the mid-eighteenth century can be found in various technologies existing at the time. For example, the appearance of heavy industrial equipment such as the steam engine impressed physiologists and anatomists by what it showed about the capacities of a 'mechanism' itself, but also how it could incorporate self-regulating mechanisms such as the planetary valve.[25] They argue that the existing technologies of controlled regulated action served to make possible a psycho-physiological model of human behaviour:

. . . we use the things we find in the outside world as schemata for understanding the things we find in the inner one, thereby shaping that inner one accordingly. What scientists have sought and found in the outer world are mechanisms, and when the 'scientific psychology' behind that quest turns itself inwards, it will be no exception.[26]

The reflex model of the nervous system was attractive because of its mechanistic basis, and in particular, the reflex model's

well-defined cleavage of stimulus and response and their machine like reliability, quite early became the model of psychological analysis among theorists who favoured a mechanistic approach, for they seemed to be the atoms out of which more complex molecules of behaviour were composed.[27]

These authors make good points about the particular take-up of cell theory in neuro-biology, and that the theorising of the reflex arc allowed for a fresh problematising of action independently of will. Their work also underlines psychology's debt to physiology, a point often downplayed in the histories of psychology. The particularities of Berry's work on the reflex arc, however, were that a new 'space' was brought into existence by means of the inscription devices at hand – the pathology report, the microscopic slide, the tables and diagrams – rather than a re-presentation of existing models.[28] We might add that this new space becomes a surface of emergence for new ways of knowing individuals and managing them, but also a new site in which individuals can come to know and govern themselves.

Physiology and the reflex arc

Reflexology, the study of the reflex nervous system, provided the basic 'atom' or unit by which behaviour could begin to be counted. Just as the cell was the basic structural unit, so the functional co-ordination of sensory, central and motor neuronic cells into a simple arc was regarded as the 'unit of behaviour'.[29] A new kind of non-voluntary behaviour came into focus which had nothing to do with being 'out of one's mind' or 'overcome by passions'. The brain presented itself as one component in a functional network whose entirety became the domain of a psycho-physiological focus. Charles Mercier's *Nervous System and the Mind*, published in 1888, outlined the basic premise:

By the psychological function of the nervous system is not meant its connection with Mind – with mental states or consciousness. At present we are dealing with objective psychology only, and objective psychology is not at all concerned with consciousness. It deals, as has been said, with matter and motion. The subjects which it treats are the dispositions and movements, molecular and molar, of parts of the organism with respect to one another, or of the organism as a whole with respect to its environment.[30]

Leaving out the mind, as it were, allowed a concentration on the way certain kinds of behaviours could circumvent the brain entirely and become entirely independent of the will, yet still be measurable. Take the classic 'knee-jerk reaction'. In physiological terms, the arc from the stimulus (a blow to receptor cells in the knee) to the response (the motor cells cause the knee to jerk) does not have to reach the brain at all – it is a non-cerebral action, automatic and independent of will. Williams

(1944) produced a diagram of the first and second level responses in reflex actions, according to relative engagement of spinal cord and brain. In Australia, Berry's work on the neuronic arc and his theory of the development of cerebral structure was first published in 1924 under the title 'The correlation of recent advances in cerebral structure and function with feeblemindedness and its diagnostic applicability.'[31] His work represents an important transitional stage for the emergence of a psychological interest in feeblemindedness and the subsequent category of psychopathic personality, and for this reason deserves a closer inspection.

Berry divided brain development into an evolutionary history of layering, the five epochs or types of 'neuronic arcs', so that as humankind becomes more sophisticated (speaking in an evolutionary sense) the circuit becomes longer and more complex. First the effector response, an immediate response, something like the sea sponge; second the epoch of the reflex, forming 'the basis of many visceral responses in man'; third the epoch of the intersegmental reflex neurone, purposeful, unconscious and usually immediate. The neuronic machinery of the fourth epoch, that of the 'supra-segmental reflex' consisted of an enormous bundle of neurones between receptor and effector:

In the higher animals such an immediate response to the stimulus would often be disadvantageous to the animal's welfare and it becomes, therefore, essential . . . to have a period of latency . . . as it were, for reflection and allows of a selection of the most advantageous motor reaction . . . The new element which so produces the period of latency by holding in check the effector response to the stimulus until the most favourable moment has arrived . . . provides the important factor of inhibition or delay in response.[32]

At this stage of the development of neuronic machinery, behaviour cannot be any longer a matter of instantaneous impulse, but is made subject to a certain degree of supervisional review guided by a primitive form of judgement which may be taken to mark the beginning of psychic life. The fifth epoch, the addition of the psycho-associational neurone of the supra-granular cortex, was responsible for the receptive, the psychic and the voluntary psychic. Berry linked, or co-related, the achievement of epochs with brain functioning. So low-grade or 'more marked dements' showed a decrease in the depth of the infra-granular cortex ('the brain of the animal instincts') and hence idiots and imbeciles were 'unable to carry on the ordinary animal functions'. High grade amentia (feeblemindedness) had all the animal instincts intact but an insufficient neuronic development of the supra-granular layer – the site of reflection and control (prudence). Thus, the degrees of self-management as outlined in documents such as the Royal Commission were here given a grounding in biology. A kind of biological foundation to self-government – the ability to manage one's affairs – was able to be read from the epochal layering of brain cells.

At one stage in the outline of his results, Berry observed the existence of an 'immense gulf' between the primitive type of brain structure and the highly complex brain of man. Differentiating the various grades of deficiency/efficiency meant, in effect, assigning a position on a scale from the primitive to the higher and more complex which again was associated with the number of cells which formed the arc between stimulus and response. It was this length or space or dimension that delayed action and allowed for judgement. The delay factor made it possible to identify the biological and physiological space of morality. And it was precisely this dimension or space which Berry's colleague Stanley Porteus had sought to measure with his maze test, which he developed in 1912 while teaching at the special school for feebleminded children in Fitzroy in Melbourne. This type of test was quite different in its scope from the ordinary tests of intelligence, and was seen as such. Porteus modelled the test on the maze-like streets of inner-suburban Fitzroy, which he had discovered posed a more or less onerous challenge to his students finding their way about to do errands.[33] The space for forethought, judgement and prudence was calculable in the performance of charting one's way through a maze, in the same way as one might calculate the time and distance from stimulus to response across the neuronic arc. Porteus clearly differentiated his work from other types of tests, particularly intellectual and scholastic tests. Later, in his position as lecturer in experimental education at Melbourne University, he measured 1,000 children firstly using the Binet scale to cover a range of intellectual activities, and then using his own 'motor intelligence tests' which assessed 'prudence, foresight and mental alertness generally'.[34] His assessment of what the maze measured was supported by his medical and psychiatric colleagues. Ralph Noble claimed that powers of foresight, planning and ability to concentrate were measured, as well as 'the capacity of the child for success in the social world rather than in school attainments'.[35] And Berry made the connection with 'social diagnosis' quite plain:

The inference is . . . that in this case we are dealing with a boy of under-neuronic development who is incapable of exercising control over his neuronic effector responses. That this inference is correct is supported by the failure of the boy at the Porteus tests and is borne out by the personal history that he is 'mischievous, destructive and wants constant watching' . . . The boy has no planning capacity, no foresight . . .[36]

With the creation of a specific location for morality, intelligence testing comes to occupy less prominence, in favour of a means of identification of those who may approximate normal intelligence but who have a moral defect. Indeed, as I have already suggested, the development of new governmental designs on the high grade defective were prompted by the failure of existing techniques of measurement properly to grasp and incorporate it.

Berry's expertise was concentrated around the connection between the reflex and categories of feeblemindedness. Though non-volitional behaviour might itself be outside the bounds of the rational, it could, thanks to the 'unit of behaviour' provided by the reflex arc, be thought of as able to be rationally analysed, numerically graded and hierarchically ordered. For Berry, different grades of mental defectiveness could be constructed which corresponded to the network of neuronic arcs, and his hierarchical scale of idiot, imbecile and high-grade moron were directly proportional to the intricacy of the neuronic arcs – or pathways – involved from stimulus to response. Hence his belief that cranial capacity existed in direct proportion to mental capacity.[37] According to Berry's schema, the high grade moron, or moral imbecile, was the outcome of a physiological defect – a truncated pattern of neuronic pathways, which, though less gross than other grades of defectiveness, narrowed the gap between stimulus and response, that gap in which the 'moral' qualities of prudence, forethought and judgement could take place. The model took in behaviour which might be seen to circumvent rational or prudent judgement. An example of reflexivity in the extreme was Cleckley's version of psychopathic personality in *The Mask of Sanity* (1941); the psychopath was not a 'complete' man at all, but something resembling 'a subtly constructed reflex machine which can mimic the human personality perfectly'.[38]

As we have seen, these transmutations allowed for the possibility of being deficient in capacity and permitted, through the development of such tools, the 'mentally deficient' to become known. Psychological measurement's ties to physiological measurement also explain the virtual interchangeability, during much of this early period, of the terms 'mentally defective' – an account of (physiological) structure, and 'mentally deficient' – an account of (psychological) capacity. The category of moral imbecility was different however. Although this group was initially calculable on a grid of the 'mentally deficient/defective' and was able to be known, through these tools of calculation, as a group distinct from the insane, the means for knowing the defective eventually proved to be inadequate to grasp the moral imbecile. This 'failure' was first observed in the recognition that the moral defective might score average or even above-average in intelligence. But the conditions of possibility for different means of calculation of moral defect lay once again in the administrative and spatial arrangements put in place for this group. There is perhaps no better place to document the setting out of these arrangements than Tasmania, which became the first state of Australia to introduce legislation.

The space for personality

The Tasmanian Mental Deficiency Act was passed in 1920 and proclaimed in 1922, after which a Mental Deficiency Board and a State Psychological Clinic were established. Perhaps the influential presence of E. Morris Miller as Director of Public Health made the difference, but Tasmania was certainly well ahead of every other state in moving down the path which the English Act had taken. In the first volume of the *Australasian Journal of Psychology and Philosophy*, the head of psychology at Sydney University, H. Tasman Lovell, congratulated the Tasmanians on recognising the necessity for an ongoing 'mental survey' of the people. Now that the instrument had been delivered into the hands of scientific psychology, the state could exercise its responsibilities towards those found to be defective, especially the low-grade moron, the imbecile and the idiot. The Act had recognised the problem as a scientific rather than moral one, and Lovell commented at length about the social improvement it would bring, in terms of making mentally deficient people healthier and happier and the likely reduction in antisocial acts.[39] Indeed, the antisocial and possibly dangerous among the mentally deficient held far more interest for the professional practitioners. The Mental Deficiency Board reported in its first year that extensive surveys of the entire school population had begun and several avenues of supervision, care and training had been opened up. The Psychological Clinic had also begun its diagnosis and classification of '. . . exceptional children . . . those who deviate from the normal, positively or negatively', those who

. . . are retarded in schoolwork, mentally dull and backward; who manifest abnormal or aberrant trends, resent reasonable discipline, show undue signs of obduracy or stubbornness, misbehave as psychopaths, delinquents, truants or inferiors, reveal marked instability and want of control during puberty and adolescence; in fact, who are in any way maladjusted to the ordinary conditions of life whether in the home, school, or community. In short, the clinic is concerned with the mental hygiene of childhood.[40]

In charge of public health, E. Morris Miller realised he was walking in an 'untrodden field' in Australia. Prior to his appointment, he took leave for a detailed study tour of institutions and psychological clinics in the

United States and Canada, including the Bureau of Juvenile Research in Columbus, Ohio under H. H. Goddard, the Judge Baker Foundation in Boston under Healey, the Bureau of Juvenile Research in Chicago under H. M. Adler, and a number of children's courts and detention homes in Philadelphia, New York and Toronto. He also visited Vineland, Letchworth Village and other institutions and colonies for the residential care of defectives and epileptics, as well as a number of psychological clinics attached to universities. The focus of the study tour and also of the first report of the new body made it clear that the clinic was not concentrated on the problem of chronic mental defectives, who could be registered and then farmed out to an institution for special training. The Act had given the clinic certain duties regarding the legally enforceable placement of defective individuals but the major interest for the emergent psychologists was not with classifying and batching out the imbeciles and idiots, but rather with building a firmer knowledge base for the mental status and functioning of children who deviated from the norm, but not too far:

. . . especially in cases where normality is latent or maturity of mind is delayed; where aberrant or deviating trends are manifest; where advice is desired concerning corrective pedagogics for special abilities; where an analysis of the mental factors involved in delinquencies is necessary.[41]

So the Act itself and the charter for Australia's first state psychological clinic showed, at the very least, some degree of convergence of the problem of deficiency on the one hand, and the problem of the delinquent and the dangerous, the 'unstable and the psychopathic', on the other. The Act prompted special training at the Teachers' College in the psychology of these 'exceptional children'.[42] Later, in some states, psychological clinics were established under similar Acts, such as in Victoria in 1939. It is worth noting that most, such as Queensland in 1938, established provisions for 'backward persons' under amended mental hygiene legislation and under the control of the Director of Mental Hygiene. In the Victorian Act, which was passed in 1939 but not proclaimed until many years later due to lack of accommodation, two changes were made to the list of definitions. The category of idiot disappeared entirely and its mental age classification was added to that of imbecile; and the definition of moral imbecile stipulated that such a person must be above the age of sixteen years.[43] This latter move reflected a weakening of the inheritability or 'constitutionality' aspect of the category of moral imbecility and a recognition that its appearance may be more dependent on events to do with childhood than simply with heredity.

But there was by now clear evidence that the tool which had allowed the moral imbecile to share beds with the mental defective proved too narrow to obtain a read-off of the dimension of the 'moral'. More 'space', or rather some other kind of space, was needed to incorporate a group previously but inadequately known as 'defective' or 'deficient' whose administration had early been recognised as a problem. That pioneer of educational measurement, Alfred Binet, observed in 1905 the limitations of the intellectual measure for knowing this group:

> . . . in the definition of this state, we should make some restrictions. Most subnormal children, especially those in schools, are habitually grouped in two categories, those of backward intelligence, and those who are unstable. This latter class, which certain alienists call moral imbeciles, do not necessarily manifest inferiority of intelligence: they are turbulent, vicious, rebellious to all discipline; they lack sequence of ideas, and probably power of attention . . . It would necessitate a long study, and probably a very difficult one, to establish the distinctive signs which separate the unstable from the undisciplined. For the present we shall not take up this study.[44]

So here, from the inception of the intelligence test, a group was recognised that although generally conceived as sitting atop the hierarchy of mental defectiveness-deficiency nevertheless sat in an uneasy relation to the overall category. Measurements of mental capacity, rather than leading to a thorough knowledge of this liminal group, tended to put a question-mark over its identifiability, progressively hewing it off from the main population of defectives/deficients. This group was unable to be known and governed using the existing technology applied to the overall classification.

But how to capture this problem group whose identity was not fixed and arrested by intelligence tests? How to capture a group of 'defectives' who were not 'truly defective'? Danziger has argued that through the proliferation of tools created to identify more knowledge of the useful components of 'normal' individuality, psychology forged that space it comes to know as personality. However, there is available to us a different kind of argument resulting from some of the continuities of historical argument outlined in this book. The appearance of the term personality is clearly significant given the demand to seek a measure of the dangerously defective within the confines of the more-or-less normal. The reader will recall that the dangerousness of the defective was thought to increase as it approximated the norm (and approximated the appearance of the normal). A calculable field came to extend over the entire body of the population rather than with a more limited investigation of the body of the anomaly at the extreme edge. Everyone, after all, has a personality. Moreover, it seems on the basis of the sorts of historical evidence reviewed here that the 'origins' of personality as a governable field can be found not so much from the 'something more' needed to make up the deficiencies of intelligence tests on the normal population (from the demands, for example, that something other than intellect needs to be known if we wanted to choose the right person to be a bank manager, for example, or a colonel in the army), but rather from the 'something else' that was required to calculate that space where dangerous moral defect resided but could no longer be calculated. The 'content' of personality would seem, on this account, to derive from an already existing space carved out by the physiology of disorder, a space where morality seemed to reside but was no longer calculable, rather than, as Danziger argues, from the cultural preconceptions of an 'ordered' personality derived from the inventors of personality tests. The fabrication of the space in which personality as a structured whole would come to occupy developed as a response to a governmental problem of managing the 'problem' individual – the individual which needed to be governed. Nikolas Rose argues this way in relation to the more general application of the 'psy-disciplines' under liberal forms of government; that is to say, that which was normal did not need to be governed.[45]

A plea for that 'something' with which to know the 'not truly defective' defective began to appear from the late 1920s, accompanied by the gradual abandonment of the term defective and its replacement with the term 'psychopathy'. In the late 1920s, Harris in the United Kingdom talked about 'temperamental anomalies or psychopathy' occurring at every level of intelligence and the need to draw a line 'below which subnormality complicated by psychopathy is allowed to constitute defect'. In other words, to use the term moral imbecility in the case of a psychopath of normal or super-normal intelligence was simply 'to stretch the term "mental deficiency" until it ceases to have any significance':

... In the case of the most troublesome of all maladjusted individuals, the psychopaths who are only slightly subnormal, one might term them 'unstable subnormals' or even use the American term 'constitutional psychopathic inferiority', but they are not defectives, and should not be treated or segregated with defectives.[46]

So the use of the term 'psychopath' signals the beginning of a splitting off of a group from the mentally deficient-defective category, confirming that the technology associated with the administration of this group can no longer incorporate it. Moreover, the invention of psychopathic personality allows a grid of calculability over the entire population, whose chief defining characteristic is the government of defective morality.

There is a fundamental change in inscription processes as we move from the measurement of performance capacities to that of personality. With the multiplication of performance tests, the individual was able to occupy a position on multiple grids or lines representing multiple ratings for different abilities or characteristics, rather than merely on a single line of intelligence. It was possible to expand the register of human capacities (and, for that matter, the work of psychology) with multiple lines gauging multiple performances. But if left this way, the result is an unwieldy criss-cross of lines *ad hoc* and *ad infinitum*. In order to serve the twin goals of turning this kind of work into a bounded knowledge of psychology *and* transforming a loose aggregate of inscribed gauges of performance capacities into a bounded space nameable by psychologists as personality, it was necessary to find some way of relating these lines to one another. Here, as we have argued, the problem requiring government (and knowledge of the population in order to govern) had to do with the disordered rather than the normal. What are the other inscription devices utilised for this kind of shaping and binding? Let us consider just two which appear to be significant for subsequent studies of personality: Galton's normal distribution held the beginnings of a technology of charting the individual's relative position in space; and Spearman's work marked the earliest attempts at breaking up the single gauge into a multiplicity.

Spearman spoke of the problem of identifying a 'something more' or something 'else' in the single indicator of intelligence:

The main cause of trouble, probably, is that current mental testing has never been built up on any general theoretical foundation. In consequence no means have been available for ascertaining how much of any correlation does derive from 'g' and how much remains over to be attributed to anything else.[47]

Spearman's work on the so-called 'general' or 'g' factor was concerned with finding relations between different gauges and thus transmuting them into a bounded field by plotting their interconnectedness. The Australian psychologist Jorgensen made the point that Spearman's ideas about specific and general abilities were not new but did put the theory on a definite scientific basis: 'the obtaining of all the intercorrelations of all the abilities under consideration . . . for the purposes of ascertaining whether or not more than one factor, "g", has been in operation to cause the correlations'.[48] Once this transmutation from multiple dislocated knowledges into a space of interconnectedness has occurred, a new 'whole' can emerge, amenable to measurement. Indeed, the very possibility of its emergence depended on the measurability of its constituent parts. This became clear in John Bowlby's subsequent reworking of Spearman's ideas on factor analysis in his chapter of 'measuring personality'.[49] Bowlby noted that activities such as writing, dotting, tapping and so on were able to be measured and then correlated with 'salient features in the personality of the subject'. Motor tests could be used to isolate and measure certain general factors:

These cannot be immediately correlated with superficial personal qualities but they probably do represent some fairly fundamental factor in the make-up of personality. This work gives much promise and may well be of great importance in the future, as it appears to be measuring something more profound and constant than superficial characteristics.[50]

This kind of work, and the proliferation of knowledge of it, was incremental in creating the possibility of speaking of personality as a whole entity or structure, whose components lent themselves to measurement. Although Bowlby was alert to the kind of objections typically laid against any attempt to describe human personality, and the claim that 'the person' is always more than the sum of his traits, he nevertheless defended the statistical method for the purposes of comparison:

. . . so long as we concentrate on the whole, comparison is almost impossible. The great advantage of the entirely artificial method of breaking a personality up into a number of traits for descriptive purposes is that it makes comparison relatively easy . . . It must never be forgotten, however, that a list of traits present or absent is only a partial description, an index of personality.[51]

Bowlby manifested the psychiatrist's nervousness about psychology's failure to 'feel into' the person (the way Hans Eysenck described it),[52] that is, really to know the 'inside' of the person. But there is a strong argument to say that psychology was not born out of a set of practices concerned with knowing the person in this way. Rather, it was born out of a set of administrative problems to do with where individuals might be located *in relation to other individuals* – in institutions, in the company, the army, the school, and so on. Jorgensen's remarks on the usefulness of the Spearman factor outlined the problem of and for psychology as primarily one of predicting performance 'on the job'. Psychology's own view of itself simply took for granted its status as a helpful tool of administration and management. While the concept of a countable unit of behaviour may be rooted in physiology, psychology's own primitive implement is the report card and the test result, not the microscope slide or the scalpel. In this sense then, psychology was born out of problems to do with charting 'the social' – the spaces between individuals – and thus about the synchronic co-ordination of knowledges across space rather than time. Binet himself spoke of his method as a study in synchronics, as against the interests of medicine in the case history of the individual: 'we should therefore study his condition at the time and that only. We have nothing to do with his past history or with his future.'[53] For Binet, the measure of intelligence was to gauge the relation between 'self' and 'circumstances' as played out, in this case, in the practical administrative context of schooling. He was at pains to point out that his work was framed by administrative considerations of the here-and-now, and a concern with the comparative fit between individuals and institution.

The space called personality, as produced out of a multiplicity of individual measurements, and forged eventually into 'co-relations', was not the internal space of an individual psyche but a synchronic mapping of the social – the spaces between individuals. With this emphasis on the synchronics of administration, psychology can be viewed as a kind of economics, bolstered by other discourses of efficiency of the day. Psychological processes became the means to achieve the desired success with the least expenditure of effort, such as increasing the efficiency of children in school, or the level of efficiency of the organisation through personnel selection. The investigative interests of psychology led to the development of a new field of psychological research concerned with the so-called economy of learning.[54] H. H. Goddard, at this stage director of research at the Bureau of Juvenile Research in Ohio, expressed the orientation of the research as follows:

. . . the great advantage of having every man doing work on his own mental level would prove fundamental. Testing intelligence is no longer an experiment or of doubted value. It is fast becoming an exact science. The facts revealed by the army tests cannot be ignored. Greater efficiency, we are always working for. Can these new facts be used to increase our efficiency? No question! We only await the Human Engineer who will undertake the work.[55]

Emerging from the separated group of defectives and deficients came the 'psychopathic personality', but it too comes to be understood with yet another set of tools, this time provided by the psychology of personality. As we have argued, this category of person emerged out of the category of the defective, but it also became inscribed in legislative and administrative arrangements taking shape during this period. Successive entries in the *Annual Reports* of the New South Wales Mental Hygiene Authority began with a call in 1934, under the heading 'Mental Defectives Act', for special legislation to deal effectively with mental defectives and for building institutions for mental defectives, in the name of the 'integrity of the mental and physical standard of the race'.[56] In the following year, provision for criminal patients was deemed inadequate in that 'many persons who should have been dealt with in hospitals have been required to remain in gaols', and consequently a new hospital for criminals was opened at Morisset. The next year saw the arrival of a special institution at Morisset, with the emphasis on transferring mental defectives out of psychiatric institutions and providing them with educational services. The word 'control' is used repeatedly, not 'care' or 'treatment', indicating the shift of this category of persons outside of the medical framework of understanding. From 1937 until 1940 there were repetitions of earlier calls for adequate legislation and institutions to deal with the mental defective, but with a new emphasis on the 'control of higher grade mental defectives' who were beyond the ambit of education or child welfare. There was also now mention of the Mental Defectives (Convicted Persons) Act 1939, still under the Lunacy Act but with the unequivocal recognition that this group is 'not insane'.[57] Hence, there was legislation in place to treat convicted persons who were mentally defective as a distinct group, but no general Act – mental defectives still fall under the Lunacy Act, even though they are recognised as 'mental defective but not insane'. The rhetoric slides between 'control' of the defective – the word control being the pivotal signifier of the penal system – and 'care and treatment' – as the signifiers of the hospital system. In this bringing together in the one report of the 'control' of the higher grade defective on the one hand, and the 'care and treatment' of the mentally defective prisoner on the other, we begin to see the congealing of a problem group. It is defined as beyond the parameters of education and child welfare and exists somewhere between 'control' and 'treatment', between the prison and the hospital. That is to say, there is a blur, a lack of definition, around the question of their institutional and administrative location. It is noteworthy that the task of administering and reporting on this emergent group falls between both prison and mental hospital staff. By 1946 however, there was an attempt at clarifying and delimiting a group which to that point still defies definite classification:

The definition of a 'mentally defective person' laid down by the [Mental Defective (Convicted Persons)] Act is somewhat narrow, implying only the criterion of inherent intellectual defect. The Act should be amended so as to embrace individuals neither mentally defective nor insane, but who come within the category of psychopathic personalities.[58]

The move to personality as a grid for measuring dangerousness involved a shift of inquiry from the internal structure of individuals to a relative position of an individual to others in an external field. This move from individual structure to relative position was prefigured in shifts within psychological medicine itself, in particular, the lack of surety about the importance of knowledge of 'physical structure' within studies of personality. The shift was articulated in Tredgold and Tredgold's *Manual of Psychological Medicine* (1953) with the recognition that internal physiological makeup was the outcome of a highly complex set of metabolic conditions which made individual structure itself unique and peculiar and hence impossibly difficult to categorise, such that 'it is more than doubtful whether the mass of mankind can at present be divided into the clear-cut categories claimed by some writers'.[59] These authors spoke then of psychopathic personality as highly variable, and that the one characteristic they had in common was the 'tendency to various kinds of misconduct'.

At this mid-point of the twentieth century there is a turning away from the dictum that knowledge is to be found in the structure of the individual, and the introduction of the notion that what is needed is knowledge of the relative position of the individual in a field. Diagnosis has then to rely on statistical co-relation of actions, behaviours and conducts. What arrives in 1952 is 'sociopathic personality disturbance, anti-social type' presented under a listing of 'Personality disorders – disorders of psychogenic origin or without clearly defined tangible cause or structural change', inscribed into the first edition of the *Diagnostic and Statistical Manual* of the American Psychiatric Association. It was no longer possible to assess dangerousness on the basis of a calculation of the individual body.

The space for psychology

As we move into the mid-twentieth century it is possible to indicate the differences between the kind of models for behaviour in general, and personality in particular, which have emerged. It is possible to depict two distinctive approaches, one which relates to what might be called the neuro-psychiatric model used by Lind and Berry from as early as the 1910s, and another most clearly identified with the work of Hans Eysenck from the 1940s which identified a physiological or 'constitutional' basis to personality. Each of these models has different implications and certainly different tools for knowing personality. By examining the differences between these models it is possible to see psychiatry's need for a guarded incorporation of the tools of the psychologist for the total picture of personality to emerge.

The kind of neuro-psychiatric model according to which Lind and Berry operated was fairly self-contained, confining itself to brain cells and nervous pathways. Both Lind and Berry believed that structural defects in brain 'architecture' could be discovered which would explain the behaviour of the defective. Lind used this phrase in his reports on the pathology laboratory, as in 1913: 'out of 37 cases of idiocy about 33 per cent show abnormality of brain architecture through developmental defects'.[60] It was possible that if one dug deeply and deployed an array of fine enough tools, the small and elusive physical stigmata could be revealed. The reader will recall that for Berry 'the neuron is really the one important item and it is very small and very elusive'.[61] After Bolton, Watson, Mott and Cajal on 'the neuron and its significance', Berry asserted that in order to know the feebleminded one must first know the brain cell. The brain cell was the basic architectural unit, and differences in the arrangement of nervous pathways accounted for any defect in social control. The more complex the arrangement of cells and their connecting pathways, the more the anatomical structure served as a disciplinary mechanism. The space for prudence, forethought and 'supervisional review' was created as the impulse made its way through this architectural complex. The higher level of operations was to be seen in the neuronic machinery of the fourth epoch, the 'supra-segmental reflex', whereupon

behaviour is thus no longer a matter of instantaneous impulse, but is made subject to a certain degree of supervisional review, guided by a primitive form of judgement which may be taken to mark the beginning of psychic life.[62]

The architectural model of defectiveness provided an understanding of how a group whose problem is defective conduct (the moral imbecile or the psychopath) comes to emerge out of the mental defective (as distinct from the mentally disordered). As we have seen, the notion in Berry's work of a defect in brain architecture causing problems in behaviour or conduct, lingers as medical orthodoxy right through to the mid-twentieth century. We note, for example, the mechanistic analogy deployed in the Tredgold and Tredgold text, where the condition of 'moral defect' is due to an organic abnormality in the brain:

The condition is not due to lack of training and opportunity, but to an organic abnormality of the higher levels and structures of the brain. The moral defect is one who is in certain respects over-engined and who is at the same time devoid of adequate brakes.[63]

The alternative model which Hans Eysenck has a hand in developing began with a commentary on what he described as a lack of integration between psychiatry and psychology in the field of personality studies.[64] Eysenck was critical of the lack of rigour in personality studies and points to the advantages of learning theory in providing the standard of proper inquiry. When psychology ordinarily tries its hand at personality theory, in Eysenck's view, it abandons the appeal to facts and the questions of proof and disproof and resorts instead to pre-scientific modes of argumentation '. . . to persuasion, and to reference to therapies'.[65] Eysenck is clearly impressed with the strides which learning theory has made since to the work of Pavlov and the theoretical lines developed by Hull, Tolman, Guthrie, Spence and others:

The question . . . arises whether an attempt should not be made at this stage to bring together in one general framework the theory of learning and the theory of personality in the hope that the dynamic laws of the former may be able to account for the derivative principles of the latter.[66]

The problem with the model that derives from Pavlov was that the nerve cell, and the nervous system in general, was no longer that neatly bounded mechanism of containment that appears in Berry's work. The old architectural model deployed by Berry and Lind, with its nice straight lines, began to spill over with leakages. The cells and pathways model evolved into a leaky system, with a spill over between cells, into the blood stream, the lymph and the glands. These kinds of spaces took on new importance in understanding issues to do with the control of behaviour.

After Pavlov, a model developed focusing on the interrelationship between the nervous system, which took on the complexities of the central and autonomic systems, and what was to become the endocrine system. The nervous system loses the simplicity of an architectural model of control and containment evident in the work of Lind and Berry. A model of control of behaviour develops which is far more complex, interconnected and diffuse. The autonomic nervous system emerges (nerve impulses beyond the control of the will which manage the vital organs), as does the importance of glandular secretions. The nervous system connects up with various secretory mechanisms. Eysenck's discussion of Mowrer clearly shows the importance of the autonomic nervous system in his work. Mowrer started with identifying the two main response systems, the skeletal muscles and the smooth muscles and glands. Responses mediated by the first are called behavioural and belong to the central nervous system, while those mediated by the second are called physiological and belong to the autonomic nervous system. Mowrer emphasised that the two nervous systems were radically different, and that it was not unreasonable to suppose that the responses which they mediate were subject to very different learning processes. In parallel with this basic dichotomy was the differentiation between voluntary and involuntary responses. Without exception, the visceral and vascular responses were beyond direct voluntary control while all of the skeletal responses were capable of being brought under voluntary control. Eysenck cites Mowrer as follows:

By and large, the solutions to individual problems involve the central nervous system and the skeletal musculature, whereas the solutions to social problems involve the autonomic nervous system and the organs which mediate emotional responses. Intrinsically, it is hardly helpful to the individual to be told, 'Thou shalt not do thus and so', but it may be socially very necessary, and, in the long run but not in any immediately discernible psychological sense, also advantageous to the individual.[67]

Eysenck records that this acquisition of socially useful responses is equivalent to the concept of socialisation, and called 'training' by Mowrer, and then goes on to link this relationship of physiology to learning theory with the study of personality.

The importance of Pavlov's work is that, through an extension of reflexology, it complicates any notion of a simple linear pathway between stimulus and response. Pavlov himself speaks about how his work on the conditioned reflex opens up the simple concrete linearity of earlier models. Let's rehearse the central feature of Pavlov's experiments on the reflex. A dog will salivate if offered food. But if you offer food frequently enough, without giving it to the dog, it will no longer salivate. The latter is a conditioned reflex. Likewise, if you offer food and ring a bell frequently enough, then the dog will salivate just with the ringing of the bell. This is also a conditioned reflex. The breaking apart of the architectural model and its replacement with a more fluid, open-ended approach is prefigured in Pavlov:

. . . at the basis of each conditioned reflex . . . there lies an unconditioned reflex . . . Then it must be assumed that the point of the central nervous system which during the unconditioned reflex becomes stimulated, attracts to itself weaker impulses arriving simultaneously from the outer or inner worlds at other points of this system, i.e. thanks to the unconditioned reflex, there is opened for all these stimulations a temporary path leading to the point of this reaction. The circumstances leading to the opening or closing of this path in the brain are the internal mechanisms of the action or inaction of the signalising properties of the objects, and they represent the physiological basis of the finest reactivity of the living substance, the most delicate adaption of the animal organism, to the outer world.[68]

While the body of work which came to be known as endocrinology took off from Pavlov's work, the implications do not seem to have been recognised by psychology for some years. This is evidenced in Eysenck's discussion of Mowrer. Although Pavlov speaks with confidence of the promise of the objectivity of biology further to explore this reactivity of the organism, his own descriptions to do with the temporary, the fine and the delicate tend to undermine neuro-psychological faith in the solidarity and permanency of the earlier architectural model. It is no longer possible to use the metaphor of the solidarity of architecture when dealing with the temporary and liquid secretions of the organism.

We can pick up on the status of the growing science of endocrinology by reference to standard textbook knowledge in the period in which

Eysenck begins his research. Williams' *Textbook of Anatomy and Physiology*,[69] for example, does not represent cutting-edge science but rather reflects a certain givenness about the role of the autonomic nervous system and the broader movement away from a mechanistic model of conducting pathways. The term 'autonomic' proposed by Langley was given to those nerves and ganglia situated outside the spinal cord which regulated the activities of the glands and 'smooth muscle'; and further study had shown a close relation between emotional states and activity in the autonomic system. The descriptions by Williams of the increasing diversity of effects of the autonomic nervous system and the role of emotions indicate a change in conceptualising of the relations away from structure and towards a more complex set of relations. Similarly, Tredgold and Tredgold's *Manual of Psychological Medicine* voices the new lack of surety that accompanied advances in physiology, where doubt is cast upon the importance of the knowledge of 'physical structure' and the vocabulary moves from 'structure' to 'factor'. Kretschmer's work is reported on as an attempt to 'correlate personality types . . . with peculiarities of physical structure'. Berman's work, for example, signalled a complexity of interdependencies between the structure and physiological reactions of the body and the nature and balance of endocrine secretions, the result then coming to bear on personality types, including adrenal, pituitary, hyperthyroid, subthyroid and thymus personality. Tredgold and Tredgold sum up:

While the personality which we regard as normal is the resultant of the adequate and harmonious development and integration of many factors, there is no doubt that in many individuals one or other of these factors tends to predominate, and if this is so to a marked degree it results in a distinctive type. It may also be admitted that the endocrine secretions, and probably other metabolic conditions, exert an influence upon the intelligence and disposition of the individual in the same way that they do upon his physical constitution. But, as we have seen, the mental and physical factors which go to the make-up of the personality are so many and numerous, that each individual is really a personality peculiar to himself. While, therefore, a differentiation into personality types is possible in certain cases, it is more than doubtful whether the mass of mankind can at present be divided into the clear-cut categories claimed by some writers.[70]

There is a recognition, in other words, of the need for a new way of thinking the relationship between 'individual' and the 'mass of mankind', of knowledge of the individual in relation to the rest of the population rather than knowledge of individual internal structure. This is also the case with the 'psychopathic personality':

A type about which much has been written in recent years is the so-called psychopathic personality. This term really includes a variety of quite different types and the only characteristic they have in common is a pronounced tendency to various kinds of misconduct.[71]

Like Berry, Eysenck grounds the truth of his account of personality in physiology. But unlike Berry, for whom physiology provides the tools for a certain kind of knowledge of the internal architecture of the individual, Eysenck turns to physiology to question the possibility or the need to 'get inside' the individual in order to know the personality. As we have already observed, this is the point where Eysenck distinguishes himself from his colleagues in the profession, who would seek to obtain the evidence of personality 'from the patient on the couch' and with recourse to 'pre-scientific modes of argumentation, to persuasion, and to reference to therapies'.[72] Eysenck the scientist is interested in studying personality using the kind of approach which colleagues like Miller and Mowrer had adopted in relation to learning theory: an appeal to facts and experiments designed to prove or disprove their claims. In an extended discussion in the introduction to *The Scientific Study of Personality*, Eysenck speaks about two kinds of psychology differing in both aim and method. 'Common sense' psychology seeks to understand, and it is often stated that the good psychiatrist or psychologist must possess 'empathy' which enables him to 'feel himself into' his patient. But the aim of science is different, and here Eysenck draws out the distinction in his approach to knowledge as towards Einsteinian relativity rather than a knowledge of mechanistic structure. It is more important for science to chart an object's relative position in the field rather than to know its internal structure. So the aim of science is description, or to be more precise, 'to make the primary data intelligible by exhibiting their mode of connection'.[73] The kind of description deployed by science is at a somewhat higher level than simply giving a description of a blade of grass or a table. Just as would occur if we described the movement of planets in terms of parabolas, or the behaviour of electric particles in terms of field theory, we give a scientific level of description by giving 'the individual fact a place in a unified, consistent system of description':

. . . more than this science does not attempt to do. If it is clearly understood that the term 'explanation' does not carry any overtones of intuitive or empathetic understanding, no anthropomorphic 'feeling oneself into' things, but stands merely for the abstract level of description, there is probably no great danger in using that term . . .[74]

Eysenck's approach thus places emphasis on the mode of connection of data, on charting the movement and spaces between objects, and the place of an object in a field. So while not presenting Eysenck as a prime mover in the development of personality theory, he nevertheless does stand as exemplary of a kind of paradigmatic shift which occurred during the period from the physiology of Berry in Australia and Hughlings Jackson in the United Kingdom a generation before.

The physiological basis of behaviour

Eysenck's notion of a constitutional basis to personality is largely informed by the second kind of model outlined above, which emphasises the role of a physiological autonomy which is diffuse and independent of the will – that is, the autonomic nervous system. This emergent 'leaky model' of behaviour control does not, as Eysenck mentions, sit easily with traditional psychiatric models. Here, he is referring to similarities in the accounts of physiology offered by 'the arch-Atomist Pavlov' and the 'arch-Gestaltist Kohler'. Both attempt to account for their molar principles in terms of molecular (physiological) principles which, according to Eysenck, have not been accepted by physiologists and neurologists because of their unorthodox nature.[75] Pavlov's model operates at the molecular level, and a molecule is not simply a smaller unit compared with the cell, but in addition is a concept belonging to physics and only exists at the level of abstract calculation. In other words, to derive a model which has its basis at the 'molecular level' is not merely to go deeper in the search for the smaller, more subtle, more elusive stigmata. It represents a switch in registers. It is akin to moving from mechanics to physics. It may be possible in fact to suggest that the movement from one model to the other is precisely the movement from mechanics to physics.

Eysenck makes clear that he does not wish to imply acceptance of the physiological theories associated with Pavlov, and that while such theories are 'interesting and important, they are not strictly relevant to a psychological theory of the kind developed here, which remains throughout at the molar level'.[76] ('Molar' is the physicist's term for 'acting on or by masses'). He does however indicate that the processes which are the object of investigation do operate at a molecular level, well beyond the architectural concerns of traditional neurological anatomy. For Eysenck, the precise point of continuation from Pavlov is the conception of experimental neurosis, developed by Pavlov in 1927, in which it was proposed that different forms of disturbance could be produced in dogs depending on the animal's nervous system. A more 'resistant' nervous system could lead to excitation, while in dogs with the less resistant system a predominance of inhibition could be observed. These two variations in the pathological disturbance of cortical activity were comparable to the two forms of neuroses in man, which in pre-Freudian terminology were neurasthenia and hysteria. The first was associated with an exaggeration of the excitatory and a weakness of the inhibitory process, and the second with a predominance of the inhibitory and weakness of the excitatory process. These observations of Pavlov are discussed at length by Eysenck, who claims that they have been largely neglected by psychiatry and psychology alike. He picks up instead on what he calls a 'general psychological law' proposed by Hull, namely the law of reactive inhibition:

Whenever any reaction is evoked in an organism, there is left a condition or state which acts as a primary negative motivation in that it has an innate capacity to produce a cessation of the activities which produce the state . . . All responses leave behind in the physical structure involved in the evocation, a state or substance which acts directly to inhibit the evocation of the activity in question. The hypothetical inhibitory condition or substance is observable only through its effect upon positive reaction potentials.[77]

It is upon this concept that Eysenck builds a more complex, open-ended physiological theory of personality, when stood up against the older architectural model. Whenever a stimulus–response connection is made in the central nervous system, according to Eysenck, there are created both excitory and inhibitory potentials. The algebraic sum of these potentials determines the amount of learning that takes place, and through it the particular reaction the organism makes whenever the stimulus is presented again.

As a consequence of Eysenck's revision of these older models, differences in the responses of organisms may have their basis in physiological 'structure' or 'constitution', but they no longer can have their basis in structure if this is understood as an anatomical architecture. It is not that the stigmata of difference have become smaller and harder to read but that they no longer exist as concrete structural defects. Difference becomes only a matter of degree, having a quantitative and quantifiable dimension rather than a qualitative one.

Having taken Hull's law of inhibition as his point of departure, Eysenck proposes what may be called a postulate of individual differences: human beings differ with respect to the speed with which reactive inhibition is produced, the strength of the reactive inhibition produced, and the speed with which reactive inhibition is dissipated. These differences themselves are properties of the physical structures involved in the evocation of responses. Eysenck again:

Mental abnormality (including mental deficiency, neurosis, psychosis) is not qualitatively different from normality, in the sense that a person with a broken arm, or a patient suffering from haemophilia, is different from someone not ill:

different types of mental abnormality constitute the extreme ends of continuous variables which are probably orthogonal to each other.[78]

Thus, difference can only be measured in comparative terms and new tools are required to chart the total picture. It is no longer possible to build the picture up from the basic anatomical structure, as if putting more and more flesh on the skeleton. It will be with the tools of the psychologist, those '400 tests that can be made on patients' and the fragments of information about the relational, comparative position of the individual, that the contours of the picture will be formed. The multi-dimensional space that comes to be called personality is the calculated product of relations between different sets of data, as in the shape of orthogonal dimensions that emerge from Eysenck's scatter-grams. The space of personality is, literally, figurative. It ought to be apparent that the 'total picture of the patient's personality' cannot exist without the statistical tools brought in by the psychologist. Factor analysis was given birth in the biological sciences and in psychology, and only in the 1960s did it start to become a routine approach to medical research and psychiatry, announced in studies such as Hamilton and White's use of factor analysis in the classification of depression.[79] The shift from an architectural display of an anatomy to a statistical display of a space of calculations, such as we can see in a comparison of the models of Berry and Eysenck, might be seen as part of a larger epistemic or paradigmatic shift where the display no longer exists in referential relation to the object but creates the space for the concept to exist. This might be the case whether applied to atomic physics or personality studies.

It is at this time, midway through the twentieth century, that the term sociopath gains currency and enters the official register with the *Diagnostic and Statistical Manual*. In 1952 the term 'psychopathic personality' is replaced by 'personality disorders' with the subgroup 'sociopathic personality disturbance, anti-social type'. The name itself displays a certain ambivalence, oscillating between the name of a medical problem and the name of a problem for government. Perhaps its inherent instability explains its rather short life. But regardless of this, its appearance in the *Diagnostic and Statistical Manual* indicates that what is needed is knowledge of the relative position of the individual object of study in a field, an understanding of a relative location in social space.

In parallel with these changes in the models of knowledge of the individual – from the architectural model of cells and conducting path-ways and the spill-over in the physiological models of diffuse secretion – there is a discernible shift in the mode of administration of individuals which we can pick up from several sources during the 1950s, as

Australia moved further into a program of mental hygiene. To highlight those parallels, it might be possible to characterise the policy shift of the mid-twentieth century as a spilling over of the locus of mental health out of the asylum and into the community. But the terms of this shift need to be reassessed in the light of changes to systems of knowledge to which we have drawn attention in this chapter.

6 Surfaces of emergence

The outline of a field of early twentieth-century inquiry in the biological and human sciences into the problem of mental defect, provided earlier in this book, indicates how this inquiry became possible once the category of the defective is firmly separated from the category of the insane. It becomes possible to think and act upon dangerous persons as a consequence of specific techniques of calculating mental defectiveness. Two aspects of this part of the study are worth noting. First, the category of the moral imbecile produced by these techniques allows a carving out of a space or dimension which made individuals amenable to a kind of internal moral measurement. Here it was suggested, against some other accounts in the history of psychology, that certain inscription devices produced knowledge of persons and their internal dimensions as a means of seeking to manage and govern them – that certain types of person or conditions of personhood such as the moral imbecile came about as an artefact of government. Secondly, the failure adequately to grasp the measure of dangerousness through an internal gaze on the body provided the conditions for posing the problem using the conceptual machinery of 'personality'. This was a technology which permitted the mapping of the spaces between people as well as the sweeping up of whole populations within a grid of calculability. The account here suggests that personality gave up a greater widening of the potentiality for dangerousness, a way of knowing that satisfied the requirement of government to establish an economy of managing dangerousness on a broader scale.

But the conditions for the possibility of this emergence lie in several different sites. It is possible to get a fix on the category of person known as the moral imbecile within the technology of the pathology laboratory (Lind), the technology of cell structure (Berry), and the technology of the test (Porteus). We can now move on to the kind of technology in the psychological clinic of the Children's Court where the 'definitely psychopathic' is able to be read from the conduct of both parents and children as a 'problem' population in terms of conduct – delinquent, mal-adjusted, psychopathic – as this is displayed through the *activities of the clinic*, as distinct from a reading of the body. As a result of the repositioning of the mental defective out of the mental hospital and its appearance back within the penal context of the children's court but also within the activities of a para-psychiatric team, we have before us a number of surfaces of emergence of the category of psychopathic personality. The team – psychiatrist, psychologist, social worker – fixes the problem individual in a matrix, no longer bound by the walls of the asylum but in the newly psychiatrised web of relations. We can also move on to the various determinations in law, or more precisely the judgements of courts as they sought to determine answers to questions such as 'what kind of person are you? what kind of person does such a thing?', and to the changes in legislation that brought on new possibilities in person-formation.

The story is not an uncomplicated one, given that in the contexts of both the acute mental hospital and the specialist institutions for the mental defect, the birth of psychology is attended by the midwife of psychiatry who continues to maintain, protect and supervise its young ward as it steps hesitantly into the scientific world with all its rigours and pitfalls.

Psychiatry and psychology

The argument here has several parts. While turning to each of the surfaces of emergence of personality disorder, we need also to consider the historical positioning of those emergent sciences of humankind in the first half of the twentieth century that gave knowledge of the aetiology of the individual – in the school, the clinic and the court – and how it came to give this knowledge within the conceptual terrain of personality. While psychiatry and psychology might have seen each other with a competitive eye, as intimated by figures like Professor Dawson in Sydney or the Director Catarinich in Melbourne, the historical account given here tends rather to emphasise the twin movements of consolidation for these practices as they sought to interrelate. Psychiatry affiliated with medicine-as-cure while psychology became aligned with hygiene and prevention, and it was in these complementary relations that the consolidation of both occurs.

A commentary on psychology, psychiatry and the law was offered mid-point in the twentieth century by Catarinich, the rather dour and uninspiring director of mental hygiene whose career was about to suffer a major setback as a result of yet another government inquiry into mental hospital administration (the Kennedy Report). Caterinich was critical of a 'brass instrument psychology' which claimed that all kinds of abnormalities were susceptible to psychological dissection. Psychology needed to understand itself as extremely diverse, and above all, young and immature. It needed, if anything, a 'good deal of conservatism' lest it sow the seeds of unreliability and bring itself into disrepute. Psychiatry, for its part, used 'an eclectic kind of psychology' in the management of its patients, while the rather 'academical' approach by psychology was tending to indoctrinate rather than educate. Where did this advice lead? For Catarinich, it led to the view that psychiatry needed to show the way by moderating its claims and providing an impartiality in that very site where in recent times it had become particularly prominent – the legal system. The warning was a clear rebuke to psychiatrists acting as so-called impartial expert witnesses in the courts: that going down the path of psychology to pronounce on every kind of variation in conduct was counter-productive:

there has appeared a tendency in some [psychiatrists] . . . to regard any departure from what may be regarded as normal conduct as being definitely indicative of mental illness with a consequent lessened degree of legal responsibility. Apart from the difficulty of assessing just what constitutes normal conduct, one has seen such things as variability of moods, a few foolish remarks or some eccentric actions stretched to their utmost possible limits in their endeavour to prove the irresponsibility of the individual.[1]

So in the medical contexts where psychology operated and where the different categories of the mental defective were to be elaborated, psychiatry's relationship to psychology became as the leader of a team, each player given their role and function relative to the other players. Note that the team needed all to play together, as it were, in order for there to be a read-out of the category of psychopathic personality. It was not as though the psychological or social or biological would alone provide a knowledge of disorder.

The annual reports of the mental hygiene department were a vehicle for doctors' advocacy of medical support systems and branches of medicine to support the research effort on a larger scale. It was clear even from the mid nineteenth century that psychology and 'the psychological' were understood within the lunacy bureaucracy as branches of medicine. Links were made from the 1900s between pathology, the acquiring of surgical equipment for the pathology clinic and the purchase of 'a few standard works on psychological medicine'.[2] The diploma of psychological medicine began at Sydney University from 1927 under the direction of the professor of psychiatry. From 1932 lectures were compulsory in the area of Normal Psychology for third-year medical students at Melbourne University.[3] The director of Royal

Park Hospital in Melbourne was keen to see young medical practitioners take up psychological research as a profession. But by the mid-1930s, at the time of the passage of the *Mental Deficiency Bill* through the Victorian State Parliament, the specialist in psychology comes to be less identified with the medical practitioner. The most urgent need was thought to be special accommodation for the mental defective and the establishment of a psychological clinic, where specialists could make a thorough investigation of children so as to make reliable decisions about where to send them. The clinic was also seen to be of greatest value in dealing with cases from the children's courts.[4] Psychology and the psychological expert belonged to the non-curative domain of mental hygiene and made a place for itself as a consequence of the separation of the defective from the disordered.

Once the receiving house/mental hospital mechanism was established, the annexation and accumulation of related institutions began. Of special interest is the clinical pathology laboratory, because it is on this site that the 'psychopathic' first emerges in the reports of the activities of the department. Here was Dr Lind outlining the methods of investigation as he continued the quest to prove his theories of causality :

Considerable care was taken last year in investigating family histories in every particular, by means of searching interviews with relatives of patients, and at times communication with family physicians, and this, with the present laboratory methods of determining the existence of syphilis, has resulted in greater exactitude than formerly in ascribing the cause of the mental disorder. To summarise the causative factors – worry, trouble, adversity, and the like, account for 90 instances; heredity (including psychopathic and alcoholic ancestry) claims 117; excessive alcoholism, 74 cases; syphilis, 32 cases; senile changes, 72).[5]

Lind was in charge of the pathological laboratory at Royal Park by 1915 and received requests from the medical profession on the work of the department and the laboratory. One inquiry concerned the evidence of alcoholism as a cause of insanity, in particular the evidence of cirrhotic liver and kidney changes which could reasonably be connected to alcohol use. Lind pointed to the fact that nerve tissue in 'the neuropath and the psychopath . . . is very intolerant to alcohol', so there is 'no opportunity to have their splanchnics affected' before they suffered some mental derangement and are sent to a hospital.[6] We recall that a tendency or vulnerability rooted in physiology was a central theme in much of the eugenicist arguments, and here it is the disposition and susceptibility of the physiological substratum which fixed the psychopath. But the means of its calculation, although located in the laboratory and clinic, deployed techniques which problematised familial relations through analysis, interpretation and genealogical records, as well as the accounts of relatives and the expert opinion of the physician. The family became an object of inquiry into causality issues in part through the study of physiological substratum. But the effects of this inquiry shifted as psychology, social work and a range of therapeutic interventions gradually came to dominate the site of family relations well into the twentieth century.

Although the laboratory precinct clearly belonged to the doctor, the terrain was not one which fitted comfortably with either the modern mental hospital or curative medicine. By 1937 alcoholics and 'psychopathic individuals' are included within the category of 'various problems of mental disorder and defect' for a government department to deal with '. . . provided it is not inhibited by the reactionary antagonism to the growing spirit of Psychological Medicine'.[7] Indeed, a later report makes it clear that the psychopath should have no place in the domain of curative medicine:

From time to time this Department has to deal with individuals who are classified as psychopathic personalities. These persons are regarded from a medical viewpoint as being neither sane nor insane. They exhibit abnormalities both of character and conduct and are very apt to come into conflict with the law. They do not seem to exercise normal control over their impulses, and are thus likely to become persistent offenders even though they are fully capable of realising the fact that their conduct will necessarily result in punishment. Such weak-willed individuals are prone to sex offences, amongst many other forms of delinquency.[8]

The director Catarinich proposed that these individuals should be given indeterminate sentences in the courts and be overseen by neither mental hygiene nor the penal department but a separate institution under penal control, with a board advised by a medical officer to manage them.

Although there is a formal jurisdiction covered by the doctor and a continuing research interest within medicine – there was a fleeting appearance in the department's records of an individual diagnosed as having 'psychopathy' undertaking electro-convulsive therapy in 1945 but who registers a result of 'not improved' – the psychopath sat uneasily in the medical model. Eventually the category does come to inhabit an uneasy place within mental hygiene but only after a long process of disaggregation of the asylum population and the separation of the mental defective away from the mental hospital. It became possible to know the category of the 'moral imbecile' after it became possible to know the feebleminded. Insofar as moral imbecility was presumed to be

a defect rather than a disorder, it became attached to the institutions
and practices around prevention and hygiene, rather than cure.

The clinic

We are looking, then, at a range of practices which sought to develop
knowledge of individuals in order to manage them. One group carried
away from the mental hospital was a group of defects who, unlike the
more pronounced forms of feeblemindedness, did not display the
obvious stigmata of lack of intelligence. In the annual reports it is
possible to trace the solidifying of the psychopath into a psychiatric
category out of the institutions for these kinds of defects set up during
the 1920s and 1930s. In Victoria, of particular importance here is the
creation of special schools at Janefield, Pleasant Creek and Travancore.
The latter opens in 1933 originally for '. . . the reception of children
who, although mentally defective, are capable of receiving benefit from
special instruction'.[9] The beginning staff included an ex-military nurse,
a teaching staff supplied by the Education Department and medical
services supplied by the Royal Park Mental Hospital. The next year it is
described as a home for children with a particular 'intelligence range',
and should be developed as '. . . a clinic for feeble minded and problem
children'.[10] Success was recorded in terms of the improvement in
'general habits, cleanliness and general conduct' of some of the children
at Travancore; of the co-operation between the Departments of Education and Mental Hygiene in how the institution was run; that some of
the older boys, after two or three years at Travancore, had successfully
been sent on to the training farm in the town of Sale in the countryside,
where good reports had been received; and of how a waiting list for
entry to Travancore was starting to grow. These special schools and
homes opened at the same time as a formal branching-off of a sub-
department to deal with mental defectives, so that from 1936 they fall
under the Mental Defectives Branch. Later, from 1948, this is to be
called the Mental Defectives and Prevention Branch. In the 1930s'
branching off of institutions, bureaucracy and legislation for dealing
with the defective, there comes into being another clinic, this time for
the 'maladjusted'.

By 1933, Travancore was described as having three main functions:
shelter, care and education for children from five or six to age sixteen
whose mental age was from three to six years below actual age; as a
clinic for 'feebleminded and problem children'; and as a teaching and
demonstration centre for teachers and medical practitioners. In 1938,
adjoining the school was erected a small group of buildings to serve as a

clinic, where it was proposed to appoint a psychiatrist, psychologist and social worker to carry out studies of mental deficiency. Subsequently, V. P. Johnson was appointed psychiatrist, and P. M. Bachelard was appointed as psychologist. Further additional staff were proposed, based on suggestions that the clinic be made available for the examination of 'problem children and young delinquents' brought before the courts.

This of course was a far cry from the original primary role of Travancore as an institution for the mentally defective. The clinic soon takes on a life of its own, and although originally conceived as the extension of the space for mental defect – 'putting mental deficiency and mental retardation on a scientific basis' – it shifts its focus quite fundamentally to 'the examination of problem children', and by 1940 has come to specialise in this area.[11] It was claimed that over half of the children examined by the clinic were maladjusted but that the mental defect or retardation was not itself the root cause of 'behaviour problems':

. . . which are often grounded on failure and mal-adjustment in school, employment or community life, the effects of the failure usually being reinforced by criticism, ridicule and even punishment by relatives, teachers and companions.[12]

The following year's report on Travancore records that:

. . . the Clinic has many potentialities in the prevention and treatment of many and varied types of emotional mal-adjustment, which are frequently the forerunners of delinquency, crime, nervous and mental disorder and social inefficiency . . . whilst the Clinic was established to deal mainly with conditions of mental deficiency, it is evident that in the field of preventative medicine the widening of these activities is very desirable.[13]

By the time the Clinic moved temporarily to Carlow House in the city in 1942, less than ten per cent of cases were referred by the Mental Hygiene Department compared with nearly one half referred from the Children's Welfare Department and the Crown Law Department. This tendency was confirmed the following year when the clinic began to use offices in the Children's Court to carry on these activities.

In 1945, A. R. Phillips was appointed psychiatrist following Bachelard's death the previous year, and Keith Cathcart joined the clinic staff as psychologist. In this year's report, the description of the clinic's activities appeared to confirm the about-face, in that its functions '. . . have developed rapidly in the direction of treatment of nervous disorders and behavioural problems in both normal and retarded children and adolescents'.[14] In the following year, with the appointment of Patricia Holmes and Rosemary Ramsay as social workers, the staff of the clinic were described as a 'guidance team', with the regret expressed that the cases encountered by the clinic could not be followed through because no suitable institutions existed. The two types of cases cited were mental defect and 'severe conduct disorder'.[15]

The court clinic

Meanwhile, back in the mental hospital, psychology and social work had undergone considerable expansion, both straining at the leash.[16] In 1949 both the psychologist and social worker issued their own sectional reports within the Department's overall *Annual Report* devoted to Royal Park. The psychologist emphasised the need for a department which will expand into 'predictive, therapeutic and research techniques', and also emphasised the role of psychology as a science of statistics. With its expertise as a science of knowledge-gathering of large amounts of data, psychology could lend itself to the role of co-ordinating knowledge, including the kinds of knowledge coming from the medical officer. Hence, a request was made in 1949 for a research officer with psychology qualifications including psychopathology and statistics, '. . . to keep not only the records and research cards of this department, but also the research data of medical officers and the social worker'. For the psychologist, personality is of particular interest, and in the field of abnormal psychology is spoken of as something 'vast', still ill-defined and needing refined tools to identify. The mental hospital carried out initial diagnostic and basic testing on all suitable patient admissions, but almost all the tests had been developed overseas and required adjustment to take account of 'cultural differences'. Moreover, the bulk of the tests were considered

. . . relatively antique . . . and do not exploit either modern experimental techniques or modern personality and perception theories. Most have been developed by workers trained only in the clinical field, and are statistically and theoretically naive . . . vast areas of the abnormal personality, and even distinct syndromes remain uncovered by existing tests. Diagnoses can at best be only tentative until these lacunae are eliminated.[17]

An area which had been left completely untouched by testing had been the 'field of prognostics', and this was to be the first priority for research. The appointment of a further social worker would allow the type of co-operative research needed to give 'contingency factors' a predictive value. In 1949 there were now three clinics in operation under the Mental Hygiene Department – Travancore, the Psychiatric and the Observatory clinics – with a psychologist, described as a member of a 'full psychiatric team', appointed to serve all three:

Already it is becoming evident that a full psychiatric clinic team can do valuable work in the field of vocational and educational guidance, each member of the team contributing according to his training to *the total picture of the patient's personality*, and each helping him in a different, but co-ordinated way, to adjust to work or school.[18]

What this shows is that the birth and proliferation of the clinic for the problem child allows the psychopathic to take on the solidarity of a legal category. Travancore increasingly forges collaborative arrangements with the Children's Court, while in 1948 the Mental Defectives and Prevention Branch formally takes over the Psychiatric Clinic from Maternal and Child Hygiene and the Children's Court Clinic. In the same year a category appears called 'definitely psychopathic', and 'psychopathic personality' as a psychiatric classification in the report of the Children's Court Clinic:

A noticeable feature of the year's work was the large number of cases in which parental factors appeared to be the chief cause of the delinquency. Some of the parents of this group were definitely psychopathic. The children of this group were found to be either manifesting symptoms of a neurosis with feelings of anxiety and insecurity, or showing evidence of character defects arising from inadequate moral training and the bad example of their parents. Many of these cases are exceedingly difficult to treat as the abnormal parent is often non-co-operative, though requiring treatment just as much as the child.[19]

Note that the point of appearance of the category of psychopathic personality is in the description of the parents of some of the delinquent children attending the Children's Court Clinic, as 'definitely psycho-pathic'. This condition was understood to be the chief cause of the delinquency in their children.[20]

The clinic recommended policies for child guidance on a systematic scale which would allow for appropriate levels of adjustment and normality to be achieved. This kind of work would be explicitly written into the role of institutions like creches, kindergartens and schools – the terrain, that is, of the 'normal' child. To prepare them for this role, the clinic carried out an investigation of the personality attributes and level of adjustment of potential trainee kindergarteners at the request of the Maternal and Child Hygiene branch of the department. In this, questions of adjustment were put in terms of the requirement, within a strategy of preventive mental hygiene, for kindergarten teachers to have the appropriate personalities for giving guidance in the formative years and to act as emulatory figures:

the importance of having only well adjusted persons engaged in the guidance of children during the formative pre-school period in intellectual and emotional growth will be recognised by all who believe that the roots of much mental and emotional disorder in later life are established in the pre-school period.[21]

Much later, psychiatry's advance towards the 'problem family' used the concept of psychopathic to build up a series of co-relations between the functioning of families and interactions with police and the criminal justice system. This can be shown in Dax and Hagger's (1977) review of research showing that 'multiproblem families' had a concentration of social pathology, in that they were sent to prison at a rate 250 times greater than average, stole cars and had accidents 70 to 75 times more often than the average.[22] The families were rarely distinguished as a group requiring specific psychiatric assistance even though several common pathologies could be linked to them, including intellectual retardation, alcoholism, attempted suicide and aged infirmity. Multiproblem families also experienced the long-term effects of poor child rearing practices and learning difficulties. The authors expressed a wariness, however, of the implications of a psychiatric diagnosis of the family. A psychiatric construction of family members as 'patients' meant that the labels given to their 'illnesses' simply disguised their social background.[23] Nevertheless, the more common labels to describe this 'psychiatry of inadequacy' included personality disorders, the predominately inadequate psychopath, passive dependent personalities, character disorders, sociopaths, the borderline mentally retarded, the socially regressed and the simple schizophrenic. Personality disorder was the most common condition among men in these families, and the high prevalence of neuroses among women was thought to be a response to their husbands' behaviour.[24] In a disclaimer to the 'medicalisation of crime' thesis advanced by Thomas Szasz and others, Dax and Hagger claimed that few psychiatrists wished to absorb these people under the umbrella of mental illness or indeed to treat them. Rather, psychiatry wanted 'the right for them to be cared for':

the inadequacy of the family members, however it is labelled and whatever its causation, results in conduct which is sufficiently unpredictable and unusual as well as disturbing to the community, to be recognised as abnormal, though scarcely classifiable as mental illness . . . [T]he labelling of such people, especially if it is suggestive of deviancy, adds to their difficulties, yet politically at least their welfare depends upon their classification. To regard them as socially handicapped, might be a way of extending the existing services, comparable to those of the intellectually handicapped, to incorporate the group, without the problems inherent upon providing a new kind of service . . . [W]e share with other disciplines the gravest responsibility for dealing with these socially handicapped, fringe members of our community. Perhaps the first stage in the programme should be to learn more about them.[25]

We have witnessed a long shaping process of disaggregation of defect from disorder. The institutional forms at the periphery of the mental hospital, in particular the clinic, created the space which the psychopath comes to inhabit. The clinic was so far from the centre of psychiatric medical treatment and so closely related to the court that it in effect established a new zone between the psychiatric and the penal, well apart from matters concerned with insanity.

Psychological and psychiatric practices

We have considered the term personality from an historical point of view with the proposition that its increasing usage during the first half of the twentieth century, as a way of describing and measuring disorder, is contingent on developments in psychology and psychiatry, and also that the terminology used to mark out a governable space from these knowledges is far from arbitrary. The task has been to survey the topography where the invention of personality has become intimately bound up in questions of how individuals are to be governed and how they are to govern themselves.

Have we always had a personality? Raymond Williams writes that the meaning of the word has shifted, referring now to people in the context of 'leading personalities' in entertainment, the media or politics.[26] We can say that we have a personality, inasmuch as each of us is thought to have developed a more-or-less distinctive individual character. According to Williams, the supposed individual quality of personality has been recognised in the significance of the word, probably since the late fourteenth century, as the marker of being a person rather than merely 'a thing'. From the eighteenth century the significance of personality as an individualising reference was strengthened when it was defined as 'the existence or individuality of any one'. In the mid-nineteenth century Emerson used terms such as overpowering personality, weak personality and so on, reflecting a developing usage of the term to describe a particular kind of identity relative to another. The related word disposition, which derived from astrology and physiology, suggested the idea of individuality as being produced or determined. Personality and character, once an outward sign, came to be understood as 'decisively internalised, yet internalised as a possession', and therefore as something which would be displayed or interpreted.[27] So there was a time when personality became a way of thinking about and expressing individuality. As such, it also came to be understood as something evincing a 'freestanding' and 'estimable' existence; to mean, in effect, something which can be estimated or given a measure. The identification of this latter, distinctive feature of a calculable individuality is central to this study.

Historical accounts of psychology and psychiatry would locate the uptake of personality studies in the 1920s. For W. S. Dawson, the first professor of psychiatry in Australia, at Sydney University, the topic of personality bridged both psychology and psychiatry, as well as philosophy. The study of human beings had been hindered by dualistic theories of humanness, that had placed soul and spirit as entities separate from the body.[28] Dawson's review of the field, published in 1927 in the relatively new journal *Australasian Journal of Psychology and Philosophy*, presented personality studies as growing to prominence in psychological literature but still having firm links with the 'physical' aspects of the concept of personality drawn from medicine and science. His review provides a glance at a field of thinking – an organised set of concerns – that incorporated a broad sweep of thinking about the formation of personhood and the authorities which informed it, including Janet, Freud and Jung.

He begins with Janet's hierarchy of mental functions as a way of measuring 'adaption to reality and practical ends'. These included the 'function of the real' including action, attention and emotion; 'disinterested activity', including activity without full consciousness; habit, partially adapted activity and perception without certainty; the function of imagery; the level of visceral-emotional reaction; and the level of ill-adapted, useless movements. Physical components could be diagnosed on criteria such as 'sense of incompleteness' or 'sense of inefficiency' or complaints about an inability to concentrate. This lack of synthesis and harmony was evidenced in the make-up of neurotics. Neuroses could take the form of dissociated states, traces, somnambulism and the 'alternating personalities of hysteria'. In considering Freud, Dawson aligned the conception of ego, as the awareness of temporal sequence and the controller of motor discharges, with neurological conceptions of those functions of the *cortex cerebri* that maintained a contact with reality and control over the lower levels of emotional impulsive reactions. Again, the forming of the ego-ideal had links with each individual's phylogenetic endowment:

thus it is that what belongs to the lowest depths in the minds of each one of us is changed, through the formation of the Ideal, into what we value as the highest, the human soul.[29]

Jung brought us the introverts and extraverts, but Dawson considered Jung's work to be beset with problems of interpreting material that could lead to a definite category of person – particularly given that a diagnosis involved an interpretation of the person by an onlooker. More accuracy depended on correlating physical and mental qualities, and it is here that Dawson called up the work of Kretschmer, Meyer and Smuts.

Kretschmer attempted to link character or temperament to certain physical determinants, particularly the sense–brain–motor apparatus and the endocrine system, which more-or-less corresponded to Jung's two basic groups of extraverts and introverts. Kretschmer's 'two great temperament groups' are the cyclothymics and the schizothymics. The first, corresponding to the extraverts, included the open, sociable, practical individuals who are well attuned to their surroundings. The second were more complex personalities, reserved and sensitive, who find emotional rapport difficult, and exhibit qualities of stubbornness and tenacity in contrast to the fickleness and easy adaptability of the cyclothymics. Correlated to physical characteristics, the cyclothymics are most frequently thick-set, rotund individuals (the 'laugh and grow fat types' called pykniks by Kretschmer) while the schizothymics are associated with a slender build, narrow-chested slim types (asthemics) and other varieties (schizoids). Dawson was reminded of Shakespeare's comparison in *Julius Caesar* – give me the 'fat, sleek headed men' as against the 'lean and hungry look'. But he is sceptical of the usefulness of these correlations, as they tended to depend on the idiosyncrasies of the observer and often dissolve into pen-pictures of possible literary merit but doubtful practical significance. Kretschmer may have contributed some understanding of the 'sensitive constitution' and its relation to delusion formation, but this was the limit of his work in providing a physical basis to the study of personality.

Dawson approached this latter task by outlining the concept of integration. Borrowing from a lecture by Adolf Meyer, Dawson took the view accredited to the English neurologist Hughlings Jackson that the nervous system had different functional levels, and that the higher the level of integration, the greater the control of 'lower mechanisms'. The notion of integration seems to contain two main propositions: the impossibility of studying humans apart from their place 'in the world and of the world'; and the fact that these two domains are able to be connected by studying the psycho-biological operation of personality. Personality, for Dawson, was a kind of controlling relay point between human biology and social life:

When the personality is sick, disintegration occurs; lower mechanisms become released from control, consciousness (or attention) is weakened, adaptation becomes less perfect. One of the striking features of mental disorders, at any rate of the severe types known as psychoses, is the transformation and even absence of 'personality'. The mentally sick individual is like a nation in revolution without a representative head.[30]

Here, personality as a calculable entity entails the possibility of giving a measure of integration. Moreover, the study of a 'sick' personality promised to draw on roots in biology to provide a measure of (less perfect) integration. Interestingly, the arguments developed in favour of medicine's involvement in the study of personality draw upon a philosophical tendency which sought to link human evolution with an almost metaphysical conception of the achievement of humanness and freedom. Dawson cites Smuts as speaking of personology as the 'crown of all the sciences', where personality is 'the highest most evolved whole among the structures of the universe'. So the physical is laid out in terms of ever more sophisticated degrees of integration between the organs of the body and its environment, beginning with systems of glands and nerves regulating bodily processes; moving to the nervous apparatus enabling basic contact with environment through the senses; and finally, the harmonious workings of various parts of the individual with the environment in which personality develops. Dawson concludes: 'without proper integration there can be no personality'.[31]

The clear sense given in Dawson's review of personality studies was that personality provided the means for measuring something – moral development, integration, the harmonious workings of individual and environment, or whatever. One might be able to speak of these as achievements or performances in the observed behaviour of individuals, and particular achievements were made available by speaking of personality. The celebratory tone of personality studies – 'the crown of all the sciences' – is a celebration of the possibility of a scientific measurability of character, temperament, integration and any set of characteristics of personhood allowed by the concept of personality, rather than the actual 'discovery' of personality. These researchers always were drawn to return to the most problematic feature of personality studies, the question of its existence.

The terminology of personality was also adopted by moral philosophy during this period, to assist in establishing some right and proper basis for the moral upbringing of citizens. The psychology professor H. Tasman Lovell at Sydney University was comfortable about using concepts like character and personality to describe the object or location of the moral being. Lovell presented a case for the cultivation of character and personality by deliberate moulding of the habits of children, as opposed to a more 'libertarian' view at the time of allowing children to arrive at their own level of moral development through intuition, emulation and other forms of self-nurture.[32] For some of these thinkers, the received wisdom of individual psychology was that intelligence, like height, weight, musical ability or retentive memory, was unequally distributed within the population, and that it would be absurd to rely solely on the intellectual freedom of citizens themselves freely to mould their habits, attitudes and moral outlooks. The child was entitled to the experience of the older intellect, and it would be disastrous to leave this child to fate.[33] Personality and character thus became ends of a process of moral development which would later become routinised and taxonomised in the discipline of individual psychology, such as that of Kohlberg.[34] But in the moral philosophy of the early twentieth century the existence and shape of that thing which is called personality was presupposed before the effort was made to shape, influence and calculate it. The question of the existence of personality was taken up by those whose business it became to classify personality disorder.

The precursors and first editions of the *Diagnostic and Statistical Manual* were quite straightforward about the need for classification – to classify meant to bring order to the now great range of disorders. Classification has a clear and unassailable place in scientific method. The naming of a disease and its placement in a medical nomenclature was a basic requirement for recording clinical and pathological observations. Medical advances were signalled by the expansion of the nomenclature to include new terms based on new observations, and statistical classification was a way of placing a particular morbid condition in a category so that it could enable a study of disease phenomena. As the Manual of the International Statistical Classification in 1948 pointed out, this inevitably involved compromise.[35] Drawing up the categories themselves, and placing a particular disease phenomenon in a category, involved a procedure which combined etiology, anatomical site, the age of the patient and the circumstances of onset, as well as the quality of the information available in medical reports. It was also abundantly clear to the classifiers that not all conditions fitted the classification.

So from as early as 1917 the American Medico-psychological Association had adopted a plan for a uniform statistical system for use in mental hospitals, which could also be used as a nomenclature. But a major difficulty facing the authors of the first *DSM* in 1952 was due in part to a shift in the kind of patients presenting for psychiatric assistance. Prior to the Second World War the classificatory systems in use related to the needs and case load of patients typically found in the public mental hospitals. The mental problems experienced during the wartime period were quite different. The armed forces demanded an accurate account for all the causes of each and every case seen by the psychiatrist. Mental health authorities estimated that of the total cases seen by army psychiatrists only about ten per cent would be of the type ordinarily encountered in civilian life. This meant that the classificatory system in use at the time was not applicable to about ninety per cent of all the cases seen. George Raines, chairman of the committee on nomenclature and statistics for the American Association, pointed out that the 'psychoneurotic label' had been applied to men reacting briefly, and with neurotic symptoms, to the considerable stress of war. A whole range of relatively minor 'personality disturbances', which had become important only in a military setting, all had to be classified as 'psychopathic personality'. In particular, there was no provision for diagnosing psychological reactions to the stress of combat '. . . and terms had to be invented to meet this need'.[36]

There was also need for a single system of classification to replace the many in existence. Both the navy and the veterans administration adopted their own versions of nomenclature, and some agencies used one system for clinical use, another for a disability rating, and yet another for constructing a statistical charting of disorders. The issuing of a revised International Statistical Classification in 1948 was designed to clear up the confusion, and the adoption of a classification system specifically for mental disorders was adopted, drawing on the lessons learned from the army. Efforts were made to seek the views of practitioners, who cited the area of personality disorders and reactions to stress as most urgently needing attention. The practitioners also felt that the need for change was more strongly felt by those in clinics, private practice and in outpatient clinics, rather than the wards of the mental hospitals.

The International Classification Sixth Revision published in 1948 contained for the first time a major section titled 'Mental, Psychoneurotic, and Personality Disorders', eliminating from the Fifth Revision a group headed 'Chronic Poisoning and Intoxication'. The new section grouped together psychoses, disorders of character, behaviour and intelligence, which included pathological personality, immature personality, alcoholism, other drug addiction, primary childhood behaviour disorders, mental deficiency, and other unspecified character, behaviour and intelligence disorders. Pathological personality included schizoid personality, paranoid personality, cyclothymic personality, inadequate personality, antisocial personality, asocial personality, sexual deviation, and other unspecified. Within antisocial personality was constitutional psychopathic state, and psychopathic personality with antisocial trend; and within asocial personality was pathologic liar, psychopathic personality with amoral trend, and moral deficiency.[37] There were no sub-categories within mental deficiency which referred to moral states, so that the main move to notice is that the category of moral imbecility, which was attached to mental deficiency earlier in the century, had now been grouped with personality.

In 1952, the *DSM* could confidently announce that it was dealing with 'the personality structure' in its moves to classify personality disorders. On this basis, disorders were to fit into three broad groupings: personality pattern disturbance, referring to more-or-less cardinal types which 'can rarely if ever be altered in their inherent structures by any form of therapy', and where 'constitutional features are marked and obvious'.[38] The second grouping was personality trait disturbance, referring to individuals unable to maintain emotional equilibrium, developing compulsive, fixated or exaggerated character and behaviour patterns. Third was sociopathic personality disturbance, whose description contained the clear recognition of a 'social illness': '(I)ndividuals to be placed in this category are ill primarily in terms of society and of conformity with the prevailing cultural milieu, and not only in terms of personal discomfort and reactions with other individuals.'[39] Within this category was antisocial reaction, dyssocial reaction and sexual deviation. The term antisocial reaction included cases previously known as constitutional psychopathic state and psychopathic personality, with the rider that the term was intended to be more limited and more specific in its application than the two it replaced:

This term refers to chronically antisocial individuals who are always in trouble, profiting neither from experience nor punishment, and maintaining no real loyalties to any person, group or code. They are frequently callous and hedonistic, showing marked emotional immaturity, with lack of sense of responsibility, lack of judgement, and an ability to rationalize their behavior so that it appears warranted, reasonable and justified.[40]

The term dyssocial reaction took up the earlier terms pseudosocial personality and psychopathic personality with asocial and amoral trends, and was to refer to individuals who show disregard for the usual social codes 'as a result of having lived all their lives in an abnormal moral environment'.[41] Finally, sexual deviation took up an earlier class of psychopathic personality with pathologic sexuality, and the diagnosis would need to specify the type of pathological behaviour, such as transvestism, paedophilia, fetishism, sexual sadism (including rape, sexual assault and mutilation), and homosexuality.[42]

The latest edition of the Diagnostic and Statistical Manual, the *DSM–IV*, lists the following criteria for antisocial personality disorder:

A There is a persuasive pattern of disregard for and violation of the rights of others occurring since the age of 15 years, as indicated by three or more of the following:

failure to conform to social norms with respect to lawful beha-
viors, as indicated by repeatedly performing acts that are
grounds for arrest
deceitfulness, as indicated by repeated lying, use of aliases, or
conning others for personal profit or pleasure
impulsivity or failure to plan ahead
irritability and aggressiveness, as indicated by repeated physical
fights or assaults
reckless disregard for the safety of self or others
consistent irresponsibility, as indicated by repeated failure to
sustain consistent work behavior or honor financial obligations
lack of remorse, as indicated by being indifferent to or rationa-
lizing having hurt, mistreated or stolen from another

B   The individual is at least age 18 years
C   There is evidence of conduct disorder with onset before age 15
    years
D   The occurrence of antisocial behavior is not exclusively during the
    course of schizophrenia or a manic episode
    (*Diagnostic and Statistical Manual of Mental Disorders*, Fourth
    Edition, 1994)

Some authors make the point that the *DSM* gives personality a
particular importance as a category in person-description by its inclusion in the manual of mental disorders that has become the psychiatrists'
bible. Franklin argues that prior to the publication of the first edition of
the manual in 1952 by the American Psychiatric Association, a person's
diagnosis depended as much on the training and bent of the therapist as
it did on objective symptoms.[43] The various editions of the *DSM*
changed all that, writing down a changing set of rules about how one
could be mentally disordered and inscribing personality as part of an
intellectual technology for making sense of disorders that went well
outside the more narrow description of mental illness. The first edition
listed several dozen mental illnesses and rough definitions. The manual
was restructured in 1968 to follow more closely the mental disorders
classified in the International Classification of Diseases, and became
known as the *DSM–II*. Again in 1974, another revision was begun by a
team of nineteen mental health professionals headed by Robert L.
Spitzer of Columbia University, with an attempt to improve the scientific validity of the classes of disorder. The group proposed to spell out
the criteria sufficiently carefully that mental health workers in any part
of the country would diagnose a patient in the same way. The diagnostic
categories appearing in the *DSM* undergo a wide-ranging scrutiny by

sub-committees of psychiatrists, psychologists and epidemiologists before they are finally adopted by the Board of Trustees of the American Psychiatric Association. Categories appear and then disappear as they are perused and argued through. Any arbitrariness or compromise in implementing the classifications is accepted as a part of practical politics. For example, one group proposed 'paraphilic coercive disorder', a category which was meant to describe people who are sexually aroused by the coercive nature of rape, but was withdrawn because of its potential abuse as a legal defence in rape cases. Similarly, 'ego-dystonoc homosexuality' appeared in the *DSM–III* for people who are homosexual but wished they were not. This category disappeared from the *DSM–III–R* in response to opposition from gay and lesbian groups. One proposal of the sub-committees under Spitzer, 'self-defeating personality disorder', was replaced by 'sadistic personality disorder' after complaints that the first was sexist and victim blaming, but after a year of debate both were relegated to the back of the manual to indicate that they had not been agreed to. A third proposal for 'periluteal phase dysphoric disorder', the behavioural component of a condition known more commonly as severe premenstrual syndrome, was also demoted to the appendix of the manual.[44] Readers may also recall the debates surrounding the change of terminology in the *DSM* from 'hysteria' to 'histrionic personality disorder' and the close fit revealed in the Broverman studies between the description of this disorder and the descriptions given by clinicians of the 'mentally healthy woman'.[45]

This means, of course, that the politics of the clinical medical associations, teaching and academic bureaucracies, government departments and so on, all contribute to the shaping of medical and psychiatric terminology. Although much of the history of psychiatric categories throughout the English-speaking world reflects and even imitates developments taking place in England, and that the American *DSM* has tended to universalise the categories that have evolved within its papers over half a century and thus determining the range of ways in which individuals can be defined as 'mentally ill', specific political circumstances can also significantly determine the weighting and acceptability of particular categories of person. The production of the 'sexual psychopath' is a case in point. In the 1930s in many of the states in the United States, the term sexual psychopath came to dominate the 'sexualisation of risk', while in the United Kingdom the category failed to gain much acceptance. While there was a plethora of laws proposed and enacted to enable administrations in the United States, New Zealand and some of the Australian states to act decisively against the newly discovered 'sexual pervert', usually through the use of indeterminate sentences, the

English experience was different and there were no major moves to legislate under this rubric.[46] One would look, in the first instance, to variations in social and political arrangements to explain these differences. As Pratt suggests, the methods of governing particular problem populations might necessitate legislation and penal sanctions in one jurisdiction while in another, for example the United Kingdom, modes of governing providing comparatively higher levels of social assistance and care might obviate such a need:

In contrast, in the United States, with the least developed forms of welfare assistance and protection, there was the most extensive commitment to the sexual psychopath laws, as if to compensate for the greater lack of security that was to be found elsewhere in the social fabric; at the same time, this was counterbalanced by the almost total non-use of habitual criminal laws – the most materially well provided for society now had little need of them.[47]

One would look also to important regional variations within the field of psychological medicine itself, such as the relative prominence of Freudian understandings of criminal behaviour and the extent to which an intellectual colonising placed its stamp over regional inventions, training and research links and the practices of local political elites.

Underlying this politics of naming however, was the gradual adoption of the category of personality. The move to the conceptual apparatus of personality is a step taken at the number of different sites where measurement and classification of personhood in all its abnormal appearances was now taking place – the court clinic, the pathology clinic, the psychological clinic – rather than simply as a step of extending the concept of character taken up by the moral philosophers. Its key attribute became synonomous with the workings of power under advanced forms of liberalism. It allowed for a technology of measurement which would bring the whole of the (normal) population into subjection on a grid of calculability, while at the same time providing a unit of subjectification through which individuals would be incited to measure and produce themselves – to become entrepreneurs of their own normal healthy personalities.

7   Personality and dangerousness

Our earlier discussions about debates in Australia and elsewhere between law and psychiatry were to do with how personality disorders related to mental illness, criminal responsibility and issues of dangerousness. Periods of particular kinds of violence – multiple killings in homes, in public places like school playgrounds and workplaces, sometimes massive assault on individuals by persons described, in the words of Justice Cox in Tasmania about Martin Bryant, as 'a pathetic social misfit' – have taken place at the same time as new forms of intervention by government, including reforms to mental health legislation, the Crimes Act, sentencing procedures, and the institutional arrangements, on persons considered to be dangerous. In the late 1980s, groups like the Community Development Committee of the Victorian Parliament wanted to end the wrangling over the causes of dangerousness and the practice of giving medical diagnoses in order to confine people considered to be dangerous.

Much of the commentary on antisocial personality disorder takes the form of a 'fact or fiction', 'myth or reality' kind of discussion, which ultimately resolves into a scepticism about whether it is possible or even necessary to make distinctions between the 'mad or bad'. We have already encountered this view in the discussion of the passing of the Homicide Act 1959 in the United Kingdom, where it was apparent that the task of deciding on the question of diminished responsibility was an almost impossible one to give to juries. Wootton observed at the time the limits of psychiatric expertise:

the medical evidence does appear to establish . . . that certain types of personality *are more likely* to commit crimes of violence than are others. An emotionally immature person or a psychopath will be guilty of murder in circumstances in which a normal individual would merely get rather cross. That discovery, and in particular the identification of individual psychopaths, is the expert's contribution.[1]

The argument here is that psychiatry could detect abnormal propensity to crime, and it could recognise recurring patterns of behaviour. But to

143

infer diminished responsibility from increased propensity to crime was not a matter of scientific inference but instead a sheer act of faith. All that science could say is that in certain circumstances 'the psychopath *does not in fact* control his conduct . . . Any judgements as to whether he *could* do so must necessarily be governed by the philosophical position of those who make them on the eternally unresolved question of the reality of free will.' The concept of diminished responsibility could have no meaning if it was accepted that no one can behave otherwise than as he does; indeed, in these circumstances one is equally free of responsibility for everything they do. If, on the other hand, the more conventional view on the subject of free will was accepted, we are still in no position to assess the strength of another's temptations: 'on that the evidence lies buried in another man's consciousness, into which no human being can enter'.[2]

In the assessment of court proceedings following the 1959 legislation, no intelligible distinction could be drawn between psychopathy and wickedness, in terms of any meaningful concept of moral or criminal responsibility. The criteria to distinguish between the 'responsibly bad' and the 'merely irresponsible' was shown to be impossibly elusive. The description of the psychopath seemed clear enough – utterly selfish, egotistical, vain, idle, callous often to the point of brutality, devoid of normally affectionate feelings or of remorse for wrongdoing. But the question of the moral responsibility of the psychopath had to rely on unproven and unprovable assertions, such as the statement by one expert that '. . . although psychopaths know the consequences of their acts they are less able than other people to modify those acts'.[3] A paradoxical situation arose where, in the conduct of a trial, the psychopath drew for his defence on the very same qualities which in the case of the wicked would simply serve to blacken his record. The consequences of this paradox were particularly awkward in questions over the responsibility of persons whose records were less glaringly or less consistently antisocial. Moreover, the defence of diminished responsibility had allowed descriptions of the state of mind of defendants which, although not psychopathic, would most likely describe the state of mind of all but the most cold-blooded murderer: 'extreme emotional perturbation with loss of self-control and possibly confusional maniacal states'. This might be a description of what some 'normal' persons might experience, if only once or twice in their lives. The usual argument from the psychopath's history of antisocial behaviour might very well be turned upside down to provide an equally good defence of the apparently normal man of previous good character who one day commits a crime of violence. Thus, Wootton argued

Does not the fact that such a man has acted *out* of character in itself create at least as great a presumption of mental aberration as does the psychopath's consistently acting *in* character . . . In such a case the admittedly circular argument that 'he must have been mad to do it' is not to be lightly dismissed.[4]

As it stood, however, the moderately antisocial would be punished and the violently antisocial deemed irresponsible. The moderately antisocial would be punished not so much for what they had done as for the limitations of medical science. It would be possible, in theory at least, that the plea of complete and total irresponsibility to the point of insanity under the McNaghten rules involved indefinite detention (though not, perhaps, in a prison) while severe irresponsibility would incur a moderate sentence, and in the case of slight irresponsibility a heavy sentence.

The conundrum over the location of antisocial personality disorder as a mental illness continues to be problematic in law and psychiatry, and the Australian psychiatrist John Ellard has reiterated these difficulties more recently.[5] There remains confusion and uncertainty about the term personality itself, and what is currently known and understood is in fact the product of the study of personality disorder. The *DSM* had not attempted to define personality, and attempts at a definition of normality were skirted around by concentrating on abnormalities. Ellard claims this approach presents no particular intrinsic difficulties: most accumulated knowledge about speech, for example, has developed out of a study of speech pathology. The difficulties come after that: what are the differences between personality and temperament? How do we adjust for the fact that people will be viewed differently according to the background and outlook of both observer and observed? Plenty of formal definitions have been provided, by researchers from Allport to Maslow, and theoretical viewpoints ranged from the dynamic hypotheses of the various schools of psychoanalysis to the hypothetico-deductive descriptions such as the axes proposed by Eysenck. Ellard's own definition of personality – an 'elusive partial constancy' remaining above all the changes in behaviour and patterns of feeling which affect our lives – recognises that the defining takes place in a social and cultural context of meaning:

If you are a rather disagreeable small-time thief with a bad temper you are likely to be described as suffering from Antisocial Personality Disorder. If without any contrition you waste millions of dollars of other people's money and achieve nothing but notoriety you will be called an entrepreneur. No one reaches for the *DSM–IV*.[6]

Ellard also pointed to the problem of multiple diagnoses of personality disorder, as evidenced in recent studies showing that most individuals examined for disorders actually suffered from more than one disorder. The term 'co-morbidity' had come about because it was extraordinarily useful, when one is faced with the alternative proposition that the single categories currently in use have no validity at all.[7] In the end, Ellard remained the sceptic. If one used 'dubious criteria' to categorise an indefinable entity the results will only be confused and conflicting, to the point of absurdity.

Some of Ellard's colleagues in Sydney pointed out once again that how personality disorder gets to be defined – is it from behaviour and its consequences *or* is it personality traits – determines who gets to be counted in the classification. By coining the terms 'successful' and 'failed' sociopathy to differentiate the category, it can be shown that the criteria used in the current *DSM–IV* are based on criminal behaviours rather than the presence of sociopathic personality traits.[8] Thus, those picked up in the diagnostic criteria tend to be the 'readily identifiable felons or forensic psychiatric patients'. These authors draw attention to the sources of *DSM* criteria in the work of Robins (1966), who used behavioural patterns rather than personality traits as the basis for the criteria. On the other hand, Hare (1986) argued for a diagnostic schema derived from the more trait-based model of Cleckley (1941). They question whether this model generates a more valid definition than the *DSM*. The authors accentuate their point by showing how the concentration on behaviour leaves out the so-called creative sociopaths, including many successful people among business and political elites who occupy positions of power and influence. The term creative sociopath was coined in the United States in 1939 and applied to people who possessed charm and wit and an ability to carve out a career path for themselves irrespective of who got in the way. Valeria Messalina (the fourteen-year-old wife of Claudius, Emperor of Rome), Napoleon, Lawrence of Arabia, and the newspaper proprietor Robert Maxwell, could all be cited as successful sociopaths.[9] Was it possible to provide descriptors which avoided blatant or subliminal moral judgements, and which also avoided the circularity of a process, described earlier in this book, in which sociopathy becomes both explanation and cause?[10]

These difficulties in recognising psychopathy solely on the basis of behaviour and outward manifestations are matched by the difficulties of attempting to draw direct equivalence between the terms psychopathy and dangerousness. Many authors have suggested that, from a clinical point of view, it is crucial to separate the commonplace term antisocial from the strict clinical description of antisocial personality disorder. One is then directed to the study of disorder on the basis of diagnostic criteria, which may rely on an assessment of traits, neurological char-

acteristics, social and cultural factors, or a combination
One body of research has investigated the relationship b
retardation and/or moral development and delinquency,
provide additional weight to the view that mental retarc
offenders is approximately three to four times that of
population.[11] Similar studies indicate that high-mental-a
have higher moral judgement scores, suggesting the pre ...cc of a
general cognitive factor underlying moral development, and studies
showing the poor performance of sociopathic children in moral judgement support the formulation that sociopathy is related to an arrest in
moral development.[12] Alternatively, the study of possible neurological
changes in severely antisocial but otherwise normal persons began
during the 1970s. Reid reported in 1985 that initial research looking for
gross electroencephalographic changes did not prove particularly
fruitful, but that later physiological work by Hare, Mednick and others
might well be able to be used to predict a deficiency in the psychopath's
ability to learn from experience.

These problematic aspects of diagnosis relate directly to the problem
of predicting dangerousness. As Reid acknowledges, this is especially
difficult because of the absence of 'vicious intent' or of any logical
reason for guilt or anxiety in the 'true psychopath'.[13] So even though the
countryside might be laid waste with victims as a result of his behaviour,
the 'true psychopath' should be distinguished from the predatory,
crazed or neurotically driven criminal and is generally less dangerous
than those with a specific intent to cause harm. However, Monahan in
the United States suggests that there is no evidence that mental health
professionals have any special expertise in making reliable or accurate
predictions about violent behaviour. He recommended that, in keeping
with caselaw in the United States, the responsibility for criminal commitment or release of potentially dangerous persons should reside with
judges rather than psychiatrists.[14] Reid summarised the empirical
survey evidence as follows: 'we have no predictive psychiatric criteria for
the dangerousness of others which are sufficiently effective in real social
settings to allow prudent preventative measures to be taken against
individuals or groups'.[15]

Cocozza and Steadman have even charged psychiatry with promoting
the idea that there does exist a specific entity called the 'dangerous
individual' over whom psychiatry can claim expertise.[16] This 'medicalisation of dangerousness' may well have been caught up in psychiatry's
general claims to truth over the mad over the past two centuries, but
these authors argue that assessments of dangerousness are based on
empirically untested beliefs. It has been claimed, again on the basis of

empirical evidence, that the predictive value of clinical assessments of dangerousness is no greater than if they had been made by tossing a coin.[17] But in spite of these limitations, there is a reluctance to dispense with this kind of expertise when it comes to deciding the need for preventative detention in particular cases:

> As long as predictive judgements are made in the criminal justice and mental health systems, the moral obligation to persist with attempts to improve them is inescapable; but it is an open question as to how much scope for improvement there is, since it is impossible to estimate the extent to which clinical and statistical factors respectively are responsible for present indications of the state of the art. It would be unduly pessimistic to ignore the possibility of improved diagnostic procedures whether by means of improved theoretical insights and the encouragement of research and the utilisation by practitioners of its findings, or, simply, by more care in the selection and appointment of forensic psychiatrists.[18]

The principles at work here are designed to arrive at a 'just redistribution of risk',[19] that is, to distribute the risks justly as between the grave harm that may be done to the potential victims of serious offenders (in this case recidivists), and what might be called grave harm to the rights of offenders by subjecting them to the hardship of protective measures which may be unnecessary.

However, more recent attempts have been made to develop useable clinical tools to assess the likelihood of violence in recently discharged psychiatric patients. A study reported by Monahan (et al.) described a new 'actuarial' tool called the Iterative Classification Tree which displayed a high degree of accuracy and could be used for 'real-world' clinical decision-making using readily available records. Nearly three-quarters of a sample of discharged patients could be allocated to either a high-risk or low-risk category, and the rates of actually observed violence in the low- and high-risk categories were 5 per cent and 45 per cent respectively.[20] The study added further evidence that rates of violence were significantly lower among patients with schizophrenia than among patients with other, primarily personality disorder, diagnoses.

The demands by Ellard and others to rescue psychiatric practice from the error of social definition and compromise are well and good, if their interest is simply to improve the criteria for diagnosis. And sceptics such as Wootton would want to claim that such knowledge of individuality is simply impossible. However, these authors do not claim, and most likely would not wish to claim, that the social functioning of the category of antisocial personality disorder depends on its truthfulness, the validity of diagnosis, or the social outlook of those in the psychiatric and psychological professions who use the various models. As we have observed, the status of the category itself is subject to a range of governmental objectives from within and outside of psychological medicine. Present debates within psychological medicine, such as whether behaviours or traits give the true measure of disorder, ignore the contingent nature of the category itself and the work it performs regardless of its truth status. We are interested here in the invention of a category over time and the work which a category performs in capturing particular forms of personhood, rather than how well individuals fit the category once it exists.

A study of the governmental effect, as distinct from the specifically medical or legal techniques of defining disorder, entails first a consideration of the interrelations between these domains and the often mundane adjustments of administration that occur between them; secondly, an assessment of the defining moments of the category of disorder, the conditions of possibility of the category coming into existence and undergoing change and modification, which is a study prior to one which would investigate whether the category is a true index of individuality. Yet the investigation still would take its cue from present problems and current governmental moves in the realm of individuality. On this score, the account in this book has suggested a kind of synergy between the appearance of the category of antisocial personality disorder and attempts to manage dangerousness. Moves in the present become problematic in new ways, as a consequence of a history of that 'present' and the fields which it occupies. And so thirdly, a study of a governmental effect needs to consider how the discipline of disorder sets in motion a grid or framework of techniques around which individuals are obliged to seek to 'float' a personality of their own making. We take these objectifications and subjectifications in order.

The questions confronting law and psychiatry over the question of the status of antisocial personality disorder as a mental illness resurfaced in legislative changes in Australia in 1995 that paralleled the kind of changes we have seen occurring throughout the lifetime of a medical text, the *DSM*. In 1952, the *DSM–II* omitted the term mental disease found in earlier classifications, opting instead for 'mental disorder' as the generic term for mental pathology. The change was recommended because of the somatic or organic implication in the use of the term disease. Conversely, in 1995 the Australian Government introduced a Criminal Code Act which adopted the term 'mental impairment' in setting out the defences that are available in circumstances of no criminal responsibility and the whole range of legislation to do with the intersections of law and psychiatry. The new words replaced the words 'mental illness'. As we have seen, changes of this kind throughout the past 150 years have seen the separation of institutions, new kinds of disciplining and disciplines, new kinds of persons. The new Act recites the familiar section that originated in the McNaghten rules of 1843, with the exception of that small change in nomenclature:

a person is not criminally responsible for an offence if, at the time of carrying out the conduct constituting the offence, the person was suffering from a mental impairment that had the effect that:
(a) the person did not know the nature and quality of the conduct; or
(b) the person did not know that the conduct was wrong (that is, the person could not reason with a moderate degree of sense and composure about whether the conduct, as perceived by reasonable people, was wrong); or
(c) the person was unable to control the conduct . . .
    . . . "mental impairment" includes senility, intellectual disability, mental illness and severe personality disorder.[21]

The Committee (Gibbs) which recommended the changes based its decision on the difficulties experienced by courts in interpreting the McNaghten concept of 'disease of the mind', which was considered 'too narrow to encompass arrested development or mental retardation'. In a nice piece of administrative fiat, the Gibbs recommendation and all the legislation which followed managed to umbrella together conditions and types of persons that had been subject to a long-term separation from each other and different means of disposal. This move was presented in social policy terms as a progressive one insofar as it sought to expand the opportunities for individuals to become subject to the conditions for a plea under this category.

Changes were subsequently made to parallel legislation in the States and Territories in Australia. In Victoria, the Crimes (Mental Impairment and Unfit to be Tried) Act 1997 was designed to replace the common law defence of insanity with a statutory defence of impairment. The effect of these changes meant that severe personality disorder could no longer be specifically excluded from the insanity defence, and an accused's mental condition would be examined on a case-by-case basis. This position was clarified in discussions over categories in forensic psychiatry, whose genealogical roots are with the 'criminally insane'. The Community Development Committee in Victoria recommended changes to the 'Governor's pleasure' system of detaining offenders who had been found not guilty by reason of insanity, and replaced it with a sentencing and review system in the hands of courts rather than the government of the day. The Committee cited Justice Cosgrove in determining what was to be included under this defence:

It cannot be correct to say that, as a matter of law, psychopathy or anything else is a mental disease. That it can flower as such may be the inescapable conclusion from the evidence in any one case, but that conclusion is applicable only to that case.[22]

The Committee reiterated its view that persons so convicted should receive treatment in an appropriate facility, not punishment in a prison. A further amendment to the Mental Health Act 1986 passed in 1997 established the Victorian Institute of Forensic Mental Health along with a new high-security facility on the site of the original 1843 Yarra Bend Lunatic Asylum, described as a forensic hospital. It would provide inpatient psychiatric services for sentenced prisoners, a place of remand to a hospital rather than prison, and secure, highly supervised accommodation for persons with an intellectual disability and who have serious antisocial behaviour.[23] According to the Department of Psychiatric Services, it will be a centre for the care of that group who combine severe mental illness with serious offending who have never found a satisfactory place within the general psychiatric services. However, one month earlier, psychiatric services had ruled out the facility

. . . taking over every difficult and disgruntled patient. It will not be turning the clock back to establish a new long term asylum under a different name. It will not be the repository of that distressed and distressing group of patients who acquire the label of severe personality disorder.[24]

Here, of course, the decisions made for and within forensic medicine would be historically consistent with the administrative space made earlier for the criminally insane. In some important senses the personality disordered remained a problem to be governed.

Personality and government

It has become a commonplace observation that the self is an object of intense scrutiny and regulation. The self is socially and historically specific, something which is conditional for its appearance upon certain forms of social organisation and ways of knowing. I have suggested here that personality has become a key concept in the way we think about the self. Furthermore, I suggest that personality became an object of techniques 'performed upon the self' – an 'achievement' presupposing work done on the self. The space for personhood is in addition an artefact of government, increasingly subject to an extended elaboration in the human sciences and coming to acquire a specifically scientific construction.[25]

Moreover, I have shown how the language and conceptual terrain of personality emerged by means of attempts to know and act upon the disordered and unruly. Personality is not merely a set of traits or the unique characterising bundle of attributes of individuals that we might once have thought of as a character *resume*, but has in addition a connection to how persons are thought about as being governed, or requiring to be governed. Personality, that is, becomes a grid of calculability over how all individuals are governed and how they govern themselves. If it is accepted that the terrain of personality has come to acquire a recent, quite specific meaning and importance for how individuals technically go about self-formation, it might also be argued that personality has become a domain of techniques for the exercise of freedom in liberal forms of government. That is, that individuals are required to conduct their freedom – they are 'obliged to be free'[26] – by the activity of forming themselves into personhood by deploying techniques of 'making up oneself' in a constructed space known as personality. The space referred to as personality we have conceptualised within the theoretical framework of governmentality and practices of government in terms of the following schema: personality is a constructed space by means of which the macro level of politics connects with the micro level, the place for interconnections between the practices of government and practices of the self.[27] These interconnections are relayed by means of governmental attempts to know and act upon the disordered and unruly, allowing a measuring of spaces between persons on both legal and medical grids of problematic behaviours and practices.

So the category of personality is the product of governmental attempts to know and act upon the disordered and potentially dangerous individual. This argument has been contrasted with accounts which characterise the emergence of the category as either an effect of the progress of scientific knowledge or as the product of social control mechanisms. What becomes 'personality' is a particular rendering of aspects of past governmental activity and inquiry into the problem of managing disorder and inefficiency among certain groups in the population, which distilled as a kind of residue – an artefact – in the form of a space or matrix in which (self)government takes place, or, as it seems in some instances, fails to take place. Residue refers not to the content of individuality in the form of will or capacity, or to an historical residue in the sense of ideas, problematics or the accumulation of 'civilised' practices, but rather to a location or space for techniques of personal formation over which the individual becomes the entrepreneur.[28] Under distinctively liberal forms of government, rational principles of population management have sought to deploy a machinery for calculating the strengths and weaknesses in the people, and on the basis of which knowledge, populations and individuals become the objects of government. Government is thus a kind of 'action under a description'.[29] The relations between personality and government become distinctive in the sense of the actions of government carving out a space in which individuals, at a distance, will come to deploy calculative techniques in the way they go about forming their own personhood. The space for these calculative techniques, it has been suggested, was 'invented' in the context of governmental attempts to know and act upon the disordered and potentially dangerous.

The emergence of a space or dimension of individuality called personality depended on certain broader historical contingencies: the individualising and also totalising of the problem of population accomplished from the early nineteenth century; the growth of knowledges in the natural and social sciences concerned with the internal dimensions of individuality in all its complexity; and the late twentieth-century objectives of political power to regulate citizens through the advancement of norms of personal life and the forging of a desire towards the shaping and presentation of a well-adjusted self. One important implication of the study is that it disturbs the givenness of the modern categories of personality and personality disorder, and, in particular, unsettles the dichotomy of 'the biological' and 'the social' domains in which these categories are theorised.

Notes

INTRODUCTION

1 *Age*, 30 April 1996.
2 *Four Corners*, Australian Broadcasting Commission, 1 July 1996.
3 American Psychiatric Association, *Diagnostic and Statistical Manual of Mental Disorders* (fourth edn) (Washington: American Psychiatric Association, 1994), p. 645.

I   LAW, PSYCHIATRY AND THE PROBLEM OF DISORDER

1 W. Reid, 'Psychopathy and dangerousness', in M. Roth and R. Blugrass (eds.), *Psychiatry, Human Rights and the Law* (Cambridge University Press, 1985), pp. 72–80; N. Parker, 'The Gary David case', *Australian and New Zealand Journal of Psychiatry*, 25 (1991), 371–4;. K. Kissane, 'Are they mad or bad? Lawyers and psychiatrists differ on how to protect society from violent psychopaths', *Time Australia*, 135, 5 (1990), 42–3; J. Floud and W. Young, *Dangerousness and Criminal Justice* (London: Heinemann, 1981).
2 M. Foucault, 'The dangerous individual', in L. Kritzman (ed.), *Michael Foucault. Politics, Philosophy, Culture* (New York: Routledge, 1988), pp. 121–51.
3 J. O'Sullivan, *Mental Health and the Law* (Sydney: The Law Book Company, 1981).
4 A. Bartholomew and K. Milte, 'The reliability and validity of psychiatric diagnoses in courts of law', *Australian Law Journal*, 50 (1976), 451.
5 I. Campbell, *Mental Disorder and Criminal Law in Australia and New Zealand* (Sydney: Butterworths, 1988), pp. 15ff.
6 J. Cocozza and H. Steadman, 'The failure of psychiatric predictions of dangerousness: clear and convincing evidence', *Rutgers Law Review*, 30 (1976), 1084–101; P. Fairall, 'Violent offenders and community protection in Victoria – the Gary David experience', *Criminal Law Journal*, 17 (1993), 40–54.
7 J. Cocozza and H. Steadman, 'Prediction in psychiatry: an example of misplaced confidence in experts', *Social Problems*, 25 (1978), 265–76.
8 R. Blackburn, *The Psychology of Criminal Conduct. Theory, Research and Practice* (Chichester: Wiley, 1993).

9   Ibid., p. 332.
10 Ibid.
11 P. Gillies, *Criminal Law* (Sydney: The Law Book Co., 1993).
12 Ibid., p. 262.
13 Ibid., p. 264.
14 Ibid., p. 263.
15 I. Potas, *Just Deserts for the Mad* (Canberra: Australian Institute of Criminology, 1982).
16 B. McSherry, 'Revising the M'Naghten Rules,' *Law Institute Journal*, 64, 8 (1990), 725–7.
17 P. Carlen, 'Psychiatry in prisons: promises, premises, practices and politics', in P. Miller and N. Rose (eds.), *The Power of Psychiatry* (London: Polity, 1986), pp. 241–66; P. Norden, 'From whom do we need protection?', *Advocate*, 3 May (1990), 7.
18 C. Williams, 'Psychopathy, mental illness and preventative detention: issues arising from the David case', *Monash University Law Review*, 16, 2 (1990), 161–83; Victoria. Law Reform Commissioner of Victoria, *The Concept of Mental Illness in the 'Mental Health Act' 1980*, Report No. 31 (Melbourne: Law Reform Commissioner of Victoria, 1990).
19 For an excellent and comprehensive account of the relationship between concepts of dangerousness, modes of governance and sentencing legislation across a number of jurisdictions, see J. Pratt, *Governing the Dangerous. Dangerousness, Law and Social Change* (Sydney: The Federation Press, 1997).
20 Homicide Act, 1957 (London: Her Majesty's Stationary Office).
21 Wootton of Abinger, 'Diminished responsibility: a layman's view', *Law Quarterly Review*, 76 (1960), 238.
22 S. Dell, *Murder into Manslaughter. The Diminished Responsibility Defence in Practice* (Oxford University Press, 1984), p. 66.
23 Wootton, 'Diminished responsibility', 238.
24 Dell, *Murder into Manslaughter*.
25 Ibid., p. 52.
26 Ibid., p. 60.
27 A. Ashworth and J. Shapland, 'Psychopaths in the criminal process', *Criminal Law Review* (1980), 639.
28 Wootton, 'Diminished responsibility', 238.
29 Dell, *Murder into Manslaughter*, p. 60.
30 S. Trott, 'Implementing criminal justice reform', *Public Administration Review*, 45 (1985), 795–800.
31 US House of Representatives. *Hearings before the Subcommittee on Criminal Justice of the Committee on the Judiciary. Ninety-Eighth Congress. First Session on Reform of the Federal Insanity Defense*, Serial No 21 (Washington, DC: US Government Printing Office, 1983), p. 30.
32 US House of Representatives, p. 30.
33 A. Brooks, 'The merits of abolishing the insanity defense', *Annals of the American Academy of Political and Social Science*, 477 (1985), 126.
34 US House of Representatives, p. 28.
35 Ibid., p. 143ff; *Washington Post*, January 20, 1983, p. 1.

36 Trott, 'Implementing criminal justice reform', 796.
37 US House of Representatives, pp. 29, 90, 141; Brooks, 'The merits of abolishing the insanity defense', pp. 126–31; G. Geis and R. Meier, 'Abolition of the insanity plea in Idaho: a case study', *Annals of the American Academy of Political and Social Science*, 477 (1985), 72–83.
38 Trott, 'Implementing criminal justice reform', 796.
39 Victorian Parliament. Social Development Committee. *Interim Report: Strategies to Deal with Persons with Severe Personality Disorder who Pose a Threat to Public Safety* (Melbourne: Government Printer, 1990).
40 Williams, 'Psychopathy, mental illness', 162.
41 W. Glaser, 'Commentary: Gary David, psychiatry, and the discourse of dangerousness', *Australian and New Zealand Journal of Criminology*, 27 (1994), 46–9.
42 Victoria. Sentencing Act 1991, 905.
43 Victoria. Sentencing (Amendment) Act 1993, 684.
44 Ibid., 685.
45 J. Malpas and G. Wickham, 'Government and failure: on the limits of sociology', *Australian and New Zealand Journal of Sociology*, 31, 3 (1995), 37–50.
46 *Age*, Melbourne, 30 June 1996.
47 Victoria. Law Reform Commissioner of Victoria, *Diminished Responsibility as a Defence to Murder*, Working Paper No. 7 (Melbourne: Law Reform Commission of Victoria, 1981); Victoria. Law Reform Commissioner of Victoria, *Murder: Mental Element and Punishment*, Working Paper No. 8 (Melbourne: Law Reform Commission of Victoria, 1984); Victoria. Law Reform Commissioner of Victoria, *Mental Malfunction and Criminal Responsibility*, Discussion Paper No. 14 (Melbourne: Law Reform Commission of Victoria, 1988); Victoria. Law Reform Commissioner of Victoria, *The Concept of Mental Illness*.
48 D. Wood, 'A one man dangerous offenders statute – the Community Protection Act 1990 (Vic)', *Melbourne University Law Review*, 17, 3 (1990), 497–505.
49 Law Reform Commissioner of Victoria (1988), p. 5.
50 A. Borsody and J. Groningen, 'A reply – madness and badness', *Legal Service Bulletin*, 15, 3 (1990), 116–17.
51 Borsody and van Groningen, 'A reply', 23; see also C. Lewis, 'The humanitarian theory of punishment', in W. Hooper (ed.), *God in the Dock: Essays on Theology and Ethics* (Grand Rapids, MI: Eerdmans, 1949), pp. 287–94.
52 Law Reform Commissioner of Victoria, *The Concept of Mental Illness* (1990), pp. 16–17.
53 W. Glaser, 'Morality and medicine', *Legal Service Bulletin*, 15, 3 (1990), 114.
54 Glaser, 'Morality and medicine', 115–16.
55 B. Blaskett, 'The right to liberty *vs* the right to community protection: changing Victoria's Mental Health legislation', *Health Issues*, 23 (1990), 39–41.
56 D. Thompson, 'Civil liberties aspects', *News and Views*, 5, 6 (1990), 7–16.

57 Thompson, 'Civil liberties aspects', 11.

58 Williams, 'Psychopathy, mental illness', 182.

59 D. Wood, 'Dangerous offenders and civil detention', *Criminal Law Journal*, 13, 5 (1989), 326.

60 M. Ray, 'Legislative problems and solutions, *News and Views*, 5, 6 (1990), 26.

61 Home Office / Department of Health, *Managing Dangerous People with Severe Personality Disorder. Proposals for Policy Development* (London: Stationery Office, 1999).

62 Borsody and van Groningen, 'A reply', 11.

63 McSherry, 'Revising the M'Naghten Rules', 726.

64 Williams, 'Psychopathy, mental illness', 175.

65 P. Miller and N. Rose, 'The Tavistock Programme: the government of subjectivity and social life' *Sociology*, 22, 2 (1988), 171–92; see also P. Miller and N. Rose, 'Governing economic life', *Economy and Society*, 19, 1 (1990), 1–31.

66 L. Craze and P. Moynihan, 'Violence, meaning and the law: responses to Gary David', *Australian and New Zealand Journal of Criminology*, 27 (1994), 30–45; G. Coffey, 'Madness and postmodern civilisation. The Burdekin Report and reforming public psychiatry', *Arena Magazine* (1994), April–May, 32–7.

67 R. Kennedy, 'The dangerous individual and the social body', in P. Cheah, D. Fraser and J. Grbich (eds.) *Thinking Through the Body of the Law* (Sydney: Allen and Unwin, 1996), pp. 187–206.

68 A. S. Ellis, *Eloquent Testimony: The Story of the Mental Health Services in Western Australia* (Nedlands: University of Western Australia Press, 1983).

69 Ellis, *Eloquent Testimony*, pp. xvii–2.

70 M. Foucault, *Madness and Civilisation. A History of Insanity in the Age of Reason*, trans. R. Howard (New York: Vintage, 1965).

71 P. Conrad and J. Schneider, *Deviance and Medicalization. From Badness to Sickness* (St Louis: The CV Mosby Company, 1980).

72 D. Howard, *The English Prisons: Their Past and their Future* (London: Methuen, 1960).

73 D. Rothman, *The Discovery of the Asylum. Social Order and Disorder in the New Republic* (Boston: Little, Brown and Co., 1971).

74 A. Scull, *Museums of Madness: The Social Organisation of Insanity in Nineteenth Century England* (London: Allen Lane, 1979).

75 J. Minson, 'Review of Andrew Scull *Museums of Madness: The Social Organisation of Insanity in 19th Century England*', *Sociological Review*, 28, 1 (1980), 195–9.

76 Minson, Review of Andrew Scull, 198.

77 D. Russell, 'Psychiatry: making criminals mad', *Australian Left Review*, 92 (1985), 20–3, 32–3.

78 Russell, 'Psychiatry: making criminals mad', 21.

79 J. Ellard, 'The history and present status of moral insanity', in G. Parker (ed.), *Some Rules for Killing People* (Sydney: Angus and Robertson, 1989), pp. 115–31.

80 Prichard, cited in Ellard, 'The history and present status', 121.

81 Ellard, 'The history and present status', 125.
82 Ibid., 129.
83 Williams, 'Psychopathy, mental illness'.
84 W. Glaser, 'Commentary: Gary David', 46.
85 K. Danziger, *Constructing the Subject. Historical Origins of Psychological Research* (New York: Cambridge University Press, 1992).
86 Danziger, *Constructing the Subject.*, p. 161.
87 N. Rose, *Governing the Soul. The Shaping of the Private Self* (London: Routledge, 1990), p. 217.
88 Pratt, *Governing the Dangerous.*
89 P. Miller and N. Rose, 'Governing economic life', *Economy and Society*, 19 (1990), 1–31; N. Rose, 'Governing "advanced" liberal democracies', in A. Barry, T. Osborne and N. Rose (eds.) *Foucault and Political Reason* (London: University College London Press).
90 N. Rose, 'At risk of madness. Risk, psychiatry and the management of mental health', unpublished paper, Goldsmiths College, London, cited in P. O'Malley, 'Risk societies and the government of crime, in M. Brown and J. Pratt (eds.) *Dangerous Offenders. Punishment and Social Order* (London, Routledge, 2000), p. 32.
91 Foucault, 'The dangerous individual', 140.
92 Ibid., 25.
93 M. Foucault, *Madness and Civilisation*; see also E. Midelfort, 'Madness and civilisation in early modern Europe: A reappraisal of Michel Foucault', in B. Malament (ed.) *After the Reformation: Essays in Honor of J. H. Hexter* (University of Philadelphia Press, 1980), pp. 247–65; P. O'Brien, 'Michel Foucault's history of culture', in L. Hunt (ed.) *The New Cultural History* (Berkeley: University of Califoria Press, 1989), pp. 25–46.
94 G. Gutting, 'Foucault and the history of madness', in G. Gutting (ed.), *The Cambridge Companion to Foucault* (Cambridge University Press, 1994), pp. 47–70.
95 M. Foucault, 'Questions of method', in G. Burchell, C. Gordon and P. Miller (eds.), *The Foucault Effect. Studies in Governmentality* (London: Harvester Wheatsheaf, 1999), pp. 73–86.
96 C. Gordon, '*Histoire de la folie*: an unknown book by Michel Foucault', *History of the Human Sciences*, 3 (1990), 3–26.
97 G. Burchell, 'Liberal government and techniques of the self', in A. Barry, T. Osborne and N. Rose (eds.), *Foucault and Political Reason. Liberalism, Neo-Liberalism and Rationalities of Government* (London: University College London Press, 1996), 19–36.
98 M. Foucault, in C. Gordon (ed.), *Power/Knowledge: Selected Interviews and Other Writings by Michel Foucault, 1972–1977* (New York: Pantheon, 1980); see also J. Weeks, 'Foucault for historians', *History Workshop*, 14 (1982), 106–19.
99 G. Deleuze, *Foucault*, trans. S. Hand (University of Minnesota Press, 1993).
100 D. Garland, 'The limits of the sovereign state', *British Journal of Criminology*, 36, 4 (1996), 445–71; P. O'Malley, 'Volatile and Contradictory Punishment', *Theoretical Criminology*, 3, 2 (1999), 175–96.

2 HISTORIES OF PSYCHIATRY AND THE ASYLUM

1 Michel Foucault, *Madness and Civilisation*; P. Hirst and P. Woolley, *Social Relations and Human Attributes* (London: Tavistock, 1982), pp. 164–96.
2 *Historical Records of Australia*, Series 1 Governors' Despatches to and from England, vol. 1, 1788–96 (Sydney: The Library Committee of the Commonwealth Parliament, 1914), pp. 2–8; C. Cummins, *The Administration of Lunacy and Idiocy in NSW, 1788–1855* (Sydney: University of NSW School of Hospital Administration, 1968), p. 3.
3 Cummins, *The Administration of Lunacy*, p. 15.
4 R. Castel, *The Regulation of Madness. The Origins of Incarceration in France*, trans. W. Hall (Berkeley: University of California, 1988), p. 26.
5 Castel, *The Regulation of Madness*, pp. 26ff.
6 Michel Foucault, *Histoire de la folie* (Paris: 1992); N. Rose, 'Of madness itself: Histoire de la folie and the object of psychiatric history', *History of the Human Sciences*, 3, 3 (1990), 377.
7 M. Lewis, *Managing Madness. Psychiatry and Society in Australia 1788–1980* (Canberra, 1988), p. 4.
8 W. Blackstone, *Commentaries on the Laws of England* (New edition adapted to present state of the law by Robert M. Kerr, LLD) Ch. 28: 'Of the Matters Cognizable in Courts of Equity' (London: John Murray, 1857), pp. 480ff.
9 Robert Castel, '"Problematisation" as a mode of reading history', trans. P. Wissing, in J. Goldstein (ed.) *Foucault and the Writing of History* (Oxford: 1994), 242.
10 *Public General Statutes of NSW 1838–1846*, Sydney 1861, pp. 1394–97. In the context of its usage with 'gaol', the word 'dangerous' needs to be treated with some care, in that it seems to refer not to a figure such as the public nuisance for whom gaol might seem an appropriate placement, but rather on a grid of 'self managing' where the 'danger' is to oneself or others through an incapacity for self-control.
11 R. Hughes, *The Fatal Shore* (New York: Vintage, 1987), p. 105.
12 E. Cunningham Dax, 'The first 200 years of Australian psychiatry', *Australian and New Zealand Journal of Psychiatry*, 23, 1 (1989), 105; see also E. Cunningham Dax, 'Crimes, follies and misfortunes in the history of Australasian psychiatry', *Australian and New Zealand Journal of Psychiatry*, 15 (1981), 257–63.
13 Dax, 'Crimes, follies and misfortunes', 259.
14 Bostock, *The Dawn of Australian Psychiatry* (Sydney: Medical Publishing Company, 1968), p. 16.
15 Ibid., p. 20.
16 Ibid., p. 20.
17 M. Foucault, *Madness and Civilisation*, pp. 270ff.
18 Bostock, *The Dawn of Australian Psychiatry*, pp. 21–35.
19 Ibid., p. 35.
20 Ibid., p. 21.
21 John Richie (ed.), *The Evidence of the Bigge Reports. New South Wales under Governor Macquarie, Vol. 1: The Oral Evidence* (Melbourne: Heinemann, 1971), pp. 143–5.

22 W. Neil, *The Lunatic Asylum at Castle Hill. Australia's First Psychiatric Hospital 1811–1826* (Sydney: Dryas, 1992), pp. 48–9.

23 J. T. Campbell to Dr Bland, cited in Heritage Council of New South Wales, *Castle Hill: Archaeological Report*, Sydney 1984, p. 48.

24 Campbell, in *Archaeological Report*, p. 47.

25 Neil, *The Lunatic Asylum at Castle Hill*, p. 11.

26 Bostock, *The Dawn of Australian Psychiatry*, pp. 25–6.

27 C. R. D. Brothers, 'Archives of Victorian Psychiatry', *Medical Journal of Australia*, 16 (1957), 342.

28 W. Neil, *The Lunatic Asylum at Castle Hill*, pp. 48–9.

29 Lewis, *Managing Madness*, p. 6.

30 D. McDonald, '"This essentially wretched asylum": the Parramatta Lunatic Asylum 1846–1878', *Canberra Historical Journal* (September 1977), 57.

31 Bostock, *The Dawn of Australian Psychiatry*, p. 31.

32 British Parliamentary Papers, cited in N. Megahey, 'More than a minor nuisance. Insanity in colonial Western Australia', in C. Fox (ed.), *Historical Refractions. Studies in Western Australian History*, 14 (Perth: University of Western Australia, Centre for Western Australian History, 1993), p. 48.

33 Megahey, 'More than a minor nuisance', 50.

34 S. Zelinka, 'Out of mind, out of sight: public works and psychiatry in New South Wales, 1810–1911', in L. Coltheart (ed.), *Significant Sites. History and Public Works in New South Wales* (Public Works Department, Sydney: Hale and Iremonger, 1989), p. 102.

35 Bostock, *The Dawn of Australian Psychiatry*, p. 39.

36 Lewis, *Managing Madness*, p. 220.

37 Bostock describes the Retreat at York, established in 1792 by William Tuke, as a place where 'patients could be treated without concealment and in the spirit of kindness . . . at the retreat they sometimes have patients brought to them frantic and in irons, whom they at once release, and by mild arguments and gentle arts reduce almost immediately to obedience and orderly behaviour' (Bostock, *The Dawn of Australian Psychiatry*, p. 10). Bostock takes care to itemise Digby's shopping list of restraints, again to signal the extent of the problem of the pre-psychiatric regime.

38 Bostock, *The Dawn of Australian Psychiatry*, pp. 67–8.

39 Ellis, *Eloquent Testimony*, p. 5.

40 Bostock, *The Dawn of Australian Psychiatry*, p. 99.

41 Ibid., p. 104.

42 Zelinka, 'Out of mind', 107.

43 Ibid., 107.

44 C. Brothers, *Early Victorian Psychiatry 1835–1905* (Melbourne: Government Printer, 1957), p. 29.

45 I. Hacking, 'Making up people', in T. Heller, et al. (eds.), *Reconstructing Individualism: Autonomy, Individuality and the Self in Western Thought* (Stanford University Press, 1986), pp. 222–36.

46 W. Dawson, *Annals of Psychiatry in New South Wales 1850–1990* (Sydney (typescript) 1965), pp. 7–8.

47 Dawson, *Annals of Psychiatry*, p. 9.

48 R. Virtue, 'Lunacy and social reform in Western Australia 1886–1903', *Studies in Western Australian History*, 1 (1977), p. 29.

49 Virtue, 'Lunacy and social reform', 30.

50 S. Foster, 'Imperfect Victorians: insanity in Victoria in 1888' (*Australia 1888*, Bulletin No. 8, 1981), pp. 97–116.

51 Foster, 'Imperfect Victorians', 105.

52 G. A. Tucker, *Lunacy in Many Lands* (Sydney: Charles Potter, 1887).

53 Ibid., pp. 16–17.

54 Ibid., p. 17.

55 B. Harman, 'Women and insanity: the Fremantle Asylum in Western Australia, 1858–1908', in P. Hetherington and P. Madern (eds.), *Sexuality and Gender in History: Selected Essays* (Perth: University of Western Australia, Centre for Western Australian History, 1993), p. 174.

56 Harman, 'Women and insanity', p. 181.

57 W. Isdale, 'The rise of psychiatry and its establishment in Queensland', *Journal of the Royal Historical Society of Queensland*, 14, 12 (1984), 496 (emphasis added); Aubrey Lewis, *The State of Psychiatry* (London: Routledge and Kegan Paul, 1967).

58 S. Garton, '"Bad or mad?" Developments in incarceration in NSW 1880–1920', in Sydney Labour History Group (eds.) *What Rough Beast: The State and Social Order in Australian History* (Sydney, Allen and Unwin, 1982), p. 89.

59 S. Garton, 'Freud and the psychiatrists: the Australian debate 1900–1940', in Brian Head and James Walter (eds.), *Intellectual Movements and Australian Society* (Melbourne: 1988), p. 173.

60 Garton, 'Freud and the psychiatrists', p. 162.

61 Lewis, *Managing Madness*, p. 8.

62 Ibid., p. 9.

63 Virtue, 'Lunacy and social reform', 30.

64 L. Coppe, 'Insane or greatly injured? The Captain Hyndman case', *The Push from the Bush*: 1838 Volume Collective of the Australian Bicentennial History (Canberra: Collective, 1986).

65 Dawson, *Annals of Psychiatry*, p. 7.

66 Bostock, *The Dawn of Australian Psychiatry*, p. 30.

67 Ibid., pp. 89–90.

68 Manning, cited in G. Edwards, 'Causes of insanity in nineteenth century Australia', *Australian and New Zealand Journal of Psychiatry*, 16 (1982), 55.

69 Edwards, 'Causes of insanity', 59.

70 F. Manning, 'Statistics of insanity in Australia', *Journal of Mental Science*, 25 (1879), p. 174.

71 W. Barker, *Mental Diseases. A Manual for Students* (London, Paris, New York, Melbourne: Cassell and Company, 1902), p. 71.

72 Barker, *Mental Diseases*, p. 73.

73 Bostock, *The Dawn of Australian Psychiatry*.

74 A. Tolson, 'Social surveillance and subjectivity: the emergence of "subculture" in the work of Henry Mayhew', *Cultural Studies*, 4 (1960), 113–27; P. Hirst, 'The genesis of the social', *Politics and Power*, 3 (1981).

75 Brothers, *Early Victorian Psychiatry*, p. 29.

76 Ibid.
77 Ibid., p. 343.
78 D. McCallum, 'Problem children and familial relations', in D. Meredyth and D. Tyler (eds.), *Child and Citizen. Genealogies of Schooling and Subjectivity* (Brisbane: Center for Cultural Policy Studies, 1993), pp. 129–52.
79 Zelinka, 'Out of sight', 108–10.
80 Virtue, 'Lunacy and social reform', 32.
81 Lewis, *Managing Madness*, p. 6.
82 Surgeon Bland to Colonial Secretary, 11 October 1814, cited in Heritage Council of New South Wales, p. 50.
83 Dax, 'Crimes, follies and misfortunes', p. 259.
84 Bostock, *The Dawn of Australian Psychiatry*, pp. 188–90.
85 Cummins, *The Administration of Lunacy*, p. 3.
86 Ellis, *Eloquent Testimony*, p. 5.
87 E. Cunningham Dax, *Asylum to Community: The Development of the Mental Hygiene Service in Victoria, Australia* (Melbourne: Cheshire, 1961).

3   THE BORDERLAND PATIENT

1   Dawson, 'Psychology and psychiatry', *Australasian Journal of Psychology and Psychiatry* (1927), 258.
2   Queensland. Report (Woogaroo) with Minutes of Evidence taken before the Royal Commission appointed to inquire into the Management of the Woogaroo Lunatic Asylum and the Lunatic Reception Houses of the Colony (Brisbane, Government Printer, 1877).
3   Ibid., pp. 1139–42; 1163.
4   Ibid., p. 1015.
5   Ibid., p. 298.
6   Report of the Acting Inspector of Lunatic Asylums on the Hospitals for the Insane for the Year ended 1873 (Melbourne: Government Printer, 1874), p. 17.
7   Report of the Inspector for the Year ended 1899 (1900), p. 15.
8   Ellis, *Eloquent Testimony*, p. 53.
9   Report of the Inspector for the Year ended 1907 (1908), p. 34.
10 Ross, 'The treatment of the insane', 205–8.
11 Report of the Inspector for the Year ended 1910 (1911), p. 25.
12 Ibid., p. 32.
13 Report of the Director of Mental Hygiene for the Year ended 31 December 1942 (Melbourne: Government Printer, 1943), p. 25.
14 Report of the Inspector-General of the Insane for the Year ended 31 December 1907 (1908), p. 26.
15 Report of the Inspector-General for the Year ended 1911 (1912), p. 44.
16 J. Springthorpe, 'The treatment of early mental cases in a general hospital', *Intercolonial Medical Journal* (1902), 197–202.
17 Report of the Acting Inspector for the Year 1873, p. 15.
18 W. Holman, "Department of Public Health, New South Wales: Institutions for insane and infirm', *Australasian Medical Congress: Transactions*, 10th Session (Auckland, NZ: Government Printer, 1914), p. 63.

19 Report of the Inspector for the Year ended 31 December 1901, p. 14.

20 W. Ernest Jones, 'Methods of early treatment of insanity', *Australasian Medical Congress: Transactions*, 10th Session (Auckland, NZ: Government Printer, 1914), 730–6.

21 Report of the Director of Mental Hygiene for the Year ended 31 December 1949 (1950), p. 25.

22 Report of the Director for the Year ended 1955.

23 Bostock, *The Dawn of Australian Psychiatry*.

24 Queensland. Legislative Assembly. Votes and Proceedings. Report from, and Evidence taken before, the Commissioners appointed to inquire into the Lunatic Asylum, Woogaroo (Brisbane, Government Printer, 1868–9).

25 Woogaroo Report, 1868–9, p. 695.

26 Ibid., p. 733.

27 Ibid., pp. 975, 977, 979.

28 Ibid., pp. 749–761.

29 Ibid., p. 955.

30 Ibid., p. 695.

31 Ibid., pp. 950–1.

32 Ibid., p. 953.

33 NSW Dangerous Lunatics Act 1843.

34 S. Dance, J. Funstan and A. Rubbo, 'The Sunbury Mental Hospital', B. Arch. thesis, University of Melbourne, 1963.

35 Brothers, *Early Victorian Psychiatry 1835–1905*, pp. 154–5.

36 McCallum, *The Social Production of Merit. Education, Psychology and Politics in Australia 1900–1950* (London: Falmer Press, 1990), pp. 19–20.

37 N. McI. James, 'On the perception of madness', *Australian and New Zealand Journal of Psychiatry*, 27 (1993), 192–9.

38 James, 'Perception of madness', 96.

39 R. Castel, *The Regulation of Madness*.

40 D. Ingleby, 'Mental health and social order', in S. Cohen and A. Scull (eds.), *Social Control and the State* (New York: St Martins Press, 1983), p. 152.

41 Castel, '"Problematization" as a mode of reading history', p. 242.

42 J. Weeks, 'Foucault for historians'.

43 N. Rose, *Inventing Our Selves: Psychology, Power and Personhood* (Cambridge University Press, 1996), chapter 1.

44 I. Hacking, *The Taming of Chance* (Cambridge University Press, 1990), chapter 1.

4 COUNTING, EUGENICS, MENTAL HYGIENE

1 H. Rusden, 'The survival of the unfittest', *Australasian Association for the Advancement of Science. Proceedings*, 1893, 523–4.

2 J. Blum, *Pseudoscience and Mental Ability: the Origins and Fallacies of the IQ Controversy* (New York: Monthly Review Press, 1978).

3 M. Booth, 'Report of Central Committee of the Australian Medical Congress on the care and control of the feeble-minded', *Australian Medical Journal* (1913), 929; J. Yule, 'Report by the Victorian Committee', *Australian Medical Journal* (1913), 929.

4 B. Simon, *Intelligence, Psychology and Education: A Marxist Critique* (London: Lawrence and Wishart, 1971); L. Kamin, *The Science and Politics of IQ* (Harmondsworth: Penguin, 1978); Blum, *Pseudoscience and Mental Ability*; B. Evans and B. Waites, *IQ and Mental Testing. An Unnatural Science and its Social History* (London, Macmillan, 1981); N. Rose, *The Psychological Complex. Psychology, Politics and Society in England 1869–1939* (London: Routledge, 1985); McCallum, *The Social Production of Merit*.

5 N. Rose, 'Beyond the public/private division: law, power and the family', *Journal of Law and Society*, 14 (1987), 61–76.

6 A. Gaynor and C. Fox, 'The birth and death of the clinic. Ethel Stoneman and the State Psychological Clinic, 1927–1930', in C. Fox (ed.) *Historical Refractions* (Perth: University of Western Australia Centre for Western Australian History, 1993), pp. 87–101.

7 Gaynor and Fox, 'The birth and death of the clinic', 98.

8 P. Miller and N. Rose (eds.), *The Power of Psychiatry* (London: Polity, 1986).

9 P. Miller, 'Critiques of psychiatry and critical sociologies of madness', in Miller and Rose, *The Power of Psychiatry*, pp.12–42.

10 N. Rose, *Governing the Soul*.

11 M. Foucault, 'Governmentality', trans. P. Pasquino, in G. Burchell, C. Gordon and P. Miller (eds.), *The Foucault Effect. Studies in Governmentality* (London: Harvester Wheatsheaf, 1991), pp. 87–104.

12 Burchell, 'Liberal government and techniques of the self', 20.

13 J. Minson, *Questions of Conduct. Sexual Harassment, Citizenship, Government* (London: Macmillan, 1993), p. 7.

14 Miller and Rose, *The Power of Psychiatry*.

15 M. Cullen, *The Statistical Movement in Early Victorian Britain. The Foundations of Empirical Social Research* (Hassocks, Eng.: Harvester, 1975); I. Hacking, 'Making up people'; G. Reekie, *Measuring Immorality. Social Inquiry and the Problem of Illegitimacy* (Cambridge University Press, 1998).

16 Foucault, 'Governmentality'; I. Hacking, 'Biopower and the avalanche of printed numbers', *Humanities and Society*, 5 (1982), 279–95.

17 Hacking, 'Making up people', 228.

18 Ibid., 236.

19 M. Shapiro (ed.), *Language and Politics* (New York University Press, 1984); P. Miller and N. Rose, 'Governing economic life'; P. Miller and N. Rose, 'Political rationalities and technologies of government', in S. Hanninen and K. Palonen (eds.), *Texts, Contexts, Concepts: Studies on Politics and Power in Language* (Helsinki: Finnish Political Science Association, 1990), pp. 166–83.

20 M. Foucault, *Discipline and Punish. The Birth of the Prison*, trans. A. Sheridan (Harmondsworth: Penguin, 1979); M. Foucault, *History of Sexuality. Volume 1: An Introduction*, trans. R. Hurley (London: Penguin, 1984), p. 139.

21 Hacking, 'Biopower and the avalanche of printed numbers'.

22 Foucault, *History of Sexuality*, p. 143.

23 Ibid., p. 285.

24 J. Camm, *The Early Nineteenth Century Colonial Censuses of Australia*. Historical Statistics Monograph No. 8 (Bundoora: Australian Reference Publications, 1988), p. 3.

25 Hacking, 'Making Up People', p. 228.
26 Cullen, *The Statistical Movement in Early Victorian Britain;* D. Mackenzie, *Statistics in Britain 1865–1930. The Social Construction of Scientific Knowledge* (Edinburgh University Press, 1981); D. Tait, 'Respectability, property and fertility: the development of official statistics about families in Australia', *Labour History,* 49 (1986).
27 J. Dunmore Lang, *Phillipsland, or the Country hitherto designated Port Phillip: Its Present Conditions and Prospects as a Highly Eligible Field for Emigration* (London: Longman, Brown, Green and Longmans, 1847); J. Dunmore Lang, *An Historical and Statistical Account of New South Wales, from the Founding of the Colony in 1788 to the Present Day,* vol. 1 (London: Sampson Low, Marston, Low and Searle, 1875).
28 New South Wales. *Select Committee on the Condition of the Working Classes of the Metropolis.* Report, together with Minutes and Evidence. NSW Parliamentary Papers, 1859–60, IV, 1263–1465.
29 J. Donzelot, *The Policing of Families,* trans. R. Hurley (New York: Pantheon, 1979); D. Tyler, 'The development of the concept of juvenile delinquency 1855–1905', *Melbourne Working Papers,* 4 (1982–3), 1–33; Rose, *The Psychological Complex*; Rose, 'Beyond the public/private division'.
30 I. Hacking, 'How should we do the history of statistics', in G. Burchell, C. Gordon and P. Miller, *The Foucault Effect,* pp. 181–95.
31 A. Tolson, 'Social surveillance and subjectification; D. McCallum, 'The case in social work: psychological assessment and social regulation', in P. Abbott and C. Wallace (eds.) *The Sociology of the Caring Professions,* 2nd edn (London, University College London Press, 1998).
32 F. Hill, *Children of the State,* 2nd edn (London, Macmillan 1889); R. Hill and F. Hill, *What We Saw in Australia* (London: Macmillan, 1875); M. Carpenter, *Reformatory Schools for the Children of the Perishing and Dangerous Classes and for Juvenile Offenders* (London: Woburn Press, 1968. Reprint of 1851 edn).
33 D. McCallum, 'Problem children and familial relations'.
34 I. Hacking, *The Taming of Chance.*
35 Hacking, 'Making up people', p. 231.
36 M. Foucault, Afterword, 'The subject and power', trans. in part, L. Sawyer, in H. Dreyfus and P. Rabinow, *Michel Foucault. Beyond Structuralism and Hermeneutics* (Brighton: Harvester, 1982), pp. 208–26.
37 Rusden, 'The survival of the unfittest'.
38 B. Hindess, 'Interests in political analysis', in J. Law (ed.), *Power, Action and Belief. A New Sociology of Knowledge* (London: Routledge, 1988); see also C. Webster (ed.), *Biology, Medicine and Society* (Cambridge University Press, 1981); R. MacLeod and M. Lewis (eds.), *Disease, Medicine, and Empire. Perspectives on Western Medicine and the Experience of European Expansion* (London: Routledge, 1988); J. Bessant, 'Described, measured and labelled: eugenics, youth policy and moral panic in Victoria in the 1950s', in R. White and B. Wilson (eds.), *For Your Own Good. Young People and State Intervention in Australia* (Bundoora, Vic.: La Trobe University Press, 1991), pp. 8–28.
39 Rose, *The Psychological Complex,* p. 82.

40 Ibid.
41 C. Bacchi, 'The nurture–nature debate in Australia, 1900–1914', *Historical Studies*, 19 (1980), 199–212.
42 R. Selleck, *The New Education. The English Background. 1870–1914* (Melbourne: Pitman, 1968).
43 R. Gillespie, 'The early development of the scientific movement in Australian education – child study', *Australian and New Zealand History of Education Society*, 11 (1982).
44 Quoted in E. Hooper, 'Principles of the kindergarten system. Part 1: the theory of education as put forward by Froebel and other modern thinkers', *Education Gazette*, 1 (1900–1), 26.
45 J. Mitchell, 'Psychological foundations in education', *Education Gazette*, 1 (1900–1), 92.
46 Ibid., 1901.
47 Ibid.
48 'A course of lectures by Dr Stawell on the education of feeble-minded children', *Education Gazette*, 1 (1900–1), 25.
49 M. Miller, 'A study of retardation in North Newtown Practice School', *Records of the Education Society*, 6 (1910).
50 R. Noble, 'The detection and prevention of mental deficiency', *Supplement to the Medical Journal of Australia. Transactions of Congress* (1924), 401–3.
51 R. Berry, 'The correlation of recent advances in cerebral structure and function with feeblemindedness and its diagnostic applicability', *Supplement to the Medical Journal of Australia. Transactions of Congress* (1924), 393–400.
52 Rose, *The Psychological Complex*, pp. 79–84.
53 *The Australian*, 5 June 1997.
54 National Inquiry into the Separation of Aboriginal and Torres Strait Islander Children from their Families (Australia), *Bringing them Home: Report* (Sydney, Human Rights and Equal Opportunity Commission, 1997).
55 Quoted in R. Noble, 'The mental hygiene movement and its possibilities in Australia', *Australasian Medical Congress, Transactions of the Third Session, Sydney, 2–7 September 1929* (Sydney: Government Printer, 1930), p. 300.
56 J. Bostock, 'Mental hygiene', *Australasian Medical Congress. Transactions of the Third Session, Sydney, 2–7 September 1929* (Sydney: Government Printer, 1930), p. 304.
57 H. Maudsley, 'Mental hygiene in relation to the community', *Australasian Medical Congress, Transactions of the Third Session, Sydney, 2–7 September 1929* (Sydney: Government Printer, 1930), p. 305.
58 J. Wallin, *Personality Maladjustments and Mental Hygiene. A Textbook for Students of Mental Hygiene Psychology, Education, Sociology, and Counseling* (New York: McGraw-Hill, 1949), p. 43.
59 Wallin, *Personality Maladjustments*, p. 55.
60 W. Trethowan, 'Psychiatry and the medical curriculum' (The Beattie Smith Lectures), *Medical Journal of Australia*, 1 (1960), 443.
61 Trethowan, 'Psychiatry and the medical curriculum', 443.
62 Report of the Director of Mental Hygiene for the year ended 31 December 1950 (Melbourne: Government Printer, 1950), p. 43.
63 Ibid., p. 43.

64 Wallin, *Personality Maladjustments*, p. 158.
65 S. Kraines, 'Psychiatric analysis of the present day madness in the world', *Science*, 86 (1937), 2234.

5 THE SPACE FOR PERSONALITY

1 I. Hacking, *The Social Construction of What?* (Cambridge, Mass. and London: Harvard University Press, 1999), pp. 10; 122–4.
2 Report of the Inspector-General of the Insane for the Year ended 1915 (Melbourne: Government Printer, 1916), p. 37.
3 England. Royal Commission on the Care and Control of the Feeble-Minded, London: Great Britain Parliamentary Papers, 8 (1908), pp. 187ff.
4 Royal Commission on the Feeble-Minded, p. 187.
5 W. Ernest Jones, *Report of Mental Deficiency in the Commonwealth of Australia* (Canberra: Government Printer, 1929).
6 Jones, *Report of Mental Deficiency*, p. 21.
7 W. Ernest Jones, President's Address, Neurology and Psychiatry, *Transactions of the Australasian Medical Congress*, Third Session, 1929 (Sydney: Government Printer, 1930), p. 254.
8 Royal Commission on the Feeble-Minded, p. 188.
9 J. Yule, 'The census of feebleminded in Victoria, 1912', *Australasian Medical Congress. Transactions*, 10th Session, Auckland, NZ: Government Printer, 1914, 722.
10 R. Berry and S. Porteus, 'A practical method for the early recognition of feeblemindedness and other forms of social inefficiency', *Medical Journal of Australia*, 2 (1918), 87–91.
11 R. Berry, 'One of the problems of peace: mental deficiency', *Medical Journal of Australia*, 2 (1918), 485–90.
12 England. Mental Deficiency Act, cited in Berry, 'One of the problems of peace', 485.
13 'Reviews: social inefficiency', *Medical Journal of Australia*, 1 (1921), 173.
14 R. Stawell, 'The state education of mentally feeble children', *Intercolonial Medical Journal* (1900), 88.
15 J. Fishbourne, 'The segregation of the epileptic and feebleminded', *Australasian Medical Congress. Transactions, Ninth Session* (Sydney: Government Printer, 1911), p. 885.
16 E. Stevens, 'The treatment of mentally defective children from a national standpoint', *Australasian Medical Congress. Transactions, Ninth Session* (Sydney: Government Printer, 1911), p. 893.
17 W. Wood, 'Recognition, results and prevention of feeblemindedness', *Australian Medical Journal* (1912), 602.
18 Editorial, 'The control of the mentally defective', *Medical Journal of Australia* (1916), 501–2.
19 Berry and Porteus, 'A practical method', 88.
20 W. Lind, 'Venereal disease and the abnormal mind', *Supplement to the Medical Journal of Australia. Transactions of Congress* (1924), 409–12.
21 R. Berry, 'The organic factor in mental disease', *Medical Journal of Australia*, 2 (1925), 180–1.

22 Berry, 'The organic factor', 181.
23 'British Medical Association News', *Medical Journal of Australia*, 1 (1917), 536.
24 'British Medical Association News', 536.
25 G. Richards, *Mental Machinery: The Origins and Consequences of Psychological Ideas. Part 1 1600–1850* (London: Athlone Press, 1992); R. Herrnstein and E. Boring, *Source Book in the History of Psychology* (Cambridge, Mass.: Harvard University Press, 1965).
26 Richards, *Mental Machinery*, p. 396.
27 Herrnstein and Boring, *Source Book in the History of Psychology*, p. 265.
28 B. Latour, 'Visualisation and cognition: thinking with eyes and hands', *Knowledge and Society: Studies in the Sociology of Culture Past and Present*, 6 (1986), 1–40.
29 G. Allport, *Personality. A Psychological Interpretation* (London: Constable, 1937), p. 137.
30 C. Mercier, *Crime and Insanity* (London: Williams and Norgate, 1911), p. 151.
31 Berry, 'The correlation of recent advances'.
32 Ibid., p. 394.
33 McCallum, *The Social Production of Merit*.
34 'British Medical Association News', 541–3.
35 R. Noble, 'Some observations on the treatment of the feebleminded in Great Britain and America', *Medical Journal of Australia*, 2 (1924), 33.
36 Berry, 'The correlation of recent advances', p. 399.
37 Ibid., p. 397.
38 H. Cleckley, *The Mask of Sanity: An Attempt to Clarify some Issues about the so-called Psychopathic Personality* (St Louis: C. V. Mosby and Co., 1941), p. 398; J. Bleechmore, 'Towards a rational theory of criminal responsibility: the psychopathic offender. Part Two: Psychopathy, logic and criminal responsibility: some conclusions', *Melbourne University Law Review*, 10 (1975), 207–24.
39 H. Tasman Lovell, 'The Tasmanian Mental Deficiency Act', *Australasian Journal of Psychology and Philosophy*, 1 (1923), 285–9.
40 Parliament of Tasmania. Mental Deficiency Board Report for 1922–3 (Journals and Papers 89, 1923–4), Paper No. 23.
41 Parliament of Tasmania. Mental Deficiency Board Report, Paper No. 25.
42 Parliament of Tasmania. Mental Deficiency Board Report, Paper No. 19.
43 Victoria. An Act to Make Provision for the Care of Mentally Defective Persons and Mentally Retarded Children and for other Purposes (Mental Deficiency Act) No. 4704 (18th Dec) 1939, Victorian Acts of Parliament 4 Geo VI (1939), pp. 320–1.
44 A. Binet and T. Simon, *The Development of Intelligence in Children*, trans. E. Kite (Baltimore: Williams and Wilkins, 1916), pp. 37–45.
45 Rose, *Governing the Soul*, pp. 1–10.
46 H. Harris, 'Mental deficiency and maladjustment', *British Journal of Medical Psychology*, 8 (1928), 298–9.
47 C. Spearman, cited in C. Jorgensen, *An Analysis of Certain Psychological Tests by the Spearman Factor Method* (London: E. A. Gold and Co., 1932), p. 5.

48 Jorgensen, *Certain Psychological Tests*, p. 10.

49 J. Bowlby, *Personality and Mental Illness: An Essay in Psychiatric Diagnosis* (London: Kegan Paul, Trench, Trubner and Co., 1940).

50 Ibid., p. 29.

51 Ibid., p. 31.

52 H. Eysenck, *The Scientific Study of Personality* (London: Routledge and Kegan Paul, 1952).

53 Binet and Simon, *The Development of Intelligence in Children*, p. 37.

54 Danziger, *Constructing the Subject*, pp. 144–7.

55 H. Goddard, *Human Efficiency and Levels of Intelligence* (Princeton University Press, 1920), pp. vi–vii.

56 Mental Hygiene Authority, *Report for the Year ended 1934* (Sydney: New South Wales Government Printer, 1934).

57 *Report for the Year ended 1940*.

58 *Report for the Year ended 1946*.

59 A. Tredgold and R. Tredgold, *Manual of Psychological Medicine for Practitioners and Students* (London: Bailliere Tindall and Cox, 1953), p. 8.

60 Victoria. *Report for the Year ended 1913*, p. 57.

61 Berry, 'The organic factor', p. 181.

62 Ibid., p. 181.

63 Tredgold and Tredgold, *Manual of Psychological Medicine*, p. 263.

64 H. Eysenck, 'A dynamic theory of anxiety and hysteria', *Journal of Mental Science*, 101 (1955), 28.

65 Ibid., 31.

66 Ibid., 28.

67 Mowrer, cited in Eysenck, 'A dynamic theory', 42.

68 Herrnstein and Boring, *Source Book in the History of Psychology*, p. 569.

69 J. Williams, *A Textbook of Anatomy and Physiology*, Seventh Edition (Philadelphia: W. B. Saunders, 1944).

70 Tredgold and Tredgold, *Manual of Psychological Medicine*, p. 8.

71 Ibid., p. 8.

72 Eysenck, 'A dynamic theory', 31.

73 Ibid., 9.

74 Ibid., 10.

75 Ibid., 38.

76 Ibid., 38.

77 Hull, cited in Eysenck, 'A dynamic theory', 34.

78 Eysenck, 'A dynamic theory', 31.

79 R. Mowbray, 'Clinical judgement and clinical research', *Medical Journal of Australia*, 1 (1972), 762; M. Hamilton and J. White, 'Clinical syndromes in depressive states', *Journal of Mental Science*, 105 (1959), 985–98.

6   SURFACES OF EMERGENCE

1 Victoria. *Report of the Director of Mental Hygiene for the Year ended 1950*, p. 43.

2 Victoria. *Report of the Inspector-General of the Insane for the Year ended 1905*, p. 27.

3 Victoria. *Report of the Inspector-General of the Insane for the Year ended 1932*, p. 28.
4 *Report of the Director of Mental Hygiene for the Year ended 1935*, p. 27.
5 *Report of the Inspector-General of the Insane for the Year ended 1913*, p. 72.
6 *Report for the Year ended 1915*, p. 49.
7 *Report of the Director-General of Mental Health for the Year ended 1937*, pp. 25–6.
8 *Report of the Director-General of Mental Health for the Year ended 1946*, p. 38.
9 *Report of the Inspector-General of the Insane for the Year ended 1933*, p. 24.
10 *Report of the Director of Mental Health for the Year ended 1934*, p. 25.
11 *Report of the Director of Mental Health for the Year ended 1938*, p. 19–20.
12 *Report for the Year 1939*, p. 23.
13 *Report for the Year 1940*, p. 18.
14 *Report for the Year 1945*, p. 26.
15 *Report for the Year 1946*, p. 25. The term conduct disorder was later adopted in the *DSM* to describe persons under the age of eighteen years exhibiting behaviours characteristic of antisocial personality disorder.
16 D. McCallum, 'The case in social work'.
17 *Report for the Year 1949*, p. 24.
18 *Report for the Year 1949*, p. 35 (emphasis added).
19 *Report for the Year 1948*.
20 *Report for the Year 1949*, p. 33.
21 *Report for the Year 1950*, p. 35a.
22 E. Cunningham Dax and R. Hagger, 'Multiproblem families and their psychiatric significance', *Australian and New Zealand Journal of Psychiatry*, 11 (1977), 227–32.
23 Dax and Hagger, 'Multiproblem families'.
24 W. L. Tonge, D. S. James and S. M. Hillam, *Families Without Hope* (London: Royal College of Psychiatrists, 1975), Special Publication No. 11.
25 Dax and Hagger, 'Multiproblem families', 231.
26 R. Williams, *Keywords* (New York: Basic Books, 1983), p. 234.
27 Ibid., p. 235.
28 Dawson, 'Psychology and psychiatry', 258.
29 Ibid., 259.
30 Ibid., 263.
31 Ibid., 264.
32 H. Tasman Lovell, 'Character and personality', *Australasian Journal of Psychology and Philosophy*, 9 (1931), 37–48.
33 Tasman Lovell, 'Character and personality', 47–8.
34 Laurence Kohlberg, *The Philosophy of Moral Development* (New York: Harper and Row, 1981).
35 World Health Organisation, *Manual of the International Statistical Classification of Diseases, Injuries and Causes of Death*, vol. 1 (Geneva: World Health Organisation, 1948), pp. xii–xiii.
36 *Manual of the International Statistical Classification*, pp. vi–vii.
37 Ibid., pp. 112–15.
38 American Psychiatric Association, *Diagnostic and Statistical Manual of Mental Disorders*, First Edition (Washington DC, APA, 1952), p. 38.

39 Ibid., p. 38.
40 Ibid., p. 38.
41 Ibid., p. 38.
42 Ibid., p. 39.
43 D. Franklin, 'The politics of masochism', *Psychology Today* 21, 1 (1987), 53–7.
44 Ibid., 53.
45 I. K. Broverman et al. 'Sex-role stereotypes and clinical judgements of mental health', *Journal of Consulting and Clinical Psychology*, 34 (1970), 1–7; I. K. Broverman et al. 'Sex-role stereotypes: a current appraisal', *Journal of Social Issues*, 28 (1972), 59–78; see also Denise Russell, 'Making women mad', *Australian Left Review*, 97 (1986), 19–25; Denise Russell, 'Psychiatry: making criminals mad', 32–3.
46 Pratt, *Governing the Dangerous*, pp. 70–97.
47 Ibid., p. 95.

7 PERSONALITY AND DANGEROUSNESS

1 Wootton, 'Diminished responsibility', 229–30 (emphasis in original).
2 Ibid., 232.
3 Ibid., 233–4.
4 Ibid., 235.
5 John Ellard, 'Personality disorder or the snark still at large', *Australasian Psychiatry*, 4, 2 (1996), 58–64.
6 Ibid., 62.
7 Ibid., 3.
8 M. Robertson, A. Bray and G. Parker, 'Sociopathy: forever forensic?', *Medical Journal of Australia*, 164 (1996), 304–7.
9 Ibid., 306; see also D. Henderson, *Psychopathic States* (New York: W. W. Norton, 1939).
10 Robertson, Bray and Parker, 'Sociopathy', 307; see also John Ellard, 'The history and present status of moral insanity', pp. 115–31.
11 S. Hayes and R. Hayes, *Simply Criminal* (Sydney: Law Book Co, 1984); see also A. Hains and D. J. Miller, 'Moral and cognitive development in delinquent and non-delinquent children and adolescents', *Journal of Genetic Psychology*, 137 (1980), 21–35; S. Hayes and Wendy-Louise Walker, 'Intellectual and moral development in offenders: a review', *Australian and New Zealand Journal of Criminology*, 19 (1986), 53–64.
12 A. Campagna and S. Harter, 'Moral judgement in sociopathic and normal children', *Journal of Personality and Social Psychology*, 31 (1975), 199–205.
13 W. Reid, 'Psychopathy and dangerousness', in M. Roth and R. Bluglass (eds.), *Psychiatry, Human Rights and the Law* (Cambridge University Press, 1985), p. 76.
14 J. Monahan, *The Clinical Prediction of Violent Behaviour*, Washington, DC, US Department of Health and Human Services, 1981.
15 Reid, 'Psychopathy and dangerousness', p. 78.
16 Cocozza and Steadman, 'Prediction in psychiatry'.

17 B. Ennis and T. Litwak, 'Psychiatry and the presumption of expertise: flipping coins in the courtroom', *California Law Review*, 62, 5 (1974).
18 J. Floud, 'Dangerousness and criminal justice', *The British Journal of Criminology*, 22, 3 (1982), 213–28; see also Floud, and Young, *Dangerousness and Criminal Justice*.
19 Floud and Young, *Dangerousness and Criminal Justice*, p. 60.
20 J. Monahan et al., 'Developing a clinically useful actuarial tool for assessing violence risk', *British Journal of Psychiatry*, 176 (2000), 312–19.
21 Commonwealth of Australia. *Criminal Code Act 1995*, Section 7.3.
22 Victoria. Victorian Parliament Community Development Committee.
23 Victoria. Health and Community Services, Department of Planning and Development. *An Introduction to the Fairfield Institute of Forensic Psychiatry. A Proposal to Develop a Forensic Psychiatry Centre of Excellence*, Information Paper, June 1995.
24 Victoria. Health and Community Services. Psychiatric Services Branch Update, May 1995 (Melbourne: Government Printer), p. 3.
25 R. Williams, *Keywords*, p. 235; M. Valverde, 'From "habitual inebriates" to "addictive personalities"', unpublished paper, History of the Present Meeting, London, May 1996.
26 Rose, *Governing the Soul*, pp. 213–28.
27 Foucault, 'Governmentality'; Burchell, 'Liberal government and techniques of the self', p. 20.
28 C. Gordon, 'The soul of the citizen: Max Weber and Michel Foucault on rationality and government', in S. Whimster and S. Lash (eds.) *Max Weber, Rationality and Modernity* (London: Allen and Unwin, 1986), p. 300.
29 I. Hacking, 'Making up people', p. 231.

Bibliography

Aarons, B., 'Anti-psychiatry: a critique of the normal', *Australian Left Review*, 31 (1971), 65–7.

Age (Melbourne) 30 April 1996; 30 June 1996.

Allport, G., *Personality. A Psychological Interpretation*, London: Constable, 1937.

American Psychiatric Association, *Diagnostic and Statistical Manual of Mental Disorders*, Washington DC: American Psychiatry Association, 1952.

American Psychiatric Association, *Diagnostic and Statistical Manual of Mental Disorders* (third edn) Washington DC: American Psychiatric Association, 1980.

American Psychiatric Association, *Diagnostic and Statistical Manual of Mental Disorders* (third edn revised) Washington DC: American Psychiatry Association, 1984.

American Psychiatric Association, *Diagnostic and Statistical Manual of Mental Disorders* (fourth edn) Washington DC: American Psychiatric Association, 1994.

Armstrong, D., *Political Anatomy of the Body*, Cambridge University Press, 1983.
'Public health spaces and the fabrication of identity', *Sociology*, 27 (1993), 393–410.

Ashworth, A. and Shapland, J., 'Psychopaths in the criminal process', *Criminal Law Review* (1980), 628–40.

Australian, 5 June 1997.

Bacchi, C., 'The nurture–nature debate in Australia, 1900–1914', *Historical Studies*, 19 (1980), 199–212.

Barker, W., *Mental Diseases. A Manual for Students*, London: Cassell and Company, 1902.

Bartholomew, A., 'The psychiatric perspective', *News and Views*, 5 (1990), 1–6.

Bartholomew, A. and Milte, K., 'The reliability and validity of psychiatric diagnoses in courts of law', *Australian Law Journal*, 50 (1976), 450–8.

Bates, E., *Models of Madness*, St Lucia: University of Queensland Press, 1977.

Beck, U., *Risk Society: Towards a New Modernity*, London: Sage, 1992.

Berger, P. 'Towards a sociological understanding of psychoanalysis', *Social Research*, 32 (1965), 26–41.

Berry, R., *Practical Anatomy*, Melbourne: Robertson and Mullens, 1915.
'One of the problems of peace: mental deficiency', *Medical Journal of Australia*, 2 (1918), 485–90.

'The correlation of recent advances in cerebral structure and function with feeblemindedness and its diagnostic applicability', *Supplement to the Medical Journal of Australia. Transactions of Congress* (1924), 393–400.

'The organic factor in mental disease', *Medical Journal of Australia*, 2 (1925), 180–1.

Your Brain and Its Story, London: Oxford University Press, 1939.

Berry, R. and Porteus, S., 'A practical method for the early recognition of feeblemindedness and other forms of social inefficiency', *Medical Journal of Australia*, 2 (1918), 87–91.

Bessant, J., 'Described, measured and labelled: eugenics, youth and moral panic in Victoria in the 1950s', in R. White and B. Wilson (eds.), *For Your Own Good. Young People and State Intervention in Australia*, Bundoora, Vic.: La Trobe University Press, 1991, 8–28.

Binet, A. and Simon, T., *The Development of Intelligence in Children*, trans. E. Kite, Baltimore: Williams and Wilkins, 1916.

Blackburn, R., *The Psychology of Criminal Conduct. Theory, Research and Practice*, Chichester: Wiley, 1993.

Blackstone, W., *Commentaries on the Laws of England* (New edition adapted to present state of the law by Robert M. Kerr, LL.D.), Ch. 28: 'Of the Matters Cognizable in Courts of Equity', London: John Murray, 1857.

Blaskett, B., 'The right to liberty *vs* the right to community protection: changing Victoria's Mental Health legislation', *Health Issues*, 23 (1990), 39–41.

Bleechmore, J., 'Towards a rational theory of criminal responsibility: the psychopathic offender', *Melbourne University Law Review*, 10 (1975), 19–46.

'Towards a rational theory of criminal responsibility: the psychopathic offender. Part Two: Psychopathy, logic and criminal responsibility: some conclusions', *Melbourne University Law Review*, 10 (1975), 207–24.

Blum, J., *Pseudoscience and Mental Ability: The Origins and Fallacies of the IQ Controversy*, New York: Monthly Review Press, 1978.

Booth, M., 'Report of Central Committee of the Australian Medical Congress on the care and control of the feebleminded', *Australian Medical Journal*, 1913, 929.

Borsody, A. and van Groningen, J., 'A reply – madness and badness', *Legal Service Bulletin*, 15, 3 (1990), 116–17.

Bostock, J., 'Mental hygiene', *Australasian Medical Congress. Transactions of the Third Session, Sydney, 2–7 September*, Sydney: Government Printer, 1930, 302–5.

The Dawn of Australian Psychiatry, Sydney: Medical Publishing Company, 1968.

Bowie, J. Correspondence to Chief Secretary, 23 July 1862, Victorian Mental Health Services Library, Royal Park, Archives Section, Box J5.

Bowlby, J. *Personality and Mental Illness: An Essay in Psychiatric Diagnosis*, London: Kegan Paul, Trench, Trubner and Co., 1940.

Brooks, A., 'The merits of abolishing the insanity defense', *Annals of the American Academy of Political and Social Science*, 447 (1985), 126–31.

Brothers, C., 'Archives of Victorian Psychiatry', *Medical Journal of Australia*, 16 (1957), 342.

Early Victorian Psychiatry 1835–1905, Melbourne: Government Printer, 1957.

Broverman, I. K. et al., 'Sex-role stereotypes and clinical judgements of mental health', *Journal of Consulting and Clinical Psychology*, 34 (1970), 1–7.

'Sex-role stereotypes: a current appraisal', *Journal of Social Issues*, 28 (1972), 59–78.

Burchell, G., 'Liberal government and techniques of the self', in A. Barry, T. Osborne and N. Rose (eds.), *Foucault and Political Reason. Liberalism, Neo-Liberalism and Rationalities of Government*, University College London Press, 1996, 19–36.

Camm, J., *The Early Nineteenth Century Colonial Censuses of Australia*. Historical Statistics Monograph No. 8, Bundoora: Australian Reference Publications, 1988.

Campagna, A and Harter, S., 'Moral judgement in sociopathic and normal children', *Journal of Personality and Social Psychology*, 31 (1975), 199–205.

Campbell, I., *Mental Disorder and Criminal Law in Australia and New Zealand*, Sydney: Butterworths, 1988.

Caputo, J. and Yount, M., 'Institutions, normalisation, and power', in J. Caputo and M. Yount (eds.), *Foucault and the Critique of Institutions*, Pennsylvania State University Press, 1993, 3–23.

Carlen, P., 'Psychiatry in prisons: promises, premises, practices and politics', in P. Miller, and N. Rose (eds.), *The Power of Psychiatry*, London: Polity, 1986, 241–66.

Carpenter, M., *Reformatory Schools for the Children of the Perishing and Dangerous Classes and for Juvenile Offenders*, London: Woburn Press, 1968. Reprint of 1851 edition.

Castel, R., *The Regulation of Madness: The Origins of Incarceration in France*, trans. W. Hall, Berkeley: University of California Press, 1988.

'From dangerousness to risk', in G. Burchell, C. Gordon and P. Miller (eds.), *The Foucault Effect: Studies in Governmentality*, London: Harvester Wheatsheaf, 1991, 281–98.

'"Problematisation" as a mode of reading history', trans. P. Wissing, in J. Goldstein (ed.), *Foucault and the Writing of History*, Oxford: Blackwell, 1994, 237–52.

Cleckley, H., *The Mask of Sanity: An Attempt to Clarify some Issues about the so-called Psychopathic Personality*, St Louis: C. V. Mosby and Co., 1941.

Cocozza, J. and Steadman, H., 'The failure of psychiatric predictions of dangerousness: clear and convincing evidence', *Rutgers Law Review*, 30 (1976), 1084–101.

'Prediction in psychiatry: an example of misplaced confidence in experts', *Social Problems*, 25 (1978), 256–76.

Coffey, G., 'Madness and postmodern civilisation. The Burdekin Report and reforming public psychiatry', *Arena Magazine*, April–May (1994), 32–7.

Cohen, S. and Scull, A. (eds.), *Social Control and the State*, New York: St Martins Press, 1983.

Commonwealth of Australia. *Criminal Code Act 1995*.

Conrad, P. and Schneider, J., *Deviance and Medicalization. From Badness to Sickness*, St Louis: The CV Mosby Company, 1980.

Coppe, L., 'Insane or greatly injured? The Captain Hindmarsh case', *The Push from the Bush*, Canberra: 1838 Volume Collective of the Australian Bicentennial History, 1986.

Craze, L. and Moynihan, P., 'Violence, meaning and the law: responses to Gary David', *Australian and New Zealand Journal of Criminology*, 27 (1994), 30–45.

Cullen, M., *The Statistical Movement in Early Victorian Britain. The Foundations of Empirical Social Research*, Hassocks, Eng.: Harvester, 1975.

Cummins, C., *The Administration of Lunacy and Idiocy in NSW 1788–1855*, Sydney: University of New South Wales School of Hospital Administration, 1968.

Dance, S., Funston, R. and Rubbo, A., 'The Sunbury Mental Hospital', B. Arch. thesis, University of Melbourne, 1963.

Danziger, K., *Constructing the Subject. Historical Origins of Psychological Research*, New York: Cambridge University Press, 1992.

Dawson, W., *Annals of Psychiatry in New South Wales 1850–1960*, Sydney: (Typescript) 1965.

'Psychology and psychiatry', *Australasian Journal of Psychology and Psychiatry* (1927), 258.

Dax, E. Cunningham, *Asylum to Community. The Development of the Mental Hygiene Service in Victoria, Australia*, Melbourne: Cheshire, 1961.

'Crimes, follies and misfortunes in the history of Australasian psychiatry', *Australian and New Zealand Journal of Psychiatry*, 15 (1981), 257–63.

'The first 200 years of Australian psychiatry', *Australian and New Zealand Journal of Psychiatry*, 23, 1 (1989), 103–10.

Dax, E. Cunningham and Hagger, R., 'Multiproblem families and their psychiatric significance', *Australian and New Zealand Journal of Psychiatry*, 11 (1977), 227–32.

Dell, S., *Murder into Manslaughter. The Diminished Responsibility Defence in Practice*, Oxford University Press, 1984.

Deleuze, G., *Foucault*, trans. S. Hand, University of Minnesota Press, 1993.

Dennis, W. (ed.), *Readings in the History of Psychology*, New York: Appleton-Century-Crofts, 1948.

Donzelot, J., *The Policing of Families*, trans. R. Hurley, New York: Pantheon, 1979.

Edwards, A., *Regulation and Repression. The Study of Social Control*, Sydney: Allen and Unwin, 1988.

Edwards, A. and Wilson, P. (eds.), *Social Deviance in Australia*, Melbourne: Cheshire, 1975.

Edwards Hiller, A. and O'Malley, P., 'Symposium on deviance, crime and legal process', *Australian and New Zealand Journal of Sociology* 14, 1 (1978), 20–32.

Edwards, G., 'Causes of insanity in nineteenth century Australia', *Australian and New Zealand Journal of Psychiatry*, 16 (1982), 53–62.

Ellard, J., 'The dangerousness of psychiatrists', *Australian and New Zealand Journal of Psychiatry*, 23 (1989), 169–75.

'The history and present status of moral insanity', in G. Parker (ed.), *Some Rules for Killing People*, Sydney: Angus and Robertson, 1989, 115–31.

'Personality disorder or the snark still at large', *Australasian Psychiatry*, 4, 2 (1996), 58–64.

Ellis, A., *Eloquent Testimony: The Story of the Mental Health Services in Western Australia*, Nedlands: University of Western Australia Press, 1983.

England. Royal Commission on the Care and Control of the Feeble-Minded, London: Great Britain Parliamentary Papers, 8, HMSO, 1908.

Ennis, B. and Litwak, T., 'Psychiatry and the presumption of expertise: flipping coins in the courtroom', *California Law Review*, 62, 3 (1974), 693–752.

Evans, B. and Waites, B., *IQ and Mental Testing. An Unnatural Science and its Social History*, London: Macmillan, 1981.

Eysenck, H., *The Scientific Study of Personality*, London: Routledge and Kegan Paul, 1952.

'A dynamic theory of anxiety and hysteria', *Journal of Mental Science*, 101 (1955), 28–51.

Fairall, P., 'Violent offenders and community protection in Victoria – the Gary David experience', *Criminal Law Journal*, 17 (1993), 40–54.

Fishbourne, J., 'The segregation of the epileptic and feebleminded', *Australasian Medical Congress. Transactions, Ninth Session*, Sydney: Government Printer, 1911, 885–91.

Floud, J., 'Dangerousness and criminal justice', *British Journal of Criminology*, 22, 3 (1982), 213–28.

'Dangerousness in social perspective', in M. Roth and R. Bluglass (eds.), *Psychiatry, Human Rights and the Law*, Cambridge University Press, 1986, 81–95.

Floud, J. and Young, W., *Dangerousness and Criminal Justice*, London: Heinemann, 1981.

Foster, S., 'Imperfect Victorians: insanity in Victoria in 1888', *Australia 1888*, Bulletin No. 8 (1981), 97–116.

Foucault, M., *Madness and Civilisation. A History of Insanity in the Age of Reason*, trans. R. Howard, New York: Vintage, 1965.

Discipline and Punish. The Birth of the Prison, trans. A. Sheridan, Harmondsworth: Penguin, 1979.

Afterword, 'The subject and power', trans. in part, L. Sawyer, in H. Dreyfus and P. Rabinow, *Michel Foucault*, Brighton: Harvester, 1982, 208–26.

History of Sexuality. Volume I: An Introduction, trans. R. Hurley, London: Penguin, 1984.

'The dangerous individual', in L. Kritzman (ed.), *Michel Foucault. Politics, Philosophy, Culture*, New York: Routledge, 1988, 125–51.

'Truth and subjectivity'. The Howison Lecture, Berkeley (mimeo)[1980], cited in G. Burchell, 'Liberal government and techniques of the self', *Economy and Society*, 22, 3 (1993), 268.

'Questions of method', in G. Burchell, C. Gordon and P. Miller (eds.), *The Foucault Effect. Studies in Governmentality*, London, Harvester Wheatsheaf, 1991, 73–86.

'Governmentality', trans. P. Pasquino, in G. Burchell, C. Gordon and P. Miller (eds.), *The Foucault Effect. Studies in Governmentality*, London, Harvester Wheatsheaf, 1991, 87–104.

Four Corners, Australian Broadcasting Commission Television, 1 July 1996.

Franklin, D., 'The politics of masochism', *Psychology Today*, 21, 1 (1987), 53–7.

Freeman, H. 'Anti-psychiatry: a critique of the normal', *Australian Left Review*, 31 (1971), 71–5.

Fulcher, G., 'Schizophrenia: a sociologist's view of psychiatrists' views', in A. Edwards and P. Wilson (eds.), *Social Deviance in Australia*, Melbourne: Cheshire, 1975, 75–91.

Garland, D., 'The limits of the sovereign state', *British Journal of Criminology*, 36, a4 (1996), 445–71.

Garton, S., ' "Bad or mad?" Developments in incarceration in NSW 1880–1920', in Sydney Labour History Group (eds.), *What Rough Beast: The State and Social Order in Australian History*, Sydney: Allen and Unwin, 1982, 89–110.

'Freud and the psychiatrists: the Australian debate 1900–1940', in B. Head and J. Walter (eds.), *Intellectual Movements and Australian Society*, Melbourne: Oxford University Press, 1980.

Medicine and Madness: A Social History of Insanity in New South Wales 1880–1940, Kensington: New South Wales University Press, 1988.

Gaynor, A. and Fox, C., 'The birth and death of the clinic. Ethel Stoneman and the State Psychological Clinic, 1927–1930', in C. Fox (ed.), *Historical Refractions*, Perth: University of Western Australia Centre for Western Australian History, 1993, 87–101.

Geis, G. and Meier, R., 'Abolition of the insanity plea in Idaho: a case study', *Annals of the American Academy of Political and Social Science*, 477 (1985), 72–83.

Gillespie, R., 'The early development of the scientific movement in Australian education – child study', *Australian and New Zealand History of Education Society*, 11 (1982).

Gillies, P., *Criminal Law*, Sydney: The Law Book Co., 1993.

Glaser, W., 'Morality and medicine', *Legal Service Bulletin*, 15, 3 (1990), 114–116.

'Commentary: Gary David, psychiatry, and the discourse of dangerousness', *Australian and New Zealand Journal of Criminology*, 27 (1994), 46–9.

Goddard, H., *Human Efficiency and Levels of Intelligence*, Princeton University Press, 1920.

Gordon, C. (ed.), *Power/Knowledge: Selected Interviews and Other Writings by Michel Foucault, 1972–1977*, New York: Pantheon, 1980.

'The soul of the citizen: Max Weber and Michel Foucault on rationality and government', in S. Whimster and S. Lash (eds.), *Max Weber, Rationality and Modernity*, London: Allen and Unwin, 1986.

'*Histoire de la folie*: an unknown book by Michel Foucault', *History of the Human Sciences*, 3 (1990), 3–26.

Greenwood, M., *Physiology of the Special Senses*, London: Arnold, 1910.

Gutting, G., 'Foucault and the history of madness', in G. Gutting (ed.), *The Cambridge Companion to Foucault*, Cambridge University Press, 1994, 47–50.

Hacking, I., 'Biopower and the avalanche of printed numbers', *Humanities and Society*, 5 (1982), 279–95.

'Making up people', in T. Heller et al. (eds.), *Reconstructing Individualism: Autonomy, Individuality and the Self in Western Thought*, Stanford University Press, 1986, 222–36.

'How should we do the history of statistics', in G. Burchell, C. Gordon and P. Miller (eds.), *The Foucault Effect. Studies in Governmentality*, London: Harvester Wheatsheaf, 1991, 181–95.

The Taming of Chance, Cambridge University Press, 1990.

The Social Construction of What? Cambridge, Mass. and London: Harvard University Press, 1999.

Hains, A. and Miller, D., 'Moral and cognitive development in delinquent and non-delinquent children and adolescents', *Journal of Genetic Psychology*, 137 (1980), 21–35.

Hamilton, M. and White, J., 'Clinical syndromes in depressive states', *Journal of Mental Science*, 105 (1959), 985–98.

Harman, B., 'Women and insanity: the Fremantle Asylum in Western Australia, 1858–1908', in P. Hetherington and P. Madern (eds.), *Sexuality and Gender in History: Selected Essays*, Perth: University of Western Australia Centre for Western Australian History, 1993, 167–81.

Harris, H., 'Mental deficiency and maladjustment', *British Journal of Medical Psychology*, 8 (1928), 284–315.

Hayes, S. and Hayes, R., *Simply Criminal*, Sydney: Law Book Co., 1984.

Hayes, S. and Walker, W., 'Intellectual and moral development in offenders: a review', *Australian and New Zealand Journal of Criminology* 19 (1986), 53–64.

Henderson, D., *Psychopathic States*, New York: W. W. Norton, 1939.

Heritage Council of New South Wales, *Castle Hill: Archaeological Report* (Sydney: 1984).

Herrnstein, R. and Boring, E. (eds.), *Source Book in the History of Psychology*, Cambridge, Mass.: Harvard University Press, 1965.

Hill, F., *Children of the State* (second edn), London, Macmillan, 1889.

Hill, R. and Hill, F., *What We Saw in Australia*, London: Macmillan, 1875.

Hindess, B., 'Interests in political analysis', in J. Law (ed.), *Power, Action and Belief: A New Sociology of Knowledge*, London: Routledge, 1988.

Hirst, P., 'The genesis of the social', *Politics and Power*, 3 (1981).

Hirst, P. and Woolley, P., *Social Relations and Human Attributes*, London: Tavistock, 1982.

Historical Records of Australia. Series 1. Governors' Despatches to and from England, I, 1788–1796, Sydney: Library Committee of the Commonwealth Parliament, 1914, 2–8.

Holman, W., 'Department of Public Health, New South Wales: Institutions for insane and infirm', *Australasian Medical Congress: Transactions*, 10th Session, Auckland, NZ: Government Printer, 1914.

Home Office/ Department of Health, *Managing Dangerous People with Severe Personality Disorder. Proposals for Policy Development*, London: Stationery Office, 1999.

Homer, A., 'Women and the politics of "psychotherapy"', *Australian Journal of Social Issues*, 12, 2 (1977), 129.

Hooper, E., 'Principles of the kindergarten system. Part I: the theory of education as put forward by Froebel and other modern thinkers', *Education Gazette*, 1 (1900–1).

Howard, D., *The English Prisons: Their Past and Their Future*, London: Methuen, 1960.

Hughes, R., *The Fatal Shore*, New York: Vintage, 1987.

Ingleby, D., 'Mental health and social order', in S. Cohen and A. Scull (eds.), *Social Control and the State*, New York: St Martins Press, 1983, 141–88.

Isdale, W., 'The rise of psychiatry and its establishment in Queensland', *Journal of the Royal Historical Society of Queensland*, 14, 12 (1984).

James, N. McI., 'On the perception of madness', *Australian and New Zealand Journal of Psychiatry*, 27 (1993), 192–9.

Johnstone, G., 'From experts in responsibility to advisers on punishment: the role of psychiatrists in penal matters', Studies in Law Series, The University of Hull, 1996.

Jones, W. Ernest, 'Methods of early treatment of insanity', *Australasian Medical Congress: Transactions*, 10th Session, Auckland, NZ: Government Printer, 1914.

Report of Mental Deficiency in the Commonwealth of Australia, Canberra: Government Printer, 1929.

President's Address, Neurology and Psychiatry, *Transactions of the Australasian Medical Congress*, Third Session, 1929, Sydney: Government Printer, 1930, 253–5.

Jorgensen, C., *An Analysis of Certain Psychological Tests by the Spearman Factor Method*, London: E. A. Gold and Co., 1932.

Kamin, L., *The Science and Politics of IQ*, Harmondsworth: Penguin, 1978.

Kennedy, R., 'The dangerous individual and the social body', in P. Cheah, D. Fraser and J. Grbich (eds.), *Thinking Through the Body of the Law*, Sydney: Allen and Unwin, 1996, 187–206.

Kerr, J., 'Designing a colonial gaol', in L. Coltheart (ed.) *Significant Sites. History and Public Works in New South Wales*, Public Works Department, NSW History Project, Sydney: Hale and Iremonger, 1989, 40–51.

Kissane, K., 'Are they mad or bad? Lawyers and psychiatrists differ on how to protect society from violent psychopaths', *Time Australia*, 135, 5 (1990), 42–3.

Kohlberg, L., *The Philosophy of Moral Development*, New York: Harper and Row, 1981.

Kraines, S., 'Psychiatric analysis of the present day madness in the world', *Science*, 86, 2234 (1937), 372–3.

Krupinski, J. and Stoller, A. (eds.), *The Health of a Metropolis. The Findings of the Melbourne Metropolitan Health and Social Survey*, Melbourne: Heinemann Educational, 1971.

Lang, J. Dunmore, *An Historical and Statistical Account of New South Wales both as a Penal Settlement and as a Colony* (vols. I and II), London: 1840; 1852.

Phillipsland, or the Country hitherto designated Port Phillip: Its Present Condition and Prospects as a Highly Eligible Field for Emigration, London: Longman, Brown, Green and Longmans, 1847.

An Historical and Statistical Account of New South Wales, from the Founding of the Colony in 1788 to the Present Day (Vol. I), London: Sampson, Low, Marston, Low and Searle, 1875.

Latour, B., 'Visualisation and cognition: thinking with eyes and hands', *Knowledge and Society: Studies in the Sociology of Culture Past and Present*, 6 (1986), 1–40.

Science in Action: How to Follow Scientists and Engineers Through Society, Cambridge Mass.: Harvard University Press, 1987.

Lewis, A., *The State of Psychiatry*, London: Routledge and Kegan Paul, 1967.

Lewis, C., 'The humanitarian theory of punishment', in W. Hooper (ed.), *God in the Dock: Essays on Theology and Ethics*, Grand Rapids, MI: Eerdmans, 1949, 287–94.

Lewis, M., *Managing Madness. Psychiatry and Society in Australia 1788–1980*, Canberra: Australian Government Printing Service Press, 1988.

'The early alcoholism treatment movement in Australia, 1859–1939', *Drug and Alcohol Review*, 11, 1 (1992), 75–84.

Lind, W., 'Venereal disease and the abnormal mind', *Supplement to the Medical Journal of Australia. Transactions of Congress* (1924), 409–12.

Lovell, H. Tasman, 'The Tasmanian Mental Deficiency Act', *Australasian Journal of Psychology and Philosophy*, 1 (1923), 285–9.

'Character and personality', *Australasian Journal of Psychology and Philosophy*, 9 (1931), 37–48.

Mackenzie, D., *Statistics in Britain 1865–1939. The Social Construction of Scientific Knowledge*, Edinburgh University Press, 1981.

MacLeod, R. and Lewis, M. (eds.), *Disease, Medicine and Empire. Perspectives on Western Medicine and the Experience of European Expansion*, London: Routledge, 1988.

Malpas, J. and Wickham, G., 'Government and failure: on the limits of sociology', *Australian and New Zealand Journal of Sociology*, 31, 3 (1995), 37–50.

Manning, F., 'Statistics of insanity in Australia', *Journal of Mental Science*, 25 (1879), 165–77.

Matthews, J., *Good and Bad Women: The Historical Construction of Femininity in Twentieth Century Australia*, Sydney: Allen and Unwin, 1984.

Maudsley, H., 'Mental hygiene in relation to the community', *Australasian Medical Congress. Transactions of the Third Session, Sydney, 2–7 September 1929*, Sydney: Government Printer, 1930, 305.

McCallum, D., 'Problem children and familiar relations', in D. Meredyth and D. Tyler (eds.), *Child and Citizen. Genealogies of Schooling and Subjectivity*, Brisbane: Centre for Cultural Policy Studies, 1993, 129–52.

The Social Production of Merit. Education, Psychology and Politics in Australia 1900–1950, London: Falmer Press, 1990.

'Mental health, criminality and the human sciences', in A. Petersen and R. Buntine (eds.), *Foucault, Health and Medicine*, London: Routledge, 1997.

'The case in social work: psychological assessment and social regulation', in P. Abbott and C. Wallace (eds.), *The Sociology of the Caring Professions* (second edn) London: University College London Press, 1998, 73–81.

McCulloch, H. and Rogers, L., 'Medical manipulation for social control and profit', *Australian Left Review*, 71 (1979), 18–21.

McDonald, D., '"This essentially wretched asylum": the Parramatta Lunatic Asylum 1846–1878', *Canberra Historical Journal* (September 1977).

McSherry, B., 'Revising the M'Naghten Rules', *Law Institute Journal*, 64, 8 (1990), 725–7.

'Defining what is a "disease of the mind"', *Journal of Law and Medicine*, 1, 2 (1993), 76–90.

Medical Journal of Australia, Editorial, 'The control of the mentally defective', *Medical Journal of Australia* (1916) 501–2.

Medical Journal of Australia, 'British Medical Association News', *Medical Journal of Australia* 1(1917), 536–44.

Medical Journal of Australia, Review, 'Social Inefficiency', *Medical Journal of Australia*, 1 (1921), 173.

Medical Superintendent to Crown Solicitor, 13 January 1909. Victorian Mental Health Services Library, Royal Park, Archives Section, Box J5.

Megahey, N., 'More than a minor nuisance. Insanity in colonial Western Australia', in C. Fox (ed.), *Historical Refractions. Studies in Western Australian History*, vol. 14, Perth: University of Western Australia Centre for Western Australian History, 1993, 42–59.

Mercier, C., *The Nervous System and the Mind. A Treatise on the Dynamics of the Human Organism*, London: Macmillan and Co., 1888.

Crime and Insanity, London: Williams and Norgate, 1911.

Midelfort, E., 'Madness and civilisation in early modern Europe: a reappraisal of Michel Foucault', in B. Malament (ed.), *After the Reformation: Essays in Honor of J. H. Hexter*, University of Philadelphia Press, 1980, 247–65.

Miller, J., 'The latent social functions of psychiatric diagnoses', *International Journal of Offender Therapy*, 14 (1970), 148–56.

Miller, M., 'A study of retardation in North Newtown Practice School', *Records of the Education Society*, 6 (1910).

Miller, P., 'Critiques of psychiatry and critical sociologies of madness', in P. Miller and N. Rose (eds.), *The Power of Psychiatry*, Cambridge: Polity Press, 1986.

Miller, P. and Rose, N. (eds.), *The Power of Psychiatry*, London: Polity, 1986.

'The Tavistock Programme: the government of subjectivity and social life', *Sociology*, 22, 2 (1988), 171–92.

'Governing economic life', *Economy and Society*, 19, 1 (1990), 1–31.

'Political rationalities and technologies of government', in S. Hanninen and K. Palonen (eds.), *Texts, Contexts, Concepts: Studies on Politics and Power in Language*, Helsinki: Finnish Political Science Association, 1990, 166–83.

Minson, J., Review of Andrew Scull, 'Museums of madness: the social organisation of insanity in nineteenth century England', *Sociological Review*, 28, 1 (1980), 195–9.

Questions of Conduct. Sexual Harassment, Citizenship, Government, London: Macmillan, 1993.

Mitchell, J., 'Psychological foundations in education', *Education Gazette*, 1 (1900–1).

Monahan, J., *The Clinical Prediction of Violent Behaviour*, Washington, DC: US Department of Health and Human Services, 1981.

Monahan, J. et al., 'Developing a clinically useful actuarial tool for assessing violence risk', *British Journal of Psychiatry*, 176 (2000), 312–19.

Mowbray, R., 'Clinical judgement and clinical research', *Medical Journal of Australia*, 1 (1972), 760–67.

Mulder, R., 'Why study the history of psychiatry?', *Australian and New Zealand Journal of Psychiatry*, 27 (1993), 556–59.

Mullen, P., 'Mental disorder and dangerousness', *Australian and New Zealand Journal of Psychiatry*, 18 (1984), 8–17.

Myers, C., *A Text-Book of Experimental Psychology*, London: Edward Arnold, 1909.

National Inquiry into the Separation of Aboriginal and Torres Strait Islander Children from their Families (Australia), *Bringing them Home: Report of the National Inquiry into the Separation of Aboriginal and Torres Strait Islander Children from their Families* [Commissioner: Ronald Wilson], Sydney: Human Rights and Equal Opportunity Commission, 1997.

Neil, W., *The Lunatic Asylum at Castle Hill : Australia's First Psychiatric Hospital 1811–1826*, Sydney: Dryas, 1992.

New South Wales, Dangerous Lunatics Act 1843, in Public General Statutes of New South Wales 1838–46, Sydney: Government Printer 1861, 1394–7.

New South Wales. *Select Committee on the Condition of the Working Classes of the Metropolis*. Report, together with Minutes and Evidence. NSW Parliamentary Papers, 1859–60, IV, 1263–465.

New South Wales. Mental Hygiene Authority, *Annual Reports 1934–1950*, Sydney, Government Printer, 1900–50.

New South Wales. *Mental Defectives Act 1938*.

New South Wales. *An Act to make provision for the special care and treatment of mentally defective prisoners; to amend the Prisons Act, 1899, and certain other Acts; and for purposes connected therewith. (Mental Defectives [Convicted Persons] Act)*, No. 19 (24 Oct.), 1939.

Noble, R., 'The detection and prevention of mental deficiency', *Supplement to the Medical Journal of Australia. Transactions of Congress* (1924), 401–3.

'Some observations on the treatment of the feebleminded in Great Britain and America', *Medical Journal of Australia*, 2 (1924), 31–6.

'The mental hygiene movement and its possibilities in Australia', *Australasian Medical Congress. Transactions of the Third Session, Sydney, 2–7 September 1929*, Sydney: Government Printer, 1930, 300–5.

Norden, P., 'From whom do we need protection?' *Advocate*, 3 May (1990), 7.

O'Brien, P., 'Michel Foucault's history of culture', in L. Hunt (ed.), *The New Cultural History*, Berkeley: University of California Press, 1989, 25–46.

Older, J., 'Danger to freedom from the helping professions: psychiatry, psychology and social work', *Australian Journal of Social Issues*, 10, 1 (1975), 26–34.

O'Malley, P., 'Volatile and Contradictory Punishment', *Theoretical Criminology* 3, 2 (1999), 175–96.

'Risk societies and the government of crime', in Brown, M. and Pratt, J.

(eds.), *Dangerous Offenders. Punishment and Social Order*, London and New York: Routledge, 17–33.

O'Sullivan, J., *Mental Health and the Law*, Sydney: The Law Book Company, 1981.

Parker, N., 'The Gary David case', *Australian and New Zealand Journal of Psychiatry*, 25 (1991), 371–4.

Parliament of Tasmania, Paper No. 9 Education Department Report for 1922, *Journals and Papers*, 89, 1923–4.

Parliament of Tasmania, Paper No 25 Mental Deficiency Board Report for 1922–3, *Journals and Papers*, 89, 1923–4.

Pemberton, A., 'Social class and mental illness: a critical appraisal', in A. Edwards and P. Wilson (eds.), *Social Deviance in Australia*, Melbourne: Cheshire, 1975, 181–200.

Pichot, P., *A Century of Psychiatry*, Paris: Roger Dacosta, 1983.

Potas, I., *Just Deserts for the Mad*, Canberra: Australian Institute of Criminology, 1982.

Pratt, J., *Governing the Dangerous. Dangerousness, Law and Social Change*, Sydney: The Federation Press, 1997.

'Governmentality, neo-liberalism and dangerousness', in R. Smandych (ed.) *Governable Places*, Dartmouth: Ashgate, 1999, pp. 133–61.

'Dangerousness and modern society' in M. Brown and J. Pratt (eds.), *Dangerous Offenders. Punishment and Social Order*, London and New York: Routledge, pp. 35–48.

Queensland. Report from, and Evidence taken before, the Commissioners appointed to inquire into the Lunatic Asylum, Woogaroo. Legislative Assembly. Votes and Proceedings, 1868–9.

Report with Minutes of Evidence taken before the Royal Commission appointed to inquire into the Management of the Woogaroo Lunatic Asylum and the Lunatic Reception Houses of the Colony (Brisbane, Government Printer, 1877).

Ray, M., 'Legislative problems and solutions', *News and Views*, 5, 6 (1990), 24–8.

Reekie, G., *Measuring Immorality: Social Inquiry and the Problem of Illegitimacy*, Cambridge University Press, 1998.

Reid, W., 'Psychopathy and dangerousness', in M. Roth and R. Bluglass (eds.), *Psychiatry, Human Rights and the Law*, Cambridge University Press, 1985, 72–80.

Richards, G., *Mental Machinery: The Origins and Consequences of Psychological Ideas. Part 1 1600–1850*, London: Athlone Press, 1992.

Richie, J. (ed.), *The Evidence of the Bigge Reports. New South Wales under Governor Macquarie, Vol. I, The Oral Evidence*, Melbourne: Heinemann, 1971.

Robertson, M., Bray, A. and Parker, G., 'Sociopathy: forever forensic?', *Medical Journal of Australia*, 164 (1996), 304–7.

Rose, N., *The Psychological Complex: Psychology, Politics and Society in England 1869–1939*, London: Routledge and Kegan Paul, 1985.

'Beyond the public/private division: law, power and the family', *Journal of Law and Society*, 14 (1987), 61–76.

'Calculable minds and manageable individuals', *History of the Human Sciences*, 1 (1988), 179–200.

Governing the Soul. The Shaping of the Private Self, London: Routledge, 1990.

'Of madness itself: *Histoire de la folie* and the object of psychiatric history', *History of the Human Sciences*, 3, 3 (1990), 373–96.

Inventing Our Selves: Psychology, Power and Personhood, New York: Cambridge University Press, 1996.

'Governing "advanced" liberal democracies', in A. Barry, T. Osborne and N. Rose (eds.) *Foucault and Political Reason*, London: UCL Press, 1996.

'At risk of madness. Risk, psychiatry and the management of mental health', unpublished paper, Goldsmiths College, London, cited in P. O'Malley, 'Risk societies and the government of crime, in M. Brown and J. Pratt (eds.) *Dangerous Offenders. Punishment and Social Order*, London: Routledge, 2000.

Ross, C., 'The treatment of the insane in private practice', *Journal of Mental Science*, 55 (1909), 205–8.

Rothman, D., *The Discovery of the Asylum. Social Order and Disorder in the New Republic*, Boston: Little, Brown and Co, 1971.

Royal Park Mental Health Library Archives Collection. Box J5 Centenary Celebrations, Ararat and Beechworth.

Rusden, H., 'The survival of the unfittest', *Australasian Association for the Advancement of Science. Proceedings* (1893), 523–4.

Russell, D., 'Psychiatry: making criminals mad', *Australian Left Review*, 92 (1985), 20–3; 32–3.

'Making women mad', *Australian Left Review*, 97 (1986), 19–25.

Schioldan-Nielsen, J., Review of J. Ellard, 'The history and present status of moral insanity', *Australian and New Zealand Journal of Psychiatry*, 23, 1 (1989), 12–15.

Scull, A., *Museums of Madness: The Social Organisation of Insanity in Nineteenth Century England*, London: Allen Lane, 1979.

Selleck, R., *The New Education. The English Background 1870–1914*, Melbourne: Pitman, 1968.

Shapiro, M. (ed.), *Language and Politics*, New York University Press, 1984.

Sharp, G., 'The autonomous mass killer', *Arena Journal*, 6 (1996), 1–7.

Sharp, V., 'The research act in sociology and the limits of meaning: the understanding of crisis, care and control in a therapeutic community', *Australian and New Zealand Journal of Sociology*, 13, 3 (1977), 236–47.

Simon, B., *Intelligence, Psychology and Education: A Marxist critique*, London: Lawrence and Wishart, 1971.

Skultans, V., *English Madness: Ideas on Insanity 1580–1890*, London: Routledge and Kegan Paul, 1979.

Springthorpe, J., 'The treatment of early mental cases in a general hospital', *Intercolonial Medical Journal* (1902), 197–202.

Stawell, R., 'The state education of mentally feeble children', *Intercolonial Medical Journal* (1900), 82–92.

Stevens, E., 'The treatment of mentally defective children from a national standpoint', *Australasian Medical Congress. Transactions, Ninth Session*, Sydney: Government Printer, 1911, 891–3.

Storz, M., 'The social construction of mental illness. A study in the sociology of deviance', PhD thesis, Monash University, 1976.

Szasz, T., 'Curing, coercing and claims-making: a reply to critics', *British Journal of Psychiatry*, 162 (1993), 797–800.

Tait, D., 'Respectability, property and fertility: the development of official statistics about families in Australia', *Labour History*, 49 (1986), 83–96.

Thompson, J., 'Civil liberties aspects', *News and Views*, 5, 6 (1990), 7–16.

Throssell, H., 'Mental illness, social work, and politics', in H. Throssell (ed.), *Social Work: Radical Essays*, University of Queensland Press, 1975, 95–112.

Tolson, A., 'Social surveillance and subjectification: the emergence of "subculture" in the work of Henry Mayhew', *Cultural Studies*, 4 (1990), 113–27.

Tonge, W., James, D. and Hillam, S., *Families Without Hope*, London: Royal College of Physicians Special Publication No. 11, 1975.

Tredgold, A. and Tredgold, R., *Manual of Psychological Medicine for Practitioners and Students*, London: Bailliere Tindall and Cox, 1953.

Trethowan, W., 'Psychiatry and the medical curriculum', *Medical Journal of Australia*, 1 (1960), 441–5.

Trott, S., 'Implementing criminal justice reform', *Public Administration Review*, 45 (1985), 795–800.

Tucker, G., *Lunacy in Many Lands*, Sydney: Charles Potter, 1887.

Tyler, D., 'The development of the concept of juvenile delinquency 1855–1905', *Melbourne Working Papers*, 4 (1982–3), 1–33.

US House of Representatives. *Hearings before the Subcommittee on Criminal Justice of the Committee on the Judiciary. Ninety-Eight Congress. First Session on Reform of the Federal Insanity Defense*, Serial No. 21, Washington DC: US Government Printing Office, 1983.

Valverde, M., 'From "habitual inebriates" to "addictive personalities"', unpublished paper, History of the Present Meeting, London, May 1996.

Van Groningen, J., 'Dangerousness and preventative detention: a sociological approach', *News and Views*, 5, 6 (1990), 17–23.

Victoria, *Industrial Schools and Sanitary Station. First Report of the Royal Commission on Industrial and Reformatory Schools and the Sanitary Station*, Melbourne, Government Printer, 1872.

Annual Report of the Inspector-General of the Insane (Mental Health Authority), 1900–50.

Inspector of Lunatic Asylums. Annual Reports 1890–1904.

Inspector-General of Insane. Annual Reports 1905–33.

Director of Mental Hygiene. Annual Reports 1934–50.

An Act to Amend Sections Forty-four and Forty-five of the *Lunacy Act 1928*.

An Act to Amend the Law relating to the Insane (Mental Hygiene Act), No. 4157 (29 Dec.) 1933, Victorian Acts of Parliament, 24 Geo V 1933.

An Act to Make Provision for the Care of Mentally Defective Persons and Mentally Retarded Children and for other Purposes (Mental Deficiency Act) No. 4704 (18th Dec) 1939, Victorian Acts of Parliament 4 Geo VI 1939.

Law Reform Commissioner of Victoria, *Diminished Responsibility as a Defence to Murder*, Working Paper No. 7, Melbourne: Law Reform Commission of Victoria, 1981.

Law Reform Commissioner of Victoria, *Murder: Mental Element and Punishment*, Working Paper No. 8, Melbourne: Law Reform Commission of Victoria, 1984.

Law Reform Commissioner of Victoria, *Mental Malfunction and Criminal Responsibility*, Discussion Paper No. 14, Melbourne: Law Reform Commission of Victoria, 1988.

Law Reform Commissioner of Victoria, *The Concept of Mental Illness in the 'Mental Health Act' 1980*, Report No. 31, Melbourne: Law Reform Commission of Victoria, 1990.

Sentencing Act, No. 49 (25 June) 1991, Victorian Acts of Parliament, 1991.

Sentencing (Amendment) Act, No. 41 (1 June) 1993, Victorian Acts of Parliament, 1993.

Report of the Mental Hospitals' Inquiry Committee on the Department of Mental Hygiene, Its Hospitals, and Its Administration, Melbourne: Government Printer, 1949.

Report of the Mental Hygiene Authority, 1952.

An Act to Amend the Mental Hygiene Acts, and for other Purposes (Mental Hygiene [Amendment] Act No. 5923 (13 Dec.) 1955, Victorian Acts of Parliament, 1955.

Health and Community Services. Psychiatric Services Branch Update, May 1995.

Health and Community Services, Department of Planning and Development, *An Introduction to the Fairfield Institute of Forensic Psychiatry. A Proposal to Develop a Forensic Psychiatry Centre of Excellence*, Information Paper, June 1995.

Victorian Parliament. Social Development Committee. *Interim Report: Strategies to Deal with Persons with Severe Personality Disorder who Pose a Threat to Public Safety*, Melbourne: Government Printer, 1990.

Virtue, R., 'Lunacy and social reform in Western Australia 1886–1903', *Studies in Western Australian History*, 1 (1977), 29–65.

Wallin, J., *Personality Maladjustments and Mental Hygiene. A Textbook for Students of Mental Hygiene Psychology, Education and Counseling* [sic], New York: McGraw-Hill, 1949.

Washington Post, 20 January 1983.

Webster, C., *Biology, Medicine and Society*, Cambridge University Press, 1981.

Weeks, J., 'Foucault for historians', *History Workshop*, 14 (1982), 106–19.

Williams, C., 'Psychopathy, mental illness and preventative detention: issues arising from the David case', *Monash University Law Review*, 16, 2 (1990), 161–83.

Williams, J., *A Textbook of Anatomy and Physiology* (seventh edn) Philadelphia: W. B. Saunders, 1944.

Williams, R., *Keywords*, New York: Basic Books, 1983.

Wood, D., 'Dangerous offenders and civil detention', *Criminal Law Journal*, 13, 5 (1989), 324–9.

'A one man dangerous offenders statute – the Community Protection Act 1990 (Vic)', *Melbourne University Law Review*, 17, 3 (1990), 497–505.

Wood, W. 'Recognition, results and prevention of feeblemindedness', *Australian Medical Journal* (1912), 601–5.

Wootton of Abinger, 'Diminished responsibility: a layman's view', *Law Quarterly Review*, 76 (1960), 224–39.

World Health Organisation, *Manual of the International Statistical Classification of Diseases, Injuries and Causes of Death*, vol. I, Geneva: World Health Organisation, 1948.

Wundt, W., *Principles of Physiological Psychology*, trans. E. B. Tichener, New York: Macmillan, 1902.

Yule, J., 'The census of feebleminded in Victoria, 1912', *Australasian Medical Congress. Transactions*, 10th Session, Auckland, NZ: Government Printer, 1914, 722–7.

'Report by the Victorian Committee', *Australian Medical Journal* (1913), 929.

Zelinka, S., 'Out of mind, out of sight: public works and psychiatry in New South Wales, 1810–1911', in L. Coltheart (ed.) *Significant Sites. History and Public Works in New South Wales*, Public Works Department, Sydney: Hale and Iremonger, 1989, 97–120.

Index

189